# CONTENTS

## PART THREE

Every error has its consequences and venges itself unto the
seventh generation.

— Arthur Koestler, Darkness at Noon

# INTRODUCTION

It was in the early 1980s that I first met Svetlana Alliluyeva, Stalin's daughter. Our daughters were classmates at school, and the resulting contact between us developed into the beginnings of a friendship. Soon afterwards, however, Svetlana returned to the USSR, as it then was, with her daughter, and we heard nothing for two years.

Then, early one morning, my phone rang and a very Russian voice spoke. Svetlana was back in England, and suggested that we meet for lunch. This proved to be the start of a new phase of our friendship, Svetlana eventually proposing that we do a book together based on my interviews with her.

In many hours of taped conversations she took me inside her immediate family; I began to feel that I was getting to know them intimately, even though they were long since dead. Her elder step-brother Yakov and his uncle and aunt the Svanidzes; her brother Vasili; her grandparents Sergei and Olga; her Aunt Anna; Uncle Pavel, and his wife the lively Eugenia Aleksandrovna. She drew me into the heart of the family as she described with great emotion her feelings for her mother Nadya, and her complicated relationship with her father. She repeatedly declared that she wanted to set the record straight, and to tell 'the other side of the story'. As this many-skeined story of struggle, tragedy and survival unfolded I became deeply involved in the personalities and their destinies, surrounded as I was by the family pictures from Svetlana's album, which she had permitted me to have copied.

Then I found a copy of her grandfather's memoirs, together with a book that her Aunt Anna had dictated, both originally published in the mid-1940s. This took me even further back into the roots of the family, and we began to envisage an ambitious project: to tell the story of four generations of the Alliluyev family

*1*

– in their own words. This would be a unique record of one of the world's most famous families, without the overlay of Western attitudes on what is quintessentially Russian material. This book is the outcome of that idea.

The next stage was to see whether Svetlana's cousins would co-operate. She made several excited phone calls to Moscow to her family there, and they immediately agreed to speak openly to me about the past. They seldom give interviews to the media, but consented to speak to a friend of Svetlana's. I travelled to Moscow with an interpreter, and was warmly welcomed, in a fashion I can never forget, by Stalin's niece and nephews. It was an amazing week as they opened their hearts to me, speaking frankly, with emotion as well as humour, about their experiences and how they feel about their place in this extraordinary family saga.

As it developed, I began to see that this story tells us much about families anywhere in Russia at that time – and indeed wherever there is revolution, denial of human rights, and fear in political systems. Such psychological dramas are enacted by millions of families wherever oppression and corruption are the order of the day. This saga points up the pointlessness of power, its addictive quality and its sinister alchemy; the uselessness of war, and the cyclical nature of revolution, whose wake is invariably a trail of waste and tragedy. The long shadow cast by Stalin touches the family still. A dark circle, as one of them described it, has closed around them. The events of this powerful story defy belief; but truth is stranger than fiction.

The close-up view through the eyes of one family takes us from the microcosmic to the macrocosmic: it is a private statement of a public horror. This is a universal story of human tragedy, writ large.

The events of August 1991 in Russia, the *coup* which eventually toppled Gorbachev, provided my book with its completion: from the birth of communism to its demise, the revolution had come full circle. Starting in the 1890s with the optimistic ideals of the early Marxists, the fourth generation speaks its epitaph in the 1990s. Svetlana's grandfather, Sergei Yakovlevich, observed and participated in the first half of this 'glorious revolution'; he was one of the original Marxist revolutionaries of the turn of the century, a man of peasant stock who joined the underground movement in order to reform the iniquities of the system under which he laboured. He was no intellectual, but a worker who dedicated his life to changing things for the better. All surviving family members speak of him with respect and affection, and it is with his story that the book begins.

# PART ONE

*Chapter One*

# YOUNG REVOLUTIONARY

Eternal is the cruel way of life,
in which generations of mankind
Live and perish without trace,
And leave no lessons for their sons.
— Nekrasov

S ergei Yakovlevich Alliluyev was born in 1866, only five
years after the abolition of serfdom in Russia. His
daughter Anna writes:

Father was born in the village of Ramenye, in the Novohop-
ersk district of the province of Voronezh. The peasants' lot
had not been greatly improved by the abolition of serfdom.
My paternal grandfather died early from cholera leaving five
children behind. Father himself left home at the age of
twelve. He had endured enough humiliation, insults and
rebukes: the kind of things children never forget. Even at
that age he was proud, rebellious and defiant. From the age
of sixteen he worked as a casual labourer in various factories.

Although it is not the scope of this book to analyse
nineteenth-century Russian political thought, it is significant
that Sergei Alliluyev grew up at a time when dissatisfaction
at the autocratic and inefficient rule of the Romanovs had
been brewing for decades. The democratic and socialist
ideas of the European Enlightenment had been permeating
through to the Russian intelligentsia: John Stuart Mill,
Hegel and Victor Hugo were widely read, alongside Pushkin, Lermontov and Gogol. Nietzsche, re-valuer of values,
loomed large in the Russian imagination, and Dostoevski's

work owes much to his doctrines. Darwin's *Origin of Species* was later regarded as one of the causes of the movement against traditional authority.

Underpinning the development of Russian philosophy and literature in the nineteenth century was the inheritance of Peter the Great, whose early vision of the totalitarian state aspired to a nation of workers, a service state based on modernisation, grandiose industrial enterprises, total obedience to that state, and the pursuit of world-power status. Here lie the foundations of communism: each one a worker in his own field, committed to the idea that every part must be sacrificed to the greatness of the whole. 'Enormous wastes of wealth, of work, and even of human life may be necessary; but the strength of Russia, and the secret of her destiny, have always been largely made up of her willingness and ability to disregard the cost in order to obtain the final result,' says one of his biographers, Waliszewski.

Peter's obsession with duty allowed recourse to violence, a creed in which the nation acquiesced. A thousand years of autocracy, a single state imposed over 'all the Russias', which was a mixture of over one hundred ethnic groups, had rendered it more or less servile; even under the early tsars – the 'Caesars of the north' – foreign travel was a treasonable offence, so the people had no way of knowing that things were otherwise elsewhere.

The Russian people submitted. Rebellion was dealt with unequivocally in Peter's time. When conservative officers of the Streltsky guard, afraid of his innovative ideas, rebelled and sought to depose him, thousands were jailed. Peter ordered all the prisoners to be roasted alive on a spit one by one and as each one neared death his head was chopped off – the Tsar himself participating in this terminal stage of the fun. Then the heads were impaled and placed throughout Moscow to rot.

Among the most influential voices of the nineteenth century were Belinsky, father of the radical intelligentsia; Uspensky, de-romanticiser of the peasant, and Lavrov, who inspired the populist movement. These men paved the way for Tolstoy and eventually Marx. Berdyayev, religious thinker and philosopher, unorthodox Marxist and critic, wrote in his *The Origin of Russian Communism*, 1918: 'The whole history of the Intelligentsia was a preparation for Communism. Into Communism there entered the well-known traits of the Intelligentsia – thirst for social righteousness and equality, a recognition of the working classes as the highest types of humanity, aversion to capitalism and the bourgeoisie, the striving after an integrated outlook, and an integrated relation to life, sectarian intolerance . . .'

In the 1870s revolutionism was at its zenith; the ideas of Chernyshevsky had infiltrated the Russian consciousness, with their brand of socialism both scientific and Utopian. His view that nature must be subjected to the needs of man, and that socialism was a product of economic necessity, had become commonplace. This philosophy dovetails into the thinking of Marx, whose *Das Kapital* was translated into Russian in 1872. Chernyshevsky, whose thinking was favoured by Lenin, was a forerunner of the Bolsheviks: 'The road of history is not the pavement of the Nevsky Prospekt. It passes over the fields of dust or mud, over marshes, over rubbish. He who fears dirty boots must not occupy himself with public activity.'

In 1881 Tsar Aleksandr II was murdered by student revolutionaries, but the movement that demanded political amnesty and an elected constitution fell apart due to its lack of coherent organisation. Chekhov was to satirise this era of aimlessness and futility in his plays and short stories, although as it turned out the death of the old forces was also the birth of the new. By 1887 *Das Kapital* was the most widely read book among Russian students, and Viktor Chernov was formulating his triple alliance of workers to ensure the solidarity of the working classes: socialisation of the land by the plough, the factory bench and at the writing desk.

In Turgenev's *Virgin Soil* there is an engineer-manager, Solomin, a little figure of little deeds according to his critics, who is organising his men against the wishes of the mill owner. But he is a portent; a quiet man who really knows the workers, knows the job, and is a forerunner of the Bolshevik organisers. Such a man was Sergei Alliluyev, who was to become an active agent of the movement at factory-floor level, one of the original revolutionaries whose movement was to overthrow three centuries of tsardom.

'My grandfather,' says his granddaughter Svetlana, 'was never a theoretician or an important figure in the Party. He was one of the humble rank-and-file, without whom there could have been no communication between one Party group and another, nor the groundwork laid, nor the revolution itself accomplished.'

The family name, taken from 'Halleluyah', appears to have clerical antecedents. Svetlana adds: 'Grandfather came from a very poor peasant background. He didn't want to till the land like his forebears – his grandmother was a gypsy and he was not of pure Russian stock. It must have been from their gypsy blood that the Alliluyevs got their southern, somewhat exotic features, their dark eyes and flashing white teeth, their olive skins and slender frames.'


In the early nineteenth century the tsars conquered the Caucasus and Georgia lost her independence: the southern provinces were seen from the capital as buffer zones against the Ottoman empire. The Caucasus mountains, running between the Caspian and the Black seas, were regarded as a border along Europe and western Asia. An extraordinary diversity of peoples and languages, not to mention native flora and fauna, populate these lovely mountains, so beautifully depicted in Lermontov's *A Hero of our Time*.

The man who had commanded the Tsar's troops, General Yermolov, had some sympathy with political liberals, and he sheltered Pushkin, Marlinsky and other great writers, thus preparing the ground for the development of liberal and revolutionary ideas. The tsars built a great military road across the Caucasus from Vladikavkaz (now Ordzhonikidze) to Tiflis (now Tblisi), and a network of Caucasian railways. This development stimulated industrial development in the province, which in turn encouraged the spread of revolutionary ideas; for, ironically, regarding Georgia as a colony on the outskirts of the empire, the tsars chose the Caucasus as one of the places of deportation for political offenders.

Thus succeeding generations saw the growth of new socialist ideas in the Caucasian cities, particularly in Tiflis, the Georgian capital, Baku on the Persian border, and Batumi, the Black Sea port. All three felt they were culturally closer to Islam than to Christianity, they spoke their own language, not Russian, and hankered for the return of their independence from St Petersburg.

Tblisi commands a strategic position between east and west Transcaucasia and has known many masters: Persian, Byzantine, Arab, Mongol, Tartar, Turkish and finally Russian, when it was rebuilt by Yermolov along the lines of a nineteenth-century European city. Its people are lively and colourful, loving to dance and sing and drink wine in celebration of life. Against a backdrop of breathtakingly beautiful hills, the narrow cobbled streets of the old town follow the line of the winding river. The houses are stepped up steep slopes, their wrought-iron balconies overlooking tree-lined avenues. The skyline is dominated by the ruins of an old fortress, a fifth-century cathedral and the Metekhi palace of the Georgian kings of yore.

The flow of military rebels and writers of the early part of the nineteenth century was followed by agrarian socialists from the ranks of the aristocracy and civil service, then by a wave of Polish insurgents and Russian terrorists. Towards the end of the century a quite new revolutionary type emerged: the Marxist factory worker, exemplified by Mikhail Kalinin, future President of the Soviet Union, and his close friend Sergei Alliluyev, Bolshevik organiser.

Although Russian serfdom was abolished by Tsar Nicholas II in 1861, the emancipation of the Georgian peasants

*11*

did not follow for several years, and until as late as 1912 serfdom lingered in Georgia. But even the emancipated peasant was not so well off: personal freedom he was granted, but about half the land he had held as a serf was taken from him, and for what he retained he had to pay compensation way beyond his means. Lenin was to remark that 'half a century later the Russians show many more marks of slavery than the Negroes.'

Belinsky describes a 'nationality of birchbark sandals and peasant smocks' who suffered under a rigid social hierarchy, were subjected to barbarous treatment and shown no regard for human dignity in their living conditions. Deception, pretence and violence were their only weapons or means of protest. Sergei's daughter Anna writes:

> Many years later, we listened to Father telling us stories of those days. They showed us that not everything in the world was just and good.
>
> 'My father and grandfather were both serfs,' Father used to tell us.
>
> Serfs! Father's grandmother had also been a serf. She had lost all her front teeth as a young girl; the landowner had knocked them out with his snuffbox. Father's grandfather had often been flogged in the stables. He used to show his grandchildren the deep scars on his back which had not healed, even in old age.
>
> 'But you yourself were never a serf, were you, Father?' we would ask impatiently!

In Russia, the first factories were run on serf labour. Between 1887 and 1898 the output of iron and steel almost trebled, and that of textiles doubled. The gross abuses which tend to characterise early stages of industrialisation were rife: exploitation of female and child labour; enormously long hours; minimal wages; exposure to a rigorous climate; no guards on the machinery, frequent accidents with no compensation; heavy and capricious fines; housing in common barracks, or at worst, a place to sleep on the factory bench.

Bad sanitary conditions and excessive drinking were commonplace. One foreign engineer describes pre-revolutionary housing as having less than 300 square feet of floor space for more than twenty workers of both sexes and all ages – with windows that did not open. The shifts were between ten and fourteen hours long, and there were only two inspectors for the two thousand factories in the Moscow region. As in the dismal cellar described by Maxim Gorky in *Down and Out*, the beds were boards covered with rags, and there were no latrines. The workmen and women were not allowed, until the revolution of 1905, to form their own organisations.

From the 1870s onwards strikes became more frequent, usually demanding the payment of withheld wages, or protesting against excessive fines. Sergei Alliluyev's career had 'begun in the Borisoglebsk railway yards, and then in workshops in Yelets, Kovrov, and Ufa [towns in central Russia]. He wanted to settle in Moscow or Nizhni Novgorod, but could not find work. He returned to Borisoglebsk and heard from a friend about a sunny clime where working conditions were easier – so this friend alleged.'

Anna Sergeyevna continues: 'That is how father happened to come to Tiflis. This was in the 1890s. He was twenty-four years old. Here he worked for a couple of years in the rail depot, but left because he objected to paying a fine for striking an informer.' It was here that he met Olga Eugenievna Fedorenko, who became his young bride. Their life was far from easy; Sergei himself describes his working conditions at this time:

'The air in the workshops was stifling. Dazed men could barely walk across the shopfloors, exhausted from overwork, the stench and the heat. Everyone wanted to finish his work and escape from this hell. When the siren finally sounded its harsh clamour, workmen sighed with relief. But this was often premature. The siren had hardly begun its shaking wail, when the foreman would announce: "Keep the machines running. We are doing overtime!"

'Overtime was a frequent occurrence. In some workshops a number of men stood for as long as eighteen hours at the workbenches. At first the opportunity to earn extra money was welcomed. But as the overtime system spread, so pay became smaller and smaller. In the last ten years (1890–1900) wages decreased by about forty to fifty per cent. If in the nineties turners and fitters received a rouble and a half for a day's work, now they received a rouble for a full day's work, plus two or three hours' overtime.

'The turners working on carriage wheels received sixty kopeks a day. To secure a minimum living wage, every workman had to put in fifty working days a month. In other words, one had to stay for a further five or six hours at overtime. Some men did not leave the workshops for weeks on end and slept beside their machines.'

In 1887 an attempt was made to assassinate Tsar Aleksandr III. The ringleaders were executed, among them a student named Aleksandr Ulyanov. His younger brother, then aged seventeen, swore vengeance: Vladimir Ilyich Ulyanov, later known to the world as Lenin. He began to study revolutionary literature, and read Marx avidly.

Tsardom was still, after nearly three hundred years of the Romanov dynasty, an impregnable power-structure of crown, church and bureaucracy. The Tsar himself owned 95 per cent of the land in 'Holy Russia' – a country which covers one-sixth of the world's land surface. He ruled over 160 million people whose only hope and comfort was the church: their ruler was not answerable to them, he was answerable only to God. The Romanovs detested democracy; they were intent on preserving their dynasty and perpetuating the principle of autocratic rule. 'Those who believe they can share in government dream senseless dreams,' declared Nicholas II.

The peasantry, from west to east across the 7000-mile empire, were still illiterate and inarticulate and knew little or nothing of politics and revolution. Tolstoy wrote to them on his deathbed: 'You are compelled to spend all your life in want and heavy work while others who do not work at all profit by what you produce. You are slaves of these men.' Lenin, determined to change this, quickly understood that it was the factories that must become the breeding ground for new ideas.

In 1886, in a glorious ceremony in the Kremlin, Tsar Nicholas II was crowned Tsar of All the Russias. Over a thousand people were trampled to death in the crowds that followed the procession. But by the latter half of the 1890s, when Sergei Alliluyev was thirty years old, the voice of the oppressed was becoming stronger; strikes were widespread, and the workers' demands now included the limitation of hours. 1898 saw the formation, in Minsk, of the Russian Socialist Democratic Workers' Party, and Sergei Alliluyev was among its founder members.

*Chapter Two*

# Soso

> Every member of the society spies on the others, and he is obliged to inform against them. Everyone belongs to all the others, and all belong to everyone. All are slaves and equal in slavery.
>
> — Dostoevski, *The Possessed*

In 1900, rebellious workers were busy preparing the first May Day demonstrations in the Caucasus, both as a challenge to authority and to show solidarity with the workers of Europe. Four to five hundred workers assembled on the outskirts of Tiflis: a young man of twenty years old addressed the meeting, making his first public speech. His name was Iosif Vissarionovich Djugashvili, known as Soso – the Georgian diminutive for Joe – to his colleagues. After adopting a series of undercover names, he later settled on 'Stalin', man of steel. This is Sergei Alliluyev's account of that gathering.

> Spring has returned. The outskirts of the town are covered with young silky grass and the trees are in bud. Nature rejoices.
>
> In the middle of April we, members of the underground circles, were informed that a May Day meeting would be held the following Sunday.
>
> Preparations for this meeting were carried out with such meticulousness and secrecy that it was apparent that its organiser was an experienced and knowledgeable person. A *mayevka*, after all, was more than a cell meeting, where no more than ten persons met at one time; a meeting of some hundreds of workers was planned. It was a novel and incred-

ibly complex business. But despite the fact that so many people were involved in the preparations, the works' management was completely unaware that anything was happening.

Soso Djugashvili, who was in charge of the arrangements, chose a group of workers whom he asked to find a suitable place for the meeting. When the site was selected, he inspected it and approved the choice. He invited one of our friends, an amateur painter, to make a red banner. On this banner the portraits of Karl Marx and Friedrich Engels were depicted, together with slogans written in Russian, Georgian and Armenian.

I went accompanied by two friends. As soon as we reached the hills, we met a picket-leader. He glanced at us and asked quietly: 'Give the password.'

We gave him the password.

The picket indicated the way up the narrow winding path into the hills. It was still dark. Here and there a few lanterns glimmered. The pickets had equipped themselves with these lanterns which were usually carried by pilgrims making their way in the early hours of the morning to the monastery. We approached the banks of Salt Lake, about eight miles out of Tiflis.

Here, at a spot away from the road leading to the monastery, some five hundred people had gathered. As soon as the sun had risen from behind the hills dispelling the morning mist, the crowd grew animated: unconstrained, they began exchanging lively comments and arguments. I recognised many of them: some came from the railway depot where I worked, and others from Tiflis factories.

The red banner, with portraits of Marx and Engels and its stirring slogans, blazed among the trees in the sun. The *Marseillaise* rang out and was echoed back in the distance from the surrounding hills.

Like birds who had flown to freedom from narrow cages and were singing joyfully, five hundred men who had escaped to the hills also burst into a loud and thunderous refrain. Above us the red banner waved fearlessly in the breeze.

This was a new and remarkably beautiful vision! The emotion was tremendous: men surreptitiously wiped away tears of triumphant joy. One by one the speakers clambered up on to the rocky platforms. These were members of the revolutionary intelligentsia, workmen from the depot and factories. I can recall the speakers: Soso Djugashvili, Vano Sturua, Zachar Chodrishvili, and Mikho Bochoridze. They spoke of the significance of May Day as a day of international workers' solidarity, about the difficult working conditions in their factories, their humiliation, and the ill-treatment meted out to them by their bosses.

'We must fight for our rights,' the speakers proclaimed, 'we must protest, organise strikes, demand better conditions.'

This was the first time we had heard such courageous words expressed at a public meeting. Loud approval and cheers rose from all sides: 'Long live the First of May! Down with autocracy!'

Returning home from the *mayevka*, we felt happy, filled with determination to struggle and conquer.

But for all their initial euphoria, things did not turn out to be so simple. Soso Djugashvili went on to organise a wave of strikes in Tiflis between May and July 1900, but they were opposed by the majority Georgian Social Democratic Party, the Messame Dassy. Both Soso's and Sergei's careers as revolutionaries were, from now on, chequered with periods of arrest and exile.

By July the workers, driven by need and despair, were demanding higher rates of pay and the abolition of overtime. But not all of them understood the need for this. Some were afraid that the management would stop overtime, but leave their wages at the existing level. We had to explain to them that overtime led to ill-health, increased the number of unemployed, and lowered the daily wage rate. Whilst this was apparent to leading workers, the older, less educated men with large families remained unconvinced. No amount of propaganda could convince them. As a result a number of fights flared up, of an entirely unforeseen nature. The more militant among the younger workers beat up some of the older men.

Things then came to a head at the end of July and several mass-meetings were held at night in the nearby hills. At one of the meetings attended by the lathe operators, Mikhail Kalinin appeared. The question of a strike was discussed. Kalinin talked about the difficulties this would entail, particularly for workers with large families.

Mikhail Kalinin became President of the USSR from March 1919 until his death in 1946. A peasant by birth, he became an industrial worker in St Petersburg in 1893 and joined, as did Sergei, the RSDWP in 1898. He was one of the first supporters of Lenin's Bolshevik faction, and played a part in the 1905 revolution. A co-founder of *Pravda*, he served as mayor of Petrograd after the 1917 revolution. He was elected to the politburo in 1925 and held the Stalinist 'centre' with Molotov and Voroshilov. Kalinin was a popular figure, respected as a 'liberal', and was said to help frequently in hardship cases – he was affectionately known as 'Papa' Kalinin. He and Sergei had been friends from the earliest days, and Anna Alliluyeva remembers him from her childhood.

Our favourite guest was Uncle Misha, who arrived before all the others and always found time to amuse us. Our walks in the park with Uncle Misha were something we especially enjoyed; he would race with us in the open spaces and alleyways, and would run so fast that even Pavel [her elder brother] could not catch him. Then he would shake the mulberry trees and sweet mulberries would rain down on the grass.

We did not realise at the time that our adventurous playmate was an experienced clandestine revolutionary, and that the workers who gathered at our flat had much to learn from this twenty-four-year-old revolutionary . . . My father recalled how the young lathe-operator came to the depot in Tiflis, bringing all his revolutionary experience, persistence and drive, qualities which distinguished him as a member of the illegal underground.

So Kalinin, on that May Day, said to his fellow-workers:

'We must face facts. While we are getting ready to strike the police are not slumbering; they might make a few arrests to sow confusion in our ranks. Are we ready to meet this challenge?' But before he could answer his own question a dozen men replied in friendly unison, 'We are ready!'

'Yes, we are ready,' Kalinin continued decisively. 'Nothing can frighten us, and nothing will. We Social Democrats know that every struggle demands sacrifices, and that our struggle is for the cause of the working classes, the producers. It is a holy struggle.'

The preparations for the strike were undertaken by the revolutionary Social Democrats in the face of the opposition of the majority of the Messame Dassy, who tried to break the strike. Soso Djugashvili, Ivan Luzin and Mikhail Kalinin encouraged open struggle among the workers.

On 1 August 1900 Sergei Alliluyev was arrested for the first time.

I was returning home from a secret meeting. The night was very still. The heat of the day had subsided, and the air was unusually fresh. Above the town, the starlit sky looked enormous. The street was silent and deserted, but from time to time a lonely passer-by hurried along. Suddenly, policemen appeared at both ends of the street, and as they surrounded me I realised that arrest was inescapable. Among them I noticed a police inspector.

'Alliluyev?' he asked, half-affirmatively, and without waiting for my reply ordered his policemen, 'Seize him.'

## Chapter Three

# PRISON AND UNDERGROUND

Russia is a culturally backward country. There is a barbaric darkness there, a dark, chaotic, Asiatic elementalism. Russia's backwardness must be overcome by creative activity and cultural development. The most original Russia will be the coming Russia, and not the old, backward Russia.

— Berdyayev, *The Fate of Russia*, 1918

Sergei Yakovlevich was taken to the Metekhi prison fortress, his first of many experiences of arrest and imprisonment: he was arrested seven times before 1912. Here he was interrogated by the captain of gendarmerie, in a manner which makes a pointed contrast to later such interrogations under his future son-in-law Stalin during the 1930s and 40s.

He lifted his dull black eyes, and said, smiling faintly: 'You're Alliluyev, aren't you?' He pushed a cigarette case in my direction. 'Help yourself.'

'I don't smoke.'

'Oh, you don't?' the police captain said. 'How about some tea?'

'I've just had some.'

'You probably know why you were arrested. We've no wish to keep hundreds of people in prison. We'll let you out,' he continued, 'if you give us the names of the strike organisers. Well, what about it?'

I looked at the thin, saturnine face and unprepossessing figure, and felt nauseated.

'I don't know anyone,' I said . . .

The public prosecutor, who had entered during the

interrogation and had remained silent until now, suddenly asked, 'Do you have a family?'

I told him I had a wife and three children.

The prosecutor shrugged his shoulders, appearing to be baffled. 'You're an intelligent, grown-up man, yet you treat your family so brutally. It's incredible!' he exclaimed. 'Your refusal to talk may have unfortunate consequences for your family. You should try to understand . . .' Lowering his voice, the prosecutor continued: 'No one will know anything about it. You name the strike leaders and we'll leave you alone.'

The prosecutor's words infuriated me, but I controlled myself and remained silent. The police captain thrust the indictment at me, saying through clenched teeth, 'Never mind, you'll talk.' Then summoning one of his policemen, he said, 'Put him in solitary.'

When I returned to my cell, I was in pretty bad shape and thoroughly depressed. Bad news reached me from outside. The management at the rail depot had sacked all workers who had failed to turn up on time. The railway police authorities also issued an order stating that all persons who had been arrested for taking part in the strike had lost the right of employment on any railway establishment in the whole of Russia.

To make matters worse, a number of landlords demanded that the families of arrested men should vacate their houses and apartments. My family found themselves in that predicament.

While Sergei languished in jail, his family moved in with his wife Olga's mother, the children's grandmother. Anna remembered: 'We had to make ourselves as comfortable as we could in two small rooms which we shared with Granny, her eldest son and four daughters.' It was not long, however, before Sergei was released in November 1900, although he was under police surveillance and had to take the utmost care when meeting friends or going to secret meetings. He found work as a foundry foreman in a small engineering concern.

Anna continues: 'The year 1901 is a memorable one for everyone connected with the revolutionary movement in Tiflis. New people bring a ferment of ideas: among these is Soso, as Stalin was called at this time. Another name is frequently mentioned in our house, that of Kurnatovsky. Father speaks of him with special regard . . . He often expressed his indebtedness to Kurnatovsky for introducing him to Lenin's ideas. He was one of those Russian intellectuals who interpreted faithfully the works of Marx to the workers . . . I vaguely remember a tall, gaunt man, dressed in an unbuttoned jacket, his head bent forward to the person talking to him, since he was hard of hearing.'

Kurnatovsky was a couple of years younger than Sergei. He was a friend of Lenin, who had sent him to Tiflis to encourage the socialist movement there. He became a legendary hero of the 1905 revolution, arrested in 1906 and sentenced to penal servitude for life. He escaped from Siberia to Japan, and died in hospital in Paris in 1912, supported to the end by Lenin.

'At the beginning of spring 1901 the Tiflis police tracked down Kurnatovsky. He was arrested along with other comrades. The gendarmerie adopted a decision to prosecute Stalin, whom they had failed to arrest, and examine him on "the degree of political unreliability of members of the Social Democratic circle of intellectuals in Tiflis, under the State Security Act."

'But despite these arrests, barely a month later preparations went ahead for the May Day celebration. Father took part in this demonstration, which was organised, from underground, by Soso Djugashvili and Kurnatovsky.'

Sergei describes the 1901 *mayevka*:

However clandestine the arrangements, the police succeeded in learning about them. We were warned to take precautions; we were certain that a clash with the police was inevitable. Some of the workers appeared to be unseasonably dressed, in heavy overcoats and Caucasian sheepskin caps.

'What's the meaning of this get-up?' I asked in astonishment.

'Soso's orders.'

'Whatever for?'

'We're supposed to head the demonstration . . . We'll be the first to receive the blows from the Cossacks' whips. The coat and cap should soften the blow. You follow?'

. . . It was a sensible plan, since police reinforcements had gathered in every backyard from Golovinsky Prospekt to Palace Street.

'Long live the first of May!' the crowd roared in unison. 'Down with autocracy! Long live freedom!' We marched to the centre of the city, singing. Cossacks suddenly galloped up and the fight began. They began shoving, pushing and beating up the demonstrators and onlookers. The crowd began to roar out its slogans.

The police hurled themselves, with drawn sabres, on the man holding the banner. But the banner was passed from hand to hand. Whenever the police charged, the banner reappeared in a different part of the crowd. A bloody riot ensued. Cossack whips whistled through the air, sabres flashed: the workers replied with sticks and stones. It was a desperate encounter. Many workmen were wounded, the police also suffered casualties. The banner was taken off its pole, and carried off by women. It is now preserved in a museum.

I was dismissed from my employment . . . I had expected as much.

Lenin's revolutionary magazine *Iskra* (The Spark) said, in a later editorial, 'The event that took place on Sunday 22 April in Tiflis is of historic import for the entire Caucasus: this day marks the beginning of an open revolutionary movement in the Caucasus.'

Soso remained underground, and some time after the demonstration Sergei found work as a senior stoker at an electrical power station in Baku. Now the fifth largest city in the Commonwealth of Independent States, Baku lies on a curving sweep of the best harbour in the Caspian Sea. Its name derives from a local word for 'bad winds', since it suffers perishing northerlies in winter.

Baku's wealth and size are based on oil, which was discovered there in the ninth century. By the beginning of the twentieth century the Baku oilfield was the largest in the world. Peter the Great captured the city in 1723, but a dozen years later it reverted to Persia. Russia finally captured it in 1806, and in 1920 it became the capital of Azerbaijan.

Sergei did not stay long in his post. He left after a quarrel with the management at the end of 1901, and found work at the Rothschild refineries of the 'Black City' district, so-called because it was constantly enveloped in smog. He describes working conditions at the refinery:

> The workers lived in barracks, sleeping on dirty plank-beds, without taking off their working clothes. But in the barracks where the Persian workmen lived there were not even planks, and the people slept on the earthen floor, on cane mats.
>
> Medical services were badly organised. Hospital beds were few, and medicines in short supply. There were no canteens and one had to eat in crowded Persian inns and teahouses.
>
> Baku had hardly any tolerable form of transport. In that large, sprawling city there was only one horse-tram line. Tired, aged nags dragged the ancient open carriages at the speed of tortoises, often dropping dead from sunstroke or sheer exhaustion. Sometimes they would stop in their tracks and no amount of whipping or whistling would budge them.

In February 1902 Sergei was arrested for the second time and charged with being associated with a subversive organisation. While in prison he heard that Soso had been arrested for organising a mass demonstration of six thousand factory workers at the Rothschild refinery in Batumi, on a gulf of the Black Sea just north of the Turkish border. A major port, Batumi was ceded to Russia by the Turks in 1878, whose oil refineries use petroleum piped from Baku. At the beginning of the century Batumi was a prime target for Soso's activities, for stirring the workers up against their employers; but his sentence was heavy. After a year in jail he was exiled to Siberia. Sergei, however, was released in the spring of 1902 for lack of evidence against him.

In the autumn of 1901 the Alliluyevs' fourth child, Nadya, was born. 'Mother returned from the natal clinic', reminisces Anna who was aged five at the time, 'and we watched fascinated as she swaddled the baby. Then Nadya would be given a bath and it was great fun to see her splashing about all pink and smiling.' This was the child who was destined further to entwine the Alliluyev family's fate with that of the future dictator of the USSR. She was to become Stalin's second wife.

When Nadya was born, Stalin, twenty-two years old and in exile in Siberia, had not even married his first wife, Yekaterina Svanidze, the sister of a friend from his seminary days in Tiflis. Trotsky wrote, 'It is possible that the wedding took place in prison in 1903. Such cases were not rare. It is also possible that the marriage took place only after his flight from exile at the beginning of 1904. If Koba's wedding took place after his exile, it can in part explain his political passivity during 1904.'

'At various periods,' continues Trotsky, in his biography of Stalin, 'and on occasions at one and the same time, he was called David, Koba, Nizheradze, Chizhikov, Ivanovitch, Stalin.' Koba means the Indomitable. It was the name of an heroic outlaw, a Robin Hood-style people's avenger in a popular Georgian epic poem, favourite reading of the youthful Stalin.

Yekaterina Svanidze was, like Stalin's mother, highly religious and indifferent to politics. Their son Yakov was born in 1908 and Yekaterina died shortly afterwards. A school friend reports that Stalin, standing by her coffin, told him, 'This creature softened my stony heart. When she died all warm feeling for people died with her.' He put his hand over his heart: 'It is all so desolate here inside, so inexpressibly empty.'

Back to 1902, and Sergei Alliluyev, a free man again, began working as a mechanic for an illegal printing operation run by Lado Ketskhoveli. Lado, the son of a priest, had attended the same theological seminary as Soso in Tiflis, and now worked closely with him. In 1900 he had been sent to Baku by the Social Democratic organisation, to produce underground newspapers and leaflets.

As soon as I left prison, comrades from the workshop arranged for me to meet Mikho Bochoridze. Mikho was pleased to see me. 'I need your help,' he said affably. 'There's a job to be done.'

The Tiflis committee had, at this time, a small printing works created by Soso Djugashvili before he left for Batumi. It was difficult to obtain the right equipment, and this was the job the committee had entrusted to me.

In order to buy a printing press and get regular supplies of paper and ink one required a licence signed by the government. We obtained a blank licence form, filled it in and signed it on behalf of the Governor. The copy of the licence was countersigned by a Baku notary, and thus we were able to obtain the necessary equipment at any time.

Finally everything was ready. Thus the first issue of *Brdzola* [The Struggle] appeared.

But the premises were not safe for long: the police were on the alert. Bochoridze chose another site, on the outskirts of Tiflis at Avlabar where the print works were housed in the basement of an unfinished house. 'The Tiflis organisation entrusted me and my assistant to equip this press, and it was for this purpose that I was employed at the Georgian "Friendship" printing works.'

But Alliluyev found himself once again under police surveillance, so he left the works and in 1903 became assistant foreman on the construction of the Baku-Batumi pipeline. But he was arrested again and for the third time found himself in the Metekhi prison, alongside his old friends Kurnatovsky and Ketskhoveli. Sergei witnessed the latter's death, shot by one of the prison guards on a pretext. 'Thus perished one of our best revolutionary comrades, a glorious son of the Georgian people, one of the closest friends and companions-in-arms of Soso. Eternal memory be his!'

Released two months later, Sergei found work in a Baku oil refinery. In December he and a fellow conspirator were ordered to go to Tiflis to bring back a hand-printing machine to Baku. Part of this machine had been hidden in the apartment of Mikho Bochoridze.

Mikho was not at home. I was greeted by his aunt: 'Mikho has gone out,' she said, 'I don't know when he'll return. He didn't say anything.'

'Mikho will be back soon,' I suddenly heard a masculine voice exclaim.

I looked around. A young man of about twenty-three or twenty-four entered from an adjoining room.

'He's one of us,' said Mikho's aunt, pointing to me.

'One of us?' the young man repeated, inviting me with a gesture into the other room.

Having seated me at a table, the young man – Soso Djugashvili – asked, 'Well, what good news have you to tell me?'

Soso Djugashvili had only recently escaped from eastern Siberia where he had been exiled for three years. He had tried to escape in the first few days of exile, but had to give up the attempt because he lacked any warm clothes. His face and ears had become frostbitten and he was forced to return. On 5 January 1904 he made his successful getaway.

Mikho returned soon and we began to talk together. Koba, as Soso was now called, took an eager part in the conversation. He asked me what kind of printing machine we had obtained and how it had been packed. I told him we had packed the printing cylinder in a soft wicker basket and covered it with provisions.

'A splendid idea,' Koba confirmed. 'But how are you going to take it?'

I told him that a friend and I were going to sit in the same railway carriage.

'That won't do. One of you should take the drum, the other the remaining parts. Sit in separate carriages and don't contact each other.

'As for the typeface,' he said after a brief pause, 'we'll send that along by another comrade a short while afterwards.'

The Avlabar press survived until April 1906, when the police, with secret agents, paid a surprise visit to the house and found the secret entrance to the cellar. The newspaper *Kavkaz* (The Caucasus) reported that apart from the illegal press, the police discovered 'blasting gelatine and other paraphernalia for the manufacture of bombs, a large quantity of illegal literature, the seals of various regiments and government institutions, as well as an infernal machine containing 15 lbs dynamite.'

This was Sergei Alliluyev's first meeting with his future son-in-law. Shortly afterwards Sergei left Baku in search of work in central Russia. In October 1904 he brought the family to Moscow.

*Chapter Four*

# EXILE

There were at that time a handful of men of an entirely new species: militant philosophers. They were as familiar with the prisons in the towns of Europe as a commercial traveller with the hotels. They dreamed of power with the object of abolishing power; of ruling over the people to wean them from their habit of being ruled.

— Arthur Koestler, *Darkness at Noon*

B y now the Russian Social Democratic Workers' Party, of which Sergei Yakovlevich was a committed member, had polarised into two camps. Generally speaking both, formed of illegal working-class groups, believed that the future lay in industrialisation and a socialist order based on the working class. But Lenin's group, named the Bolsheviks (majority) in 1903, favoured rigid discipline and looked to the peasants as a potential revolutionary force. The Mensheviks, the minority by only two, aimed at creating a mass labour movement of the Western European type. They were made up of a number of groups who by no means agreed among themselves, whereas Lenin's 'majority' stood united in their aims.

Soso's reputation as a revolutionary had reached Lenin in exile in Europe, and the two met for the first time in 1904 at a Bolshevik Party conference in Finland. Lenin described him later as 'that miraculous Georgian'.

Anna Alliluyeva describes her impressions of the family's new home:

Moscow welcomes us coldly. In November frosts appeared,

to which we were unaccustomed. The family is poverty-stricken: Father is out of work. Casual labour brings in a small income on which we barely survive. And the police continue to follow Father, who cannot get permanent employment.

We shiver in our light Tiflis overcoats. When snow covers the streets we cannot summon up courage to go out in our galoshes. We have neither furs nor valenkis [fur boots]. It is impossible to keep warm in our unheated room. Father lies ill in bed from an attack of rheumatism. I sit beside him, glancing sideways at Mother. She is at the table, feeding Nadya with a spoon. I should like to say something which lifts the hopeless, crestfallen expression on her face; something to make Father stir as he lies there silent with his face turned to the wall. But what can one say? The police continue to watch him, and he cannot find work. How cold it is in Moscow!

In 1903 the first of several general strikes paralysed the nation and indicated to the government the extent of the converging rural and urban discontent. In 1904 Tsar Nicholas II embarked on a disastrous war with Japan which earned him contempt both at home and abroad as he continued to use the people as puppets in a game of empire. Counte Witte, his finance minister from 1892–1903, wrote that 'Russia was still being played with like a toy. In the eyes of her rulers was not the Japanese campaign itself a war with toy soldiers?' A rift between the people and the court, the state machine, was fast becoming a gulf which proved fertile ground for reactionary ideas among peasantry, urban workers and intelligentsia alike. The autocracy of the tsars, once patriarchal and benevolent, had finally become a sham.'

There was widespread unrest in the countryside, including demands for land so violent that they inspired terror among landlords. Rural unemployment was high, a rise in cereal prices increased the cost of food and of seed-grain, and higher rents accompanied these price rises. Debt was widespread among farmers and landowners; but there was still one law for the peasant and another for the landlord.

Revolution has not infrequently been triggered by hunger. Sergei Alliluyev, with his fellow factory-workers, many of whom had their origins in the peasantry, emerged as protagonists of a newly articulate revolutionism, annexing the dissatisfaction of the peasantry to their cause of better working conditions. Between the turn of the century and 1905 there were increasing numbers of strikes in factories all over Russia, and more stirring of revolutionary activity. The young Lenin was teaching Marxism in the factories of St Petersburg and demanding an eight-hour day. He also began to publish articles in a daily newspaper founded by Maxim Gorky in the interests of the revolution. Gorky was to become the revolution's leading novelist, his works a savage indictment of capitalistic society.

In St Petersburg a certain Father Georgy Gapon was working as a 'police socialist' – an agent planted among workers to persuade them that the government was working in their interests. He nonetheless was genuinely moved with sympathy for their cause as he experienced the social evils and the gross inadequacies of the workplace which they were suffering. The men he moved among in the capital had just suffered a fall of one-quarter to one-fifth in their real wages. The Bolsheviks and Mensheviks were at loggerheads over a plan for a grand demonstration of workers, who looked instead to Father Gapon for leadership. He led a procession of two hundred thousand to the Winter Palace bearing a petition for a general amnesty for political offenders, a constituent assembly to be elected under universal suffrage, and an eight-hour day. They were unarmed; some carried icons.

The Tsar was not in St Petersburg that January Sunday. He had entrusted the Grand Duke Vladimir with keeping order, who decided to wait and see what happened – and then to 'give the people a lesson'. The procession was allowed to enter Palace Square, with no summons to disperse. But the Grand Duke had posted troops around the square, and on the sounding of a bugle they fired on the crowd and the cavalry charged. More than a thousand people were killed, and several thousand injured, including women and children. Bloody Sunday marked the beginning of the 1905 revolution.

Anna describes that historic day through the eyes of a child:

> One could hardly forget what happened on that bitter, confused evening of 9 January. On that day the workers in Moscow learned of the blood that had been spilt on the Winter Palace Square. Mother put us to bed earlier than usual, but we did not complain. We sensed the highly charged atmosphere of the grown-ups and tried not to irritate Mother. We knew that the Tsar had shot at people who had come to see him. Rifles and gunfire slaughtered workers, children . . . I kept imagining the blood.
>
> 'The whole square was covered in blood,' our elders are saying. We can hear their muffled voices from the room next to us. I know that they are talking about the events in Petersburg. Pavlusha [her brother Pavel] draws closer to me. 'They are writing manifestos,' he says. 'Tomorrow they will be scattered in the streets.'
>
> Father was put in charge of the distribution of the leaflets.

Violent disturbances among the peasantry followed the massacre, constituting a direct threat to the autocracy of the Tsar, whose position, since the peasantry was still regarded as the backbone of empire, was ostensibly weakened. There were strikes, workers' demonstrations and street-fighting, and over two thousand estates were wrecked. The administration was in chaos after crushing defeats in a war which had made the Tsar deeply unpopular. Among other insurrections in army and navy, the crew of the *Potemkin* mutinied. In February the Grand Duke Sergei, uncle and brother-in-law to the Tsar, was assassinated. Count Witte, now Russia's first prime minister, granted autonomy to the universities, which took advantage of their liberation to become centres of agitation. Militant workers formed a Union of Unions, and in October the first Soviet of Workers'

Delegates was formed in St Petersburg, under the vice-chairmanship of Trotsky.

In the same month another general strike was called, and it brought the country to a standstill. The result was the Tsar's October Manifesto: this promised the people civic freedom, freedom of conscience, of speech and assembly, and an elected Duma with effective legislative powers. It widened the franchise to previously excluded selected classes of workers and peasants, with the promise of general suffrage.

But although the Tsar's power to issue decrees was limited by the Manifesto, his autocracy was effectively undiminished and he continued a long-standing programme of Russification. In an attempt to wipe out widespread insurrection among the Russian peoples, his government secretly organised a pogrom as an instrument of control to bring opinion back to the centre, a device which also served as a lightning conductor for diverting discontent. Groups of 'loyalists' sought out pockets of 'disloyalty' and beat them up. The 'Black Hundreds', as these groups were called, whose appointed task was to annihilate dissenters, were similar to the Fascist groups of the 1930s. The secret police were also authorised to stir up trouble, notably against Jews who, throughout the history of Russia, have frequently been scapegoats in times of trouble.

This was a hard time for the Alliluyev family, as Anna recalls. First her father and then her mother were arrested, and the children were split up among friends while their parents stayed in prison. As soon as he was released, Sergei again went underground, and fled back to Baku with his elder son Pavel. While Anna stayed in the Caucasus for a short while before joining them, the rest of the family stayed behind in Moscow.

The first sitting of the newly elected Duma in 1906 at the Tauride Palace in St Petersburg fell short of the high hopes of the Russian masses who had elected it. However, it did become a platform for free speech for a previously silenced class, and the appetite that comes from eating, so to speak, was awakened. Yet the peasantry still did not dream of deposing the Tsar; they simply wanted land and civil rights. At this point an incompetent government was being opposed by an ineffectual revolution. But many lessons were learned in the 1905 revolution: it was a step towards 1917, not least because all respect for the state had gone, and only a fear of the repressive tactics that so often follow revolution remained. Lenin called it 'a general rehearsal'.

Although metal workers were now on a ten-hour day, just how much 'freedom' was granted to the workers by the Tsar was soon demonstrated to Sergei Yakovlevich, as Anna remembers. By now her family was reunited, and back in Baku:

Only a few months have passed since the Tsar's Manifesto. Much was promised through the Tsar's tender mercy, but little enough remained for the workers. The elections to the Duma were under way and the authorities were anxious to remove all troublemakers from the works.

One day during the lunch break the workshop was ringed by troops: thirty men were arrested, among them my father. The arrested men were hustled into the yard and taken away under armed convoy to the Ortchalsky prison some five miles away. About half way, a detachment of sharpshooters met them. The officer in charge shouted an order to the leader of the convoy, but the prisoners reacted promptly. My father who stood in the rear ranks was thrust forward into the middle and a tight circle of friends formed around him.

This was just as well, because someone had given orders to the sharpshooters to kill my father and an attempt was made to strike him. This was the usual method: a prisoner, surprised by a blow in his back, would lurch forward. A hue and cry would follow – 'Oh, so you think you can escape?' – and he would be finished off with a bullet or a bayonet in his back.

The arrested men have been threatened with court-martial. It is dreadful to think of the consequences. Pavel and Mother go off every day to try to discover the truth of the situation and find Father's whereabouts. Rumours multiply: they say that some men have been shot in the Ortchalsky prison, Alliluyev among them. The prisoners' wives cannot bear the suspense any longer. They demand to see the railway administrator on whose orders the men were arrested. Why have they been sentenced to death?

Ortchalsky prison does not resemble the familiar Metekhi prison-fortress. Low, grey buildings appear behind the walls, with barred windows and a heavy, bolted door. I begin to tremble; I had heard so much about this death house where the condemned await their last hour!

. . . Finally the prison doors open slowly and we see the yard before us. The prisoners' relatives are allowed to approach. The prisoners enter the yard. We cannot see Father. Where is he?

'Where's Sergei?' Mother asks.

But we have already seen him. All four of us cry out, 'Father!'

'Well, what's happened? Has sentence been passed?' Mother asks.

'It's nothing, nothing. Keep calm.'

The prisoners have already been told their fate. They have been sentenced to exile somewhere in the far north.

Sergei was exiled to Archangel on the Arctic coast for six months, but escaped and made his way back across the heartland of Russia into Georgia, all of two thousand miles. But when he reached Tiflis he could only stay with his family for a few days because he was constantly followed by the police. Fleeing to Baku, he was arrested at a meeting of the Bolshevik committee. He was granted bail and went underground in Baku, living under a false name.

His daughter describes the city as she remembers it from her childhood.

From the windows of our house at the electric power station we can see regular lines of oil derricks. The sea foams below the yard; on its surface thin ribbons of oil reflect all the colours of the rainbow.

Baku has been called by its Azerbaydzhan inhabitants 'the city of winds'. Early in spring and autumn the north wind shakes the walls of the house, and sand seeps through the crannies of the closed windows, covering the sills and floors with thick layers of dust.

Oil pipes ran along the streets and alleyways of the Black City district. You had to clamber over the pipes to cross the street and make your way gingerly along the narrow wooden duckboards which served as pavements.

When the oil flamed at the borings, a black cloud obscured the sky, and thick patches of oily soot fell on the town. Trees could not grow in this poisonous atmosphere, and as a result Baku lacked all greenery. This was something of a surprise for those of us who had been brought up in lush Didube.

Baku was by now a principal stronghold of Bolshevism, and the tsarist police had their work cut out. The Okhrana, as the state secret police were called, still had unlimited authority despite the workers' so-called civil liberties: anyone was liable to arrest at any time of the day or night, and correspondence was regularly examined. The freedom laws, as so often in the history of the Russian peoples, were on paper only. It also seemed that, then as later, it was impossible for the Russian police to accept in practice any limitation on their powers. Their outlook on law, as on the liberty of the people, was fundamentally different from an Anglo-Saxon one. The courts and the press lay within their control, rather than outside where they could function as custodians of liberty.

Meanwhile Lenin, back in exile, was holding Party congresses abroad, and in 1907 Stalin made his one and only trip to England, to the London Congress. Lenin gave him the task of fundraising for the Bolsheviks back home, by means of 'expropriation' – otherwise called robbing banks. On his return to Tiflis Stalin led a successful and violent raid on the Imperial Russian Bank. But the Party was divided over this: in the eyes of many, the revolution became associated with violence, and Sergei, in his memoirs, paints a black picture of the heroic wastefulness of the guerilla warfare that ensued. Later on in the history of the Party these episodes were brushed over as an aberration, a deviation in the procedure of the revolution.

Sergei Yakovlevich ends his memoirs with this story of a meeting he had with Soso, known now as Koba, in Baku in 1907.

Koba had just returned from the London Congress. I had been arrested shortly before, together with members of the Baku committee of the party, but as there was no evidence against me I had been released on bail. This was my seventh arrest and my friends advised me to hide from the police.

I talked over my problems with Koba in a clay Tartar house with a low ceiling, on the Bailov peninsula, which Koba had rented. I asked Koba what to do. I told him that I had been invited to St Petersburg, using a false identity card. Koba asked how I would make my way there, and what I intended doing there.

'Well,' he said as we parted, 'it seems you ought to leave. I wish you a safe journey.' Then he added, 'By the way, take this money, you'll need it.'

I tried to refuse, explaining that I was amply provided with funds, but Koba repeated firmly and calmly: 'Take the money: you have a large family, children. You must look after them.'

So not long afterwards Sergei took the family to St Petersburg, city of 'white nights' on the northerly Gulf of Finland. The capital of the tsars ever since Peter the Great built this visionary city, it is a mosaic of a hundred islands in the delta of the great river Neva, linked by bridges and networked with gliding canals. St Petersburg's beauty is also world-renowned as a 'museum in stone'. Between 1914 and 1924 it was renamed Petrograd, as a concession to anti-German feeling, and after Lenin's death named Leningrad in his honour until it reverted to its original name in 1992. The Alliluyevs, who never liked Moscow, were glad to be there, it was a welcome change for all of them – although, as Anna says, 'instead of changing towns, we began changing apartments.

'I knew very well that the struggle was unceasing. Our flat had long become a general meeting place, friends from the Caucasus came to visit us, as did others who lived with Father, connected with Bolshevik and working-class organisations in St Petersburg. The most stringent precautions had to be observed during those years – the entire police apparatus, fearful of revolution, placed every suspect under surveillance. It was risky to hold meetings and gatherings in our flat: it was too well known to the police who soon had it under their eye.'

Nevertheless, the Alliluyev flat was where Stalin made for when, deported to Siberia in 1909 for organising industrial strikes, he escaped after only four months' internment. Through Sergei, he got in touch with the secret Party headquarters and was given a false passport to enable him to head south for the Caucasus. However, he was recaptured, tried and sentenced to five years in jail.

Being an experienced technician, Sergei was eventually, in 1911, made head of section in an electricity station and the family's material conditions improved considerably. They now had two rooms in a house on Samsonievsky Prospekt, and another two rooms for a mechanical repair shop. His daughter gives us a glimpse of Sergei the family man at this time:

Sundays always began with Father calling us: 'Get up! get up! Breakfast's on the table! Get dressed, hurry!' He would then place our shoes which he had polished to look like glass at the foot of our beds. 'Look what I've done for you – you lazybones, all of you!'

Father insisted that everyone should sit down to breakfast at the same time on Sundays. It was gay and noisy.

'Yesterday at school . . .'

'Yesterday in the repair shop . . .'

On Sunday evenings the whole family went to the Narodny Dom [People's House, a concert and opera house]. We fell in love with the theatre that winter, but we were first attracted to opera. Mother and her sisters sang, and Uncle Vanya taught us to accompany ourselves on the guitar. We enjoyed Georgian melodies and got to know Russian music well. But in Petersburg the world of music opened up for us in a new way. We heard opera performances by such famous artists as Chaliapin, Sobiniov, Battistini and Caruso.

And then we visited the Alexandrinsky Theatre, and finally we were exposed to the cinema. The Russian 'Golden Series', a programme of early films, was being shown: Father was opposed to the 'Golden Series'. 'They have a distinctly decadent influence,' he would say.

But he softened his attitude somewhat when some of his friends advised him to see Zola's *The Miners*. The cinema was absolved and became one of our Sunday entertainments, which included the ice-rink where Nadya cut such a dash.

One day, early in September 1911, the front doorbell rang.

'Open the door, Anna!' Mother called from the next room.

I loudly expressed my pleasure at seeing our grown-up friend Sila Todria, but suddenly stopped in my tracks when I saw a stranger standing behind the shortish Todria. The stranger was very thin, in a black overcoat and a soft felt hat. When he stepped into the corridor I looked more closely at his pale face and attentive hazel-grey eyes under the thick, sharply-curved eyebrows.

'Is your father at home,' asked Sila. 'My friend and I would like to see him.'

'He should be back shortly. Come in. Mother is in the dining room,' I said.

They went into the dining room, and Sila introduced the stranger. 'Meet our comrade – Soso,' he said.

Father returned home late, but greeted his guests with

undisguised pleasure. He took Soso's hand for a long time and said something to him and Sila. Through the half-opened door the muffled voice replied mockingly, rolling out his words: 'Well, well . . . You seem to have them on the brain!'

'Take a look yourself through the window,' said father. The three of them went over to the open window which faced Saratovskaya Street.

'Well, can you see them now?' Father continued. 'They can't fool me. I recognised them as soon as I approached the house.'

'We'll have to wait a while,' said Soso.

We now knew that this was the same Soso about whom we had heard so often from our friends. Soso, the well-known revolutionary whom Father had already met in Tiflis and Baku: Soso, who had been arrested and exiled several times, but who had always managed to escape. And now he was on the run from the far north and the police were already after him . . . Our friends always spoke of him in such a way as to make us understand that Soso was one of the most important and most courageous of revolutionaries. We were just getting ready for bed when we heard Soso exchange goodbyes with Mother and Father.

A few days later Sila dropped in again. He appeared to be gloomy and worried.

'He has been arrested,' he replied to our unspoken question.

The Okhrana spies had been watching Soso closely. He was arrested, imprisoned for a few months and then deported to Vologda for three years, forbidden to visit any of the big cities. He escaped several times, and in 1912, having heard that Lenin had selected him to be a member of the Bolshevik Central Committee, he travelled under cover to St Petersburg where he became editor of the new underground Bolshevik newspaper, *Pravda*. Although relentlessly pursued by the police he once surprised the Alliluyev children as they were sledging through the winter streets:

I remember the frosts, the snowdrifts, the icy sledge paths of that winter. In February [1912] at Shrovetide, the streets were filled with low Finnish sledges decorated with ribbons and jingling bells. The stumpy little horses raced along the icy roads made hard by traffic, shaking their plaited manes, carrying their load of laughing passengers.

'Who'd like a sledge ride? Well, get dressed and hurry – we're leaving straight away!'

We all jumped up, shouting with excitement. We had just been sitting glued to the window, admiring the sledges as they raced by, and suddenly we were invited to take a ride ourselves! By none other than Koba – Soso himself!

During this visit to Petersburg he often comes to see us. We now know Soso more intimately. We know that he can be simple and gay and that, although he is usually uncommunicative and reserved, he can also laugh and joke boyishly and tell amusing stories. He sees the funny side of people and imitates them to such perfection that everyone roars with laughter.

Fedya, Nadya and I grab our fur coats and run downstairs. We take our places in the sledge. Every word that is uttered makes us laugh. Soso laughs with us at everything – at the way the driver praises his little emaciated horse, at our screams as we bump over a snowdrift, certain that at any moment we will take a tumble.

The sledge glides down Samsonievsky Prospekt, past the station. 'Stop! I'll get off here – and you can ride back home.' Jumping off the sledge, Stalin walks hurriedly to the station.

During the years of exile and escape, Stalin (he adopted the name in 1913) kept in touch with Sergei by letter, so that he knew where to find the older man should he escape. The family sent Soso food parcels and clothes, and he recalled 'how happy he was when, in his lonely exile, he unexpectedly found a note bearing greetings from us in the pocket of his jacket. We had placed this money in the jacket when we sent him a winter suit,' recounts Anna. 'He often corresponded with Father.' The only published personal

letter that Stalin wrote is in reply to one of these offerings,
addressed to Sergei's wife:

25/XI

For Olga Eugenievna:

I am more than grateful to you, dear Olga Eugenievna, for
your kind and good sentiments towards me. I shall never
forget the concern which you have shown me. I await the
time when my period of banishment is over and I can come
to Petersburg, to thank you and Sergei personally, for everything. I still have two years to complete in all.

I received the parcel. Thank you. I ask only one thing: do
not spend money on me; you need money yourselves. I
should be happy if you would send me, from time to time,
postcards with views of nature and so forth. In this forsaken
spot nature is reduced to stark ugliness – in summer, the
river, and in winter, the snow, and that is all there is of
nature here – and I am driven by a stupid longing for the
sight of some landscape even if it is only on paper.

My greetings to the boys and girls. Wish them all the very
best from me.

I live much as before. I feel quite fine. My health is good
as I have grown used to the conditions here. But nature is
pretty fierce; three weeks ago we had up to 45 degrees of
frost.

Until the next letter.
Respectfully yours,
Iosif.

## Chapter Five

# OLGA EUGENIEVNA

Olga Eugenievna Alliluyeva was only two years Stalin's senior: she was born Olga Fedorenko, in 1877. Svetlana describes her as a 'very typically Georgian woman, hot-blooded and temperamental'. Her father, Eugeny Fedorenko, married Magdelena Eicholz, who came from a family of German settlers. 'She was the perfect housewife, baking fine cakes and bearing nine children. The Fedorenko children spoke German and Georgian, and were brought up in the Protestant faith. I knew one of the brothers a little, he used to come and visit her, but the others we never saw. Two of her sisters had incipient schizophrenia.'

Svetlana's Aunt Anna, Olga's elder daughter, describes scenes from her mother's childhood:

My mother was born in Tiflis, in the same Didube quarter where I spent the early days of my life. My grandfather's house was much like any other in Didube, with an open balcony around the middle floor of the house. There was always a great deal to do. Grandmother and her eldest daughter, Olga, my mother, never ceased working: they cooked, sewed and did the washing.

Grandfather was the undisputed head of the family. His wife, a quiet woman, and children trembled before the old man. He was always inclined to be quick-tempered and stubborn, and old age did not sweeten him. But he was hardworking and tried his hand at anything. He wanted to become rich, but something always frustrated him. His profits never increased but his debts mounted. Misfortune made him even more testy and he took it out on his family.

As his eldest daughter was growing up, a friend of grandfather's, the owner of a local sausage shop, became a frequent caller at the house. Grandfather soon observed that his guest, with whom he shared a glass or two of beer, was casting attentive glances towards his eldest daughter. The sausage-shop owner was wealthy; it did not matter that he was old and ugly and had an artificial eye.

My mother's fate had been decided. She was not yet sixteen when grandfather promised her to the old man. However, a young fitter by the name of Sergei Alliluyev, who worked in the railway depot, was already a lodger in the house. Grandfather did not approve of the young man's attention to his daughter, Olga. What did this penniless worker want? He had not brought her up for the likes of him.

But there was nothing Grandfather could do about it. Olga was fascinated by the young fitter. Life was not easy for her in those formative years, bounded by the same street in Didube, the house ruled by Grandfather's iron hand, the unending chores and the constant gossip of the neighbours. And suddenly young Alliluyev turned up; he was not afraid of anyone. Once, when he saw the old man raise his fist at my mother, this penniless nobody who lived in the annexe dared to stop him. 'I won't let you settle your differences in this way,' he told the old man firmly.

Olga noticed that her father, before whom everyone trembled, retreated in front of Alliluyev.

The day for Olga's engagement with the sausage-shop owner was fixed, but the night before the celebration the bride-to-be ran away from her parents' house with the man of her choice. She tied her few possessions in a bundle and climbed out of the window. The escape had been planned with her beloved. Grandfather's room was next door. A chained watchdog slept downstairs and would not allow anyone to approach. Grandfather trusted this watchdog and lay peacefully in his bed. But the dog had long become accustomed to the young tenant's friendly attention, and did not stir when he assisted Olga to scramble out of the window.

Father's young friends at the rail depot who had helped him to elope with Olga found a flat for the young couple. Grandfather turned up at the flat shortly afterwards with a whip in his hand: he would teach his daughter a salutary lesson and bring her home. But when Father opened the door Grandfather soon realised that there was nothing to do but make peace with the young people.

From the beginning of her married life Mother was immersed in revolutionary activities. A few days after her wedding there was a loud knock on the door. The police had arrived to look for the copy-machine in which father and his friends had printed their first manifestos.

Anna has clear childhood memories of her grandmother, Olga's mother, who played a stabilising role in the early days of her daughter's revolutionary family life.

We always took our troubles to Granny Fedorenko. She would hear us out, sympathise with us, and we would dry our tears and run off with a sticky sweet in our hand, our woes left behind us.

How gentle she was whenever Father was arrested and we remained alone with Mother. Granny never passed judgement on any of her children: she was proud of them. She was also on the side of every rebel in Didube . . . If there was anything they wanted to hide, they knew they had only to ask Magdelena Yakovlievna. She never asked any questions and her house was always open to anyone persecuted by the police. 'Try the house of the old woman Fedorenko. Her relatives the Alliluyevs will look after you' – the advice of a police inspector to an unknown girl lost in Tiflis.

After Grandfather's death, Grandmother was forced to look after her large family. Her eldest son was sixteen, and the youngest children were about our own age, yet no one ever heard the old woman complain, or ask anyone for help. But all the poor of the neighbourhood turned to her for assistance and advice.

She left Didube on only one occasion, when we wanted her to get medical treatment for her eyes. But she could not endure the St Petersburg mist. How delightful Didube seemed to her then! How dear was her own sunny, green little street where she knew everyone and where everyone greeted her.

She was accidentally run over and killed by an automobile in Tiflis.

Olga the young revolutionary's bride was, according to her granddaughter Svetlana, 'a splendid wife, dedicated to the same causes as her husband; she too joined the Party well before the revolution.

'Grandpa and Grandma were very poor people. They started life with very little: they always had to work hard, they both came from poor backgrounds – Grandma's was a little better because her parents ran a *gasthof*, a roadside inn with a restaurant, which made them better off. But they had to work very hard to feed themselves and their family, and Grandma did anything from sewing to household work. They were both work-loving and looked on it as not a chore but a pleasure. Grandma had been brought up by a hard-working German mother, and was a wonderful cook and dressmaker. She eked out the meagre resources available to her as the wife of a Bolshevik who was in jail part of the time and always on the move from one town to another.'

Olga Eugenievna once described a friend of hers as: 'so energetic, so capable. . . . with such determination she could achieve anything. She never complains, and she's so full of life . . .'

'Mother,' says Anna, 'obviously did not realise it, but she had sketched her self-portrait.'

These qualities were going to stand her in good stead: years of arrest, moving from city to city, imprisonment and exile lay ahead. In 1901, when Sergei Alliluyev was in prison in Batumi, Anna records:

Mother finds it difficult to get a job right away, but a friend comes to our rescue. She obtains work from the hospital, sewing linen. She works all day at her sewing machine. We try to keep out of her way; there is always the open field for us to play in.

I still remember our instructors with gratitude: they always

47

found time for their working-class friends' children, and taught other new ways of sewing, and even made clothes for us, and did everything to encourage Mother.

In 1904 the family moved for a short while to Moscow; it was not a happy experience. Sergei could not find work, Olga fell ill, and the family were poverty-stricken. Finally, friends found Olga some work as a housekeeper in a students' communal flat, on the eve of the 1905 revolution.

Sergei, freed by now but still operating underground, was asked by the Party to go to Tula to collect cartridges, but he was so closely followed by the police that it was impossible. Olga therefore undertook to go herself. The family's room was searched in her absence, and the police found revolution manifestos in one of her coat pockets. They arrested Sergei, and put out a warrant for Olga. The family managed to get a coded message to her in time, and she returned without the cartridges; nevertheless she was arrested on Moscow station and thus both parents found themselves in prison. The children went to various friends who sheltered them, and the family were not fully reunited for some time.

Anna takes up the story, back in Baku where Sergei had returned to find work:

So at last the family is together again. Goodness, how Fedya and Nadya have grown! We discuss events in Moscow around the table. Mother sometimes forgets or omits some detail and Pavlusha and Fedya prompt her.

Mother was living in a room for herself in the wooden house belonging to a carter. In this hole there was barely room to put a bed. She brought Fedya with her, but Pavel went to Novgorod, and Nadya went to stay with the Rjevskys.

'I was working all day at the dressmaking shop,' Mother explains. 'It was terrible to leave Fedya all by himself.'

'It wasn't at all terrible. I wasn't a bit frightened!' says Fedya.

For all the freedoms promised after the 1905 revolution, Sergei had found himself in prison again, this time under imminent danger of death. Olga was finding this hard to bear; her elder son Pavel took on the mantle of his father and gave her the support she needed. His sister Anna describes his gentle concern for his mother.

Pavlusha seems to have grown more mature in these days. He carries out Mother's instructions, or prevents us from making too much noise when we grow forgetful, and when Mother pauses for a moment at her sewing machine and drops her head into her hands, he comes up to her and says softly, 'Don't, Mother . . .'

She glances up at her eldest son, straightens herself, and the sewing machine turns rhythmically again. But it is difficult for this one noisy machine to feed so many mouths. We hear that friends have found Mother a job as a sales assistant in a shop, the first co-operative store run by the railways workers. We lie in bed discussing this new development.

'We must try to help Mother,' says Pavlusha. 'Get a job packing and delivering parcels . . .'

Olga's worst fears were realised when her husband was sentenced to exile in Siberia. However, the resourceful Sergei escaped and found his way back to Tiflis, albeit briefly; no sooner had he appeared than the ever-vigilant police came to search the family rooms:

'Where's your husband?'

Mother stops turning the sewing machine at that question and lifts her head. I can see her eyes are filled with tears.

'But you know very well he's not in Tiflis. He's been exiled. Exiled! You know that, too. I am here alone with my sick children.' Mother gestures around the room – 'Look for yourselves. They are ill.'

There was something so convincing about Mother's explanation that the police merely glanced around the room and left. We did not make a move until their footsteps died out.

Father stayed in Tiflis for a few days, but it was impossible to stay longer. Someone had babbled about his return, and he had to leave.

Finally the family settles in St Petersburg:

The first winter . . . in Petersburg was not a happy one. Mother fell dangerously ill and was taken to hospital. Without her constant care . . . our apartment felt like an orphanage. Pavlusha and I did what we could to replace Mother in taking care of the younger children. We set to work feverishly doing the chores which we recalled Mother doing. Pavlusha was now in his fourteenth year, but he did not scorn to do any 'girlish' job. Good, considerate and loyal Pavel!

Fedya and I completed our primary schooling and prepared to enter a gymnasium [secondary school], which was Mother's fondest wish. She loved to repeat jokingly: 'A fortune teller once told me that you would become savants!'

Olga herself had had only four years of schooling, and was pleased to be in a position now to give her children the best education available. From 1911 onwards the family were living in relative comfort in a flat in Samsonievsky Prospekt, and once the elder children were settled into high school she decided to give herself some further education.

Every evening . . . is now devoted to study . . . Mother opens a thick volume entitled *Biology*.

'I've a whole chapter to get through,' she says anxiously, settling down to work.

For some months past she has been taking a midwifery course. She was of the firm opinion that domestic work had somehow diminished this winter. 'After all, the children are quite grown up . . .'

There was some truth in this, and Mother could have taken a brief rest. But she did not like taking things easy, and with the determination which characterised everything she did, she began to study.

'I must get to know a few things, find myself a profession. It's always been my ambition,' she would say, a little shyly.

According to her granddaughter Svetlana, on the evidence of photographs taken of her at this time Olga was a very lovely woman, with an 'oval face, large grey eyes, regular features and a small refined mouth. She had a bearing of extraordinary dignity which made her small figure seem taller. She was short, with fair skin and light hair, neat and agile. It was said that she was very attractive, with no shortage of admirers.'

So Olga studied midwifery and found work at the hospital. Then, in 1914, war came and her medical and nursing skills were in demand. By autumn 1915 Russia had lost more than one million men; in all the Great War was to claim fifteen million Russian lives, and leave countless wounded.

Mother has recently appeared in a white cap, with a red cross on her bosom. She is a Red Cross sister now: she has passed her midwifery course at the institute and is working in the hospital which was opened ceremoniously. She tells us about the growing numbers of the wounded, the crippled and suffering who talk about betrayal at the front. The impressive spectacle of the first few days of the war has turned into a bitter sham.

'Our men have a great capacity for endurance. They are ready to do anything,' says Mother. She adds bitterly, 'But they are being pushed too far!'

She was completely absorbed by her job of nursing the wounded, who had become like close friends to her, and was deeply grieved by their misery and sad condition.

'The situation at the front is appalling. Soldiers are constantly complaining. They want an end to the war. "What are we dying for?" they ask all the time,' said Mother, sharing her impressions with us. 'I look at the soldiers and I realise that they are our people, ours!'

When the wounded men got better and left hospital, they corresponded regularly with Mother. They addressed her as 'our dear little sister', and were always seeking her advice or assistance in some matter.

## Chapter Six

# A SAFE HOUSE

The tree of liberty must be refreshed from time to time with blood. It is its natural manure.

— Thomas Jefferson

While World War I was raging over the battlefields of Europe, Stalin, who was refused for military service on the grounds of his deformed left arm, was in exile in Siberia. As a small boy he had developed a blood infection from an ulcer on his left elbow, possibly as the result of a beating, and was, he later told his sister-in-law Anna, close to death. 'I don't know what saved me then, my strong constitution or the ointment of the village quack.' From then on he could not bend his arm fully and was often in pain, nor was the hand fully mobile. The deformity is visible on photographs and film taken of him later, including in his open coffin. It was this arm that he lifted in a final terrible, threatening gesture as he was on the point of death.

Anna and Nadya were busy collecting money for Bolshevik sympathisers, with which their mother bought food and clothes to be sent to Stalin and his fellow exile Sverdlov, who was later to become a member of the first Central Committee. He became titular chief of state of Soviet Russia after the October revolution, virtually controlling the Party organisation and the state bureaucracy. He died in 1919.

Stalin often corresponded with Father from exile in Siberia. From his letters which we all read, we received an impression of that distant place with its harsh winters. He lived in the hut of an Ostyak fisherman in a tiny hamlet lost in the gloomy, endless tundra.

But there was not a single word about his hardships in the letters which Stalin wrote. He asked us not to send him anything and not to spend any money on him.

'Don't forget you have a large family,' he reminded Father in his letters. 'I have everything I need,' was his usual refrain.

He sent a manuscript of his work on the nationalities question to Father and asked him to send it abroad to Lenin who was expecting the manuscript.

This was an essay on the national minorities that Lenin had asked Stalin to write, setting out Bolshevik policy for ethnic groups throughout the nation. It was the only paper that Stalin wrote in his years of exile 1914–17, and it was never published.

Russian losses in the World War I battlefields were arousing bitter discontent with the Tsar. While Lenin denounced the 'imperialist war', the Duma and the press were demanding, as early as winter 1915, a 'government commanding the confidence of the nation'. Choosing to ignore this demand the Tsar assumed supreme command of the armies in the field. He left behind in Petrograd, as St Petersburg was now called, a collection of second-rate ministers, Rasputin among them, who were unpopular with the people.

Economic conditions in Russia deteriorated: prices rose, there were serious shortages of goods, including food, and the working classes grew increasingly unhappy. By early 1917 there were, again, widespread strikes, demonstrations and food queues. Barracks mutinied, and the Tsar's troops refused to fire on the crowds of protesters. The Tsar himself still refused to form the government asked of him, so in Petrograd a Soviet of workers' and soldiers' deputies, dominated by Mensheviks and Socialist Revolutionaries, was formed.

In collaboration with the Duma this Soviet set up a provisional government with Prince Lvov as its prime minister. Its emissaries travelled to Tsar Nicholas in Pskov, where he handed them his abdication, transferring power to the Grand Duke Michael. Twenty-four hours later he too abdicated. Nicholas II arrived back in the capital alone, on an empty train, deserted by his courtiers. A thousand years of Russian tsarist monarchy came to an end that February day.

Amnesty was granted to political prisoners as soon as the Tsar relinquished power, so in no time at all Stalin made his way back to Petrograd where he resumed his editorship of *Pravda*.

I recall that Stalin dropped in on us, *writes Anna Sergeyevna*, two or three times in the morning when work had just begun in the electrical repair shop. He would sit on the sofa in the dining room, looking very tired.

'If you feel like taking a rest, Soso, go and lie down on the bed in the store-room,' Mother would tell him. 'It's no good trying to catch a nap in this bedlam!'

A bed is made up for Stalin in the dining room where Father also sleeps on the other divan. We go into the next room, our communal bedroom shared by Mother, Nadya and myself . . . We fall asleep to the sound of Father's deep, sonorous voice, interrupted now and again by Stalin's short, clipped sentences.

Soon afterwards the family decided to move closer to the centre of town, and found an apartment at number 17, 10th Rozhdestvenskaya Street. Stalin asked them to keep a room aside for him. Olga continued working at the hospital.

The task of the provisional government was to maintain order and establish some democratic reforms. Similar Soviets to the one in Petrograd were set up all over Russia, not claiming power but waiting to follow a lead from the centre. Aleksandr Fyodorovich Kerensky, a Duma deputy, became minister of justice and chief liaison man with the Soviets. Kerensky was a moderate, a prominent lawyer who had gained a reputation as an eloquent and dynamic politician of the middle left. His aim, partly achieved after the February revolution, was, in his words, 'to grant people the unshakeable fundamental of civil liberty, based on principles of true inviolability of the individual, freedoms of conscience and speech, and the right of assembly and union.'

In May 1917 public uproar over Russia's war aims forced several ministers in the provisional government to resign, and Kerensky was transferred to the post of minister of war where, however, he also failed to inspire the troops to renew their efforts. The Bolsheviks' slogan of 'Peace, bread and land' fell on willing ears. During May and June revolutionary fever rose to fever pitch, the workers demanding that power be switched to the Soviets. In July, Kerensky was appointed prime minister of the provisional government, but managed to alienate the moderates and to lose the confidence of the left wing by apparently planning to assume dictatorial powers.

In early July workers marched on the Tauride Palace, the seat of the Soviet, to submit their demands. Violent mass demonstrations were sparked by sailors from the Kronstadt naval base, and the Petrograd crowds responded to a Bolshevik appeal for a new revolution. In the ensuing days the demonstrations grew larger and more violent, until finally armed groups of the right wing destroyed Bolshevik headquarters, and wrecked the offices of *Pravda*, their principal mouthpiece. It appeared that the Bolsheviks were defeated.

The government were now after the blood of their leaders. References to Lenin could be heard on every street corner. Rumour had it that he had escaped abroad on a minesweeper, and that he was a German agent. These were the famous 'July Days', the first test of strength between the provisional government and the Party. On her return to the flat one day early in the month, Anna was introduced to a stranger. She was overwhelmed.

Vladimir Ilyich is so simple, so courteous: he asks questions and listens with such evident sincerity, that I am made to feel as if I were his equal.

'But he's wonderful, absolutely wonderful!' I tell Mother when we go into the kitchen.

'He's a splendid person, splendid. . . .' Like me, Mother finds it difficult to describe him. 'He has been here since yesterday. I met him at the Poletayevs. They were saying that it would be dangerous for Lenin to stay there, because Kerensky wants to arrest him. It was suggested that he should give himself up voluntarily, but he refused categorically. Stalin is also opposed to the idea. So it was decided that he should stay in hiding for the time being. They are searching for him all over the city. It's fortunate that we have a new address and that no one knows it.'

I ask Mother to tell me exactly how Lenin came to our place.

Mother had been the first to suggest that Lenin could best be hidden in our place. This was at Poletayev's flat. The Poletayevs were well known and the police could come at any moment.

'But no one knows where we live,' said Mother. 'We've only been here a couple of months.'

Mother had dropped in on the Poletayevs straight from her work at the hospital. She had not been home for a few days. So it was decided that she would first return to the flat, see how things were at home, and return to fetch Lenin. As there was no time to lose Mother came home immediately. She met Father in the entrance hall.

'Only we must be quite certain we can provide Lenin with a completely safe hiding place,' Father said after he had learned what had been discussed at the Poletayevs.

When Mother returned, Lenin was waiting for her. She told him that everything was in order at home.

'You'll be absolutely safe at our place, Vladimir Ilyich. I'm quite convinced,' she said.

Early next morning Lenin came by himself to our flat. There was such a reassuring calm and confidence about him, and he enquired about Mother's health with such touching concern, that one would have thought that a friend had dropped in for a moment. He was so charming and gay. But his first question was, 'Olga Eugenievna, please show me all the entrances and exits to your flat.'

He was taken through the kitchen to the staircase leading to the tradesmen's entrance. Then he went up to the attic and glanced inside. Returning to the flat, he again walked through all the rooms. And afterwards he sat down on the sofa, and smiling, with a wicked expression in his eyes, he looked at Mother:

'Well, now, Olga Eugenievna, I won't budge, even if you want to throw me out. I like everything about your home!' And suddenly he burst out laughing: 'You know what struck me? I remember the faces of some of my friends whom I visited in these last few days. Their faces became very long and their eyes grew round with fear. Well, I immediately turned around and left.'

'So he decided to stay at our place,' Mother said, concluding her account. 'We gave him Iosif's room. I think he'll be all right there. Iosif was here yesterday and we're expecting him at any moment now.'

Iosif Vissarionovich came to see Lenin a couple of times or so after that. They had tea in Lenin's room and talked together for a long while. Then Stalin had to go off on some urgent business. Before he left, he dropped into the kitchen, and taking Mother aside, said, 'Well, what's the situation with provisions? Is Ilyich eating? Do the best you can for him.'

When Stalin left, Mother burst out laughing. 'Lenin says exactly the same thing about Stalin. "How's Stalin eating? Please look after him, Olga Eugenievna, he seems to be losing weight . . ." '

Whatever else, Mother did not have to be told how to look after her friends when it came to meal times. She always approached Lenin's room as quietly as she could. He invariably left the door open. He would sit there at the writing table, reading and making notes, never lifting his hand from the paper which he filled page after page.

Mother would wait for a few seconds on the threshold. If

Lenin was engrossed in a book or was writing, and did not notice her, she would return some minutes later.

She would repeat her attempts to attract his attention a few times, until finally Lenin would lift his head. She would then address him quietly. But mostly Lenin would sense Mother's presence immediately. 'Olga Eugenievna, pray come in. You want to see me, my dear?' he would say in his inimitably courteous manner.

'Vladimir Ilyich, it's lunchtime,' Mother would remind him softly but decisively.

'But really, Olga Eugenievna, I'm not hungry, you shouldn't have bothered. I'll go on working. There's so much to do.'

'I'm sorry, Vladimir Ilyich, but you have to eat. I'll bring your lunch presently. Have a bite and then get on with your work.'

Mother's voice sounded most determined. She would approach the desk, and start moving the papers carefully to one side. Ilyich would look at her and smile good-naturedly. 'Is that an order?' he would ask, resigning himself.

'Absolutely,' Mother would reply delightedly and go off into the kitchen to fetch a plate with food which had already been prepared.

Mother always observed most carefully everything which Lenin did. From time to time she would peep into his room from the corridor to see if he required anything. Once she saw Lenin lift his head from his manuscript and pass his hands over his eyes with a tired, absentminded gesture.

'Is there anything you want, Vladimir Ilyich? You've been working since early morning. You really ought to have a break and lie down – you only went to bed at dawn.'

But Lenin had already taken up his pen.

'No, Olga Eugenievna, I must work . . . . I'll rest some-time later.'

Mother was very distressed because she could not vary Lenin's diet. Food was getting difficult to obtain in Petrograd. Sometimes Father would bring some additional item of food, and Stalin would bring something extra. We still had a reserve of dried peas which usually went in the preparation of soup or pease pudding. These Mother cooked as tastily as possible to feed Ilyich, our friends and anyone else who dropped in to see him or us.

Lenin was always embarrassed if anyone made a fuss of him, and he did not like to trouble Mother or to ask me for the smallest favour. And he always expressed his thanks for the most insignificant things we did for him. Whenever he interrupted his work, he always dropped in to the dining room or kitchen to have a friendly chat with Mother or me. Talking to him in ordinary domestic surroundings, it was difficult to imagine that he was hiding from great danger, and possibly even from death. He never spoke about it, or showed any fear or alarm.

Kerensky, restoring order with what loyal troops he could muster, had by now outlawed the Bolshevik Party. A warrant was issued for the arrest of its leaders – Lenin, Zinoviev and Kamenev. Kamenev – his adopted name means 'stone' – came from a middle-class family and had joined the Bolsheviks in 1903. In the early days he worked closely with Lenin, and when he, like Stalin, returned from Siberian exile in 1917, he joined the leadership of the Party as a moderate who advocated support of the provisional government. His approach to revolution was cautious and, along with his close friend Grigory Zinoviev, he urged coalition with other socialist parties once the Bolsheviks had come to power. In spite of this aberration, Kamenev was elected to the first politburo of the Bolsheviks.

Zinoviev also worked with Lenin before 1917 as a close collaborator and friend, and became a central figure in the Communist Party leadership of the 1920s. He had accompanied Lenin on his return to Russia from exile abroad but opposed him when he insisted on armed insurrection, feeling so strongly about it that in late 1917 he resigned, but was immediately reinstated.

Both Kamenev and Zinoviev believed that they should give themselves up and stand trial in order for their truth to be heard. Lenin, however, did not trust the justice of the provisional government, so he remained in hiding. When news came that Kamenev had accepted Kerensky's proposals, and that he was giving himself up, Lenin made a last-ditch attempt to dissuade him; he sent Olga Eugenievna on a mission to Kamenev to persuade him and his wife – who was Trotsky's sister – to change his mind. Trotsky had already been arrested.

'Olga Eugenievna, I should like to ask you a favour. Go to Kamenev and tell him that I insist categorically that he refuses Kerensky's proposals. Please go to him straight away.'

Mother went. She returned in a most distressed condition which she could not hide, and told me what had happened.

As she was going up the stairs to Kamenev's flat, she met Nogin [one of the two dozen original members of Lenin's first Central Committee] on the way down. He stopped Mother and said, 'I can guess who you are coming from and why, but I think nothing can be done.' He glanced upwards. 'They have already made up their minds.'

Mother went upstairs and rang the doorbell. Kamenev's wife answered, but when she heard that Mother had come from Lenin, she was startled.

'No, no, you can't see Kamenev. He's not well. If you tell me what it's about I'll pass on the message.'

Mother realised that she would not be allowed to see Kamenev; she therefore repeated what Lenin had said so insistently. Kamenev's wife replied with hostility, 'He knows what he's doing. He doesn't need any teachers.'

She then disappeared into a room. Through the half-closed door Mother could hear her convey Lenin's message, and then exclaim hysterically: 'You must never agree to it! We are in mortal danger. If you don't accept Kerensky's offer right away, we shall all perish!'

She then turned from threats to begging. Afterwards she came out and told Mother coldly that Kamenev had already accepted the provisional government's proposals as the authorities had been informed, and that he was giving himself up that day. [Kamenev was arrested along with Trotsky, but

released the following month when Kerensky relaxed his ban on the Bolsheviks, following a right-wing attempt by his own chief of staff General Kornilov to overthrow him.]
 Lenin listened to Mother's account without any indication of protest or anger. He merely shrugged his shoulders and said: 'I had almost expected as much . . .'

This news made it clear that it was unsafe for Lenin to hide with the Alliluyevs any longer, so Sergei suggested that he flee to a small town on the Gulf of Finland, Sestroretsk, just twenty miles north-west of St Petersburg; he knew it intimately, having worked there for many years. He drew up a plan for Lenin's escape route, and on 24 July Lenin left the apartment. Shortly before his departure Stalin came in and everyone gathered in Lenin's room to devise a way of disguising him.

Mother suggested bandaging Lenin's face and forehead. At first this proposal was accepted and Mother began to bandage Lenin's head with a wide gauze. But when Lenin looked at himself in the mirror he told Mother to stop.
 'No, Olga Eugenievna, don't bother. I'm more likely to attract attention with this bandage. It's not worth it.'
 The bandage was removed.
 'Wouldn't it be better if I shaved?' Lenin suggested. 'Take a look at me when I am without my beard and moustache.'
 Everyone agreed, and moment or two later Lenin sat with his face covered with soap. Iosif Vissarionovich acted as barber. Without his beard and moustache Lenin was unrecognisable.
 'And now let me try on your cap,' Lenin asked Father.
 It had previously been suggested that Lenin should wear Father's cap and coat. Lenin looked very much like a Finnish peasant with the cloth cap pulled down over his eyes and Father's overcoat sagging over his shoulders.

Stalin and Sergei escorted Lenin through the darkening streets to the Finland Station. He made his way unrecognised to Finland, where he wrote his major work *The State and Revolution*, outlining the main points of what has come to be known as Leninism. Its chief tenets are based on an efficient Party made up of the most advanced and resolute sections of working-class parties of all countries, an elite possessing 'consciousness of the imperatives of history'. Lenin's authoritarian bent underlies his distrust of spontaneity and lays stress on a rigid centralisation which he called democratic but which, having arrived at its conclusions, would then brook no discussion.

The Alliluyev flat became a point of contact for messages and secret correspondences between members of the underground movement in contact with their leader in exile. Stalin had landed the delicate task of maintaining a liaison between Lenin and the Central Committee. He was hesitant, therefore, about moving into the room which Lenin had vacated, and told Olga Eugenievna of his misgivings:

'I should very much like to move in with you,' said Iosif Vissarionovich, 'but I don't think this is the right time. The flat could be put under police observation, and you might get into trouble because of me.'

'Please don't worry about us, Iosif, we're accustomed to such things,' Mother answered. 'I'd be only too happy to have you in the flat, but if it's dangerous for you then, of course, we ought to hold things over for a bit.'

But when Iosif Vissarionovich dropped in about a week later, Mother told him decisively: 'No one seems to be keeping watch on the house. You'd better come to live with us, rest and sleep properly, and generally lead a more normal life.'

And so Iosif Vissarionovich came to stay with us.

Nadya, youngest of the Alliluyev children and only just sixteen, announced with sparkling eyes that she had become a Bolshevik. To her, Joseph Vissarionovich was a hero of the revolution.

# Chapter Seven

# A POLITICIAN IN THE FAMILY

'Beat, beat and beat again.'
— Stalin, advising an investigating judge on what methods to
use, according to Khrushchev.

'Nadya had always been very vivacious, open and spontaneous, and quite high-spirited in her early childhood,' writes Anna Sergeyevna in her reminiscences. She found her state-supported school, the gymnasium, 'gloomy, straight-laced and oppressive', and was frequently taken to task for her boisterous behaviour. Sergei was hauled in to see the headmistress.

'I don't find high spirits at all objectionable in children, Madam,' Father said, without being in the least put out, 'and my daughter's voice is naturally resonant. There is nothing I can do about it.'

Not long afterwards Nadya moved to a more liberal-minded high school, where she 'fell in love with music. She had a good ear and wanted to study the piano. We had no piano at home, but Nadya managed to get into a music school near our home and each evening she went there to practise.' When Joseph Vissarionovich came to stay in the Leningrad flat just before the October revolution he was already like one of the family. One day 'Nadya, who enjoyed domestic work and liked to keep the house spick and span, got up early and started heaving the furniture around to clean out the dining room and bedroom.

'Stalin, who must have been disturbed by all the commotion, poked his head out of his room. "What's going on here?" he asked, surprised. "What's all the noise?" Then he saw Nadya in her apron, with a brush in her hand. "Oh, it's you! A real housewife settles down to work!"

' "Is there anything wrong in that?" bristled Nadya.

' "Go right ahead. If the place has to be kept tidy, keep it tidy. Show 'em how it should be done." '

Nadya, as she developed through her teens, was becoming an increasingly ardent Bolshevik. Although surrounded by schoolmates who did not share them, 'she made no attempt to hide her convictions,' writes Anna Sergeyevna. ' "Let them know what I am",' Nadya told her sister.

We listened to what Stalin had to say and grasped the immensity of the work which was being done by the Bolsheviks. Sometimes Stalin did not come for some days. We would stay up at nights waiting for him to return, but when we finally lost all hope and went to bed, there would be a knock at the door.

'What, are you already in bed!' We would hear Stalin's voice. 'Get up, you sleepy heads! I've brought you some roach and bread.'

We would jump up, dress hurriedly and rush into the kitchen to make tea. Often we went into Iosif's room so as not to awake our parents who were sleeping in the dining room. And the atmosphere in his room immediately became carefree and noisy. Stalin would crack jokes, and caricature all the persons he had met that day, sometimes kindly, sometimes maliciously. He liked inventing nicknames for people, he had his own favourite collection of these. He would poke good-natured fun at us.

When he talked about the most serious and important matters, we could always see their funny side. His humour was sharp and colourful whether it related to people or to events.

Sometimes, during our evening tea-parties in his room, Stalin would pull out a volume of Chekhov from the swivel-bookcase by his bed. 'It would be rather nice to read something tonight. How would you like me to read you *A Chameleon?*'

He greatly admired both this and other stories by

Chekhov, and would stress all those incredibly funny remarks made by Chekhov's characters. We would shriek with laughter and ask him to read more. He would often read the works of Pushkin and Gorky to us.

Lenin, in hiding in Finland, heard word of how popular support for the provisional government was waning, and how the revolutionary mood of the people, inflamed by rampant inflation and worsening shortages, was igniting into action. Peasants had begun seizing and plundering landlords' estates, strikes were increasing in number, and workers seized control of their factories. The army began to crumble as peasant troops deserted to join their comrades in the countryside, and reserve units in the cities came under Bolshevik control.

The Bolsheviks, the party promising 'Peace, land and bread', stood ready to acknowledge these popular demands. They won control of key Soviets, including Moscow and Petrograd, at which point Lenin judged it timely to return to seize power, try to overthrow Kerensky's government and make the Soviets the official organs of power. However, many in the Party were not persuaded that force was needed, feeling that power was in the process of being won more or less democratically. Walking the middle path, Stalin played a watchful game, busying himself in the *Pravda* offices and keeping a relatively low profile amongst the differing factions: 'politically noncommittal' as Trotsky described him.

But things were not moving fast enough for Lenin's liking. He returned in secret to Petrograd on 7 October, to urge his policy of armed insurrection. On 10 October the Bolshevik Central Committee voted in principle – with only Kamenev and Zinoviev in opposition – 'to place armed insurrection on the agenda'. Kerensky now played into the Bolsheviks' hands by organising an abortive government crackdown. On the morning of 24 October he sent in troops to close the Bolshevik newspapers. In response, the Bolsheviks called out sympathetic troops to defend their Soviet, only to find that effective government troops were virtually non-existent: the opposition consisted of only a women's regiment, students, some cadets and a cycle regiment. By evening most of Petrograd was in Bolshevik hands: they had seized key positions in the capital – the stations, bank, strategic bridges and the telephone exchange. They proclaimed the overthrow of the provisional government and that night captured cabinet ministers in the Winter Palace. It was a virtually bloodless revolution, brought about as much by default and good fortune as by Lenin's single-minded leadership.

Kerensky, who later described the coup as 'the crucifixion of liberty', remained in hiding until May 1918, then emigrated to Western Europe where he lived until 1940. The war drove him to the USA, where he lived until his death in 1970.

Nadya, meanwhile, was growing up into a young woman. Early in 1918 she was running the household in the place of her mother, who had temporarily left her family 'because they are all grown up and anarchists and she couldn't have a life of her own'. Olga Eugenievna was soon however to return to look after her brood, and took over again from her efficient daughter.

Stalin, appointed Commissar for Nationalities in the first Bolshevik government, in his turn appointed Nadya his secretary. By February 1918 Nadya's emotions had reached an intensity which blinded her, in spite of her mother's warnings, to Joseph's character. She wrote to a friend that she had lost 20 lb in weight and had had to alter all her skirts. 'I've lost so much weight that people are suspecting me of being in love.' In March 1918 Lenin moved his capital to Moscow and Stalin had to find somewhere to house his ministry. He decided on the Great Siberia Hotel, and ordered Nadya to write out notices announcing that the Commissar for Nationalities had taken over the building.

Right from the outset the Bolshevik seizure of power was unpopular. Their new government, finding that it did not have the general support of the people, was driven to rule by decree. Private property was abolished, and land was redistributed to those who worked it. A decree on peace called for an immediate armistice in a war which was crippling the country's economy. This eventually materialised in 1918 in the Treaty of Brest-Litovsk, in which Lenin signed away the Baltic countries, Poland, the Ukraine, Finland and the Caucasus to German, Austrian and Turkish occupancy.

Workers' control in industry was legitimised, the banks nationalised, the old courts abolished and a workers' militia established. Class privileges and titles were thrown out, as was inheritance, and the sexes were given legal equality.

The country was now divided into 'Whites' – anticommunist Russians among whom were the officers of the old tsarist army, and 'Reds', the Bolsheviks under Trotsky's newly formed Red Army. Their power was resisted immediately in the Ukraine where nationalists and Don Cossacks established independent regimes. The allied powers of Europe supported the Whites, but in spite of this backing they could not match the advantages of the communists who had interior communications with which to harness the spirit of national resistance against foreign, 'imperialist' intervention. Gradually the Whites were beaten back in a bloody and terrible civil war which claimed seven million lives. Serious famine, another legacy of World War I, claimed a further five million. By 1920 any realistic challenge of counter-revolution was fading.

The Red Army now occupied much of the territory lost under the Treaty of Brest-Litovsk, and the atrocities which they perpetrated against their own people are only now coming to light. The new regime was fast becoming a communist dictatorship; Lenin established one-party rule from very early days, as an integral part of his doctrine of the dictatorship of the proletariat.

So unpopular were the Bolsheviks that a spate of assassinations followed the civil war, including an attempt on

Lenin's life. He responded with the Red Terror, a campaign which legitimised the murder of hostages and prisoners, and the execution of suspected enemies without trial. In order to buttress the power of his Party, Lenin banned all splits and oppositions by founding the Cheka or secret police, the 'hammer of the revolution', which chalked up 12,733 executions in its first year, 1922. With it went press censorship and the death penalty for 'acts of terror'. He ordered his colleagues to be merciless against the enemy – defined as anyone who was against the Bolsheviks. Between fifty and one hundred thousand 'political dissidents' were executed during the course of the civil war.

Lenin later wrote: 'The Cheka was our weapon against attempts on Soviet power from outside, from people who were always much stronger than ourselves. Capitalists and landowners have all manner of international contacts, they have international support, they have the support of governments who are much more powerful than us. You know how, in the history of conspiracy, these people behaved. You know that without relentless repression, not relying on the peasants, it was not possible to be answerable for them. This is the virtue of the Cheka.' Thus his first chief of secret police, Dzerzhinsky, looked at repression not as a punishment but as an integral part of the political struggle.

Son of a Polish nobleman, Feliks Edmundovich Dzerzhinsky's revolutionary career had earned him many periods of arrest and exile. He had played a part in the 1905 revolution and was a close follower of Lenin. Elected to the Bolshevik Party Central Committee in July 1917, he also played an active part in the October revolution and on 7 December 1917 was named head of the Cheka. He was to become a firm supporter of Stalin during the early 1920s, and in 1924 was elected to the politburo. In 1926, during a session of the Central Committee at which the country's economic policies were being heatedly debated, Dzerzhinsky collapsed and died. Stalin was a principal pall-bearer at his funeral.

The period of 'war communism', as it was known, was effectively rule by decree and firing squad; its hallmarks were centralisation, confiscation and coercion. The wealth of the countryside was harnessed to pay for rapid industrialisation; grain was requisitioned from the farms to feed workers in industry and to pay for the import of foreign machinery. To add to the beauty of this system, Trotsky proposed the idea of vast labour camps to build socialism. The original concept of social democracy was fast turning into something else; Lenin was putting into practice his statement that 'the state is an instrument for coercion', although on his deathbed he acknowledged it as 'a mistake'. Berdyayev wrote in 1918, in *The Fate of Russia*, an unheeded and prophetic sentence: 'A nation pays for the errors of its statesmen.'

In July 1918 Tsar Nicholas and his family were assassinated at Yekaterinburg on the eastern slopes of the Urals. The city was renamed Sverdlovsk in 1924 in honour of the assassin. This terrible shooting which all but wiped out the Romanov dynasty precipitated a mass emigration of two million intelligentsia, fleeing communist rule. Russia's social and cultural life never fully recovered from this exodus. And, as Svetlana later put it, 'in 1918 democracy was murdered in the cradle.'

Always in the arena of political struggle, the Alliluyev family now found itself drawn into the inner circle of power. For in 1918, when Nadya was still only seventeen, she and Joseph were married. Not that there was a ceremony, no legal niceties, that was not the fashion of those early revolutionary days. Their daughter Svetlana recalls, 'I don't think there was any wedding. My father was at the southern front of the civil war, and mother and Aunt Anna went to stay with him. That was all there was to it; and all the other leaders were the same.

'Father was marrying into his "second family" – the Alliluyevs were *home* to him, a haven, familiar, comfortable. He suffered from the insecurity of the revolutionary – always being chased and exiled. My father trusted the Alliluyevs; they had been his background from long ago – and underground revolutionaries can trust almost no one. There is always this insecurity in an extremist movement. But for him, the Alliluyevs were his family, and he loved them all.

'But on her side, Nadya married out of passion.' In those early days she saw her husband, at thirty-nine twenty-two years her senior, and of Georgian blood, through the eyes of a Russian adolescent idealist; in the heady days of revolution and the setting up of the world's first Marxist-Leninist communist state, he was right there at the centre of things, putting into action everything that her father had fought for and that she had been brought up to believe in. She thought.

In May 1918 Stalin was asked to take charge of grain collection in the south so, along with Nadya, an infantry detachment and two armoured cars, he travelled to Tsaritsyn, a fortress town on the Volga built in 1589 to defend newly acquired Russian territory. Stalin's brief was to organise the defence of the city in a major battle against the White armies, which he did with a characteristic, ruthless efficiency.

'My hand,' he wrote to Lenin, 'will not tremble, we shall treat our enemies as enemies.' He reorganised the police force which quickly uncovered counter-revolutionary plots: all the plotters – and their associates – were executed. Nadya was kept busy at her typewriter throughout. As a result of his success the city was renamed Stalingrad. It is now known as Volgograd. This, Nadya's first taste of marriage, was also her first experience of her husband's uncompromising use of power.

Late in 1918 Stalin was sent on a fact-finding mission to Siberia, where he salvaged a collapsing wing of Trotsky's Red Army. Throughout the civil war Stalin had quarrelled with Trotsky who became his arch enemy, in spite of Lenin's attempts to pacify them both. In 1919 Stalin was deployed to the defence of Petrograd, returning to Moscow early in July. Nadya now found herself a job in Lenin's secretariat, and the following year became pregnant with her first child, their son Vasili, who was born in March 1921.

By this time Stalin had been sent south, to the Caucasus. Here he made his mark, along with fellow-Georgian Sergo Ordzhonikidze, by putting down the independence movement in Georgia with a ferocity which appalled even Lenin. Stalin, the man who in 1918 had written, 'The revolution is incapable of either regretting or of burying its dead', launched a savage military attack on his own people in Tiflis, brutally crushing the nationalist movement. Lenin criticised him for his excessive use of violence and power, even taking into account his nationality; when Olga Eugenievna once complained to Lenin about Stalin's character, he replied, 'Well, he's an Asian: it's Asiatic ruthlessness.'

Stalin had indeed been reared in a culture of Asiatic ruthlessness; the Georgian tradition was that once you acquired an enemy you had not only to eradicate him, but to stamp on his grave. Ordzhonikidze was equally pitiless and shared his mountain-feud mentality. Sergo, as he was nicknamed, had taken part in the 1905 revolution in the Caucasus and by 1912 had earned a place on the Party Central Committee. In 1917 he was elected to the Petrograd Soviet, and after the October revolution became Commissar for the Ukraine. He was then transferred to the Caucasus to help Stalin establish Soviet government in Georgia, colluding with his brutal methods. The two remained close friends for many years.

In 1922 Stalin was appointed General Secretary of the Party, and his political ascent began in earnest. So did family life: their second child Svetlana was born in February 1926. Nadya and Joseph were well embarked along the path of parenthood.

Nadya's elder brother Pavel was also married in 1919, to Eugenia Aleksandrovna, a priest's daughter from Novgorod. She was vivacious, educated, intelligent and outspoken, an elegant woman renowned for her lively sense of humour. Anna Sergeyevna now married Stanislav Redens, a Polish Bolshevik and associate of Feliks Dzerzhinsky.

The new decade saw the birth of five of the next generation of seven Alliluyev children: in 1920 a daughter, Kyra Pavlovna, was born to Pavel and Eugenia. Kyra's brother Sergei Pavlovich was born in 1928, and Anna's first-born, Leonid Stanislavich, in 1928 also. Two more children followed in the early 1930s – Aleksandr (Sasha) Pavlovich in 1931, and Vladimir (Volodya) Stanislavich in 1935. These cousins were to get to know each other well during their childhood in the 1930s, brought up in close proximity and spending much of their free time together.

But the first tragedy of many that befell the Alliluyev family occurred in the early 1920s. Fyodor, the brightest intellect of an intelligent family, underwent a traumatic experience that permanently damaged his personality.

*Chapter Eight*

# FYODOR'S FATE

Comrade Stalin warned many times that our achievements also have a darker side.

— Pravda, 13 January 1953

Anna Sergeyevna's reminiscences of her younger brother Fyodor (Fedya) show a bright, lively boy who was as fervent a young revolutionary as any of them. At the age of six or seven, during the 1905 revolution, his mother found him climbing the strikers' barricades. As a young teenager, an ardent reader of the *Star* and later *Pravda*, he expressed deep admiration for a schoolmate who refused to go through the motions of mourning one of the Romanovs at a public memorial service.

Fedya was the most gifted student of his family, clever enough to win scholarships throughout his education, thus freeing his parents from paying school fees. Quick-witted and multi-talented, his especial gifts were in the field of maths, physics and chemistry. His brilliant results won him a place, before the revolution, in the *corps élite* of the Marine Guards, in a college for privileged officers. He became the pride of the family.

After the revolution, when civil war broke out, Fedya was seconded into the intelligence section of the Red Army, for which a rigorous SAS-style 'hit-troop' training was required. Trainees were subjected to ordeals in order to test their nerve. Fedya was sent to be toughened by a certain Semyon Arshakovich Ter-Petrosyan, known as 'Kamo', an Armenian commander of revolutionary fighting squads who had known Stalin in his Georgian days and who had been ordered by Lenin to create a special military detachment. Anna writes of him that he was the 'most beloved of Stalin's young pupils'. The family met him once when Stalin brought him to their home:

We looked with curiosity at our guest who shyly shook hands with all of us, smiling with his large, kind eyes. He was of medium height, squarely built, with smooth black hair and a pale, lustreless face. He spoke with a pronounced Caucasian accent. Stalin said, 'This is Kamo. You just listen to him – he's got plenty of interesting stories to tell you!'

So this was Kamo, hero of such legendary exploits! We did not notice the evening go by, we were so gripped by the adventures of this truly romantic revolutionary. In prison he feigned madness and fooled even the most experienced of doctors. He spent many years behind bars and organised several courageous escapes. We were touched by a story about a sparrow he had tamed in prison. Kamo spoke a lot about Stalin; he was his first teacher.

Kamo told us in great detail about his attempt to escape from the Kharkov prison where he was incarcerated when the revolution broke out. He had intended to simulate death and escape from the mortuary, but the February revolution released him from prison. We had the impression he was a trifle disappointed because he could not carry out his daring plan of escape.

Kamo's legendary fame was based on his robbery of a Tiflis bank in 1907 when he 'expropriated' more than a quarter of a million roubles for Bolshevik funds. He was sentenced to death four times but finally, having worked for the Cheka and the Red Army after the revolution, died in a car accident in 1922.

Kamo played out a grisly charade in front of the younger Alliluyev son: on the pretext of getting Fedya and his father Sergei Yakovlevich to deliver some money, he staged Fedya's capture by White Army troops and told him that he would be shot, along with the rest of his corps who had also been taken, unless he changed his allegiance to the enemy. He was led to a place where a body was lying covered in blood with its heart gouged out. 'Here is the heart of your commander,' they said, handing it to him.

Then they told him it was all a joke and roared with laughter.

Sergei Yakovlevich stood firm but Fedya never recovered. Only recently over an attack of typhus, according to his nephew Volodya, it left him psychologically damaged for the rest of his life. His niece Svetlana described how 'he sat in silence for a number of years, in hospital, not able to talk. He was in a total state of shock. Slowly his speech came back, and he became a human being again. But he was completely devastated, he was a sick man for the rest of his life.'

This episode is reminiscent of a grotesque farce experienced by Dostoevski when he was imprisoned for dissident activities. He was sentenced to death and led with a group of fellow-prisoners to public execution. The death sentence was read out, they were given a cross to kiss and ordered to put on white shirts. The first three men were bound to the execution posts: Dostoevski's turn was due in the second batch. Suddenly a messenger appeared on horseback to announce that the Tsar had graciously decided to grant a reprieve. The drums rolled, a retreat was sounded and the bound men were untied. Some of the prisoners fainted, two went permanently insane, and Dostoevski's epileptic fits from which he had suffered from childhood grew immeasurably worse from then on.

Fedya's elder niece Kyra has memories of 'his strange behaviour: he would suddenly explode over something. Other times he would sit and never leave. Yet he remembered his French well and he used to sing *chansons* with me, and sometimes he helped me with my maths lessons.'

For a while Fedya lived with his father, now living apart from Olga Eugenievna. Then he went to live with his mother, then 'he married a pretty Russian woman,' says

Kyra, 'but they had no children.' From the early thirties onwards they lived in the famous 'House on the Embankment'. This huge, grey block, the first Soviet high-rise, stands on the south bank of the Moskva river diagonally across from the Kremlin. Its foundation stone was laid in the year of Stalin's fiftieth birthday, 1929, and the building was completed in 1931.

The idea was to bring under one roof Lenin's closest comrades and members of his government, until then scattered all over Moscow. Old-time revolutionaries, more accustomed to prison and exile than to five-roomed apartments, got their first taste of Soviet privilege. The House incorporated a post office with telegraph, a pharmacy, movie theatre, department store, hairdresser and even an indoor tennis court. The servants' apartments, no less, were in the basement; 'house-workers' was their official denomination, because a servants' class was, in communist theory, nonexistent.

On staircase 12 lived nearly all Stalin's politburo – Molotov, Voroshilov, Ordzhonikidze, Kaganovich and, for a short while, Beria. The House welcomed actors, writers, dancers and even the head of the Red Army choir. Long black stretch-limos, Soviet ZILS, were soon to be seen in the courtyard, their chauffeurs employed to drive the children of the House to school.

As the Stalin cult grew, so did its privileges, and so, inevitably, did envy. The House nurtured a sense of hierarchy curiously at odds with Marxist-Leninist theory. Comradely love took second place to self-interest and self-gratification, as did theory to practice. With good food in their bellies, and better facilities for their children, the inmates of the House on the Embankment were insulated – until the Great Terror of the late thirties – from the troubles in the country; news of famine, starvation and the labour camps did not filter through the velvet curtains of elitism.

Fedya and his wife lived here, on his pension, in their own apartment and close to other members of the family.

But, recalls Svetlana, 'he even ate in a very messy way – he couldn't feed himself, the food fell from his hand and his clothes were always dirty, so he had to be looked after all the time. He was broken: they ruined him.

'But the intellect remained a little: he would read and write quite a lot, so evidently this portion of his brain was still working. He was a gentle person, like all of them, but he wasn't handsome like all the other Alliluyevs – although he did have their beautiful brown velvety eyes with long straight eyelashes.'

His nephew Sergei Pavlovich knew him well. 'I loved him very much, I respected him and he taught me many things. He was slightly mentally ill, in that he permitted himself to do what others do not, and often such people are liked, they meet with sympathy. He heard a word in an American film which described this kind of person – 'pig-silly' – and he kept on repeating it, delighted with it. He was a bit out of order, but in a pleasant way.'

Anna's sons, who also lived in the building for many years, remember him well. Volodya says, 'He had some strange ways, but I regarded him as a normal human being. He was given a pension because of his handicap, and he lived on this. He was always ill, although things improved a little as he got older. His wife is still alive, but suffering from senile dementia.' Leonid, Volodya's elder brother, speaks of 'his internal torment, as if his experiences in the army meant that he could not stand what was going on in the world.'

There is a faded picture of Uncle Fedya in Sergei Pavlovich's photograph album, standing behind other family members and only just discernible. It is a picture of a slight, thinnish man with a bald head and a moustache, wearing a vaguely amiable expression. Fedya died aged fifty-seven in 1955, of a heart attack. He is buried in the Novedevichy Cemetery in Moscow, alongside his parents.

*Chapter Nine*

# EARLY DAYS OF MARRIAGE

Reliable, detailed first-hand accounts of Stalin's domestic background are few.

*— Encyclopaedia Britannica*

As Nadya's husband now moved in the inner circle of government, the couple lived relatively well: they had a town apartment in the Kremlin, albeit consisting of two rooms in former servants' quarters, with some of the original furniture, a worn floor and small windows. They made up for this with a country house, a dacha just outside Moscow, where they spent most weekends. Zubalovo was named after an oil magnate who had owned refineries in Batumi and Baku. 'It was the former estate of the millionaire Zubalov,' Kyra Pavlovna reminisces, 'a large, two-storey house surrounded by large gardens. I remember guinea-fowl and peacocks walking around.' Stalin, indulging his famous enthusiasm for architecture, transformed its gothic gloom into a modern, sunlit mansion. 'Large, good rooms and a long corridor leading to the kitchen, so that smells from the kitchen would never reach the house itself; that was a luxury typical of a landlord's estate, not to be annoyed by the smells and noises from the kitchen.'

Stalin also ordered the clearing and maintenance of woodland close around the house, to let more light in. He ran the estate with livestock, beehives, kitchen gardens, orchards and a well-tended birch grove. By any standards the Stalins lived the life of a comfortable upper-middle-class family, an anomaly in social-democratic terms, and one which did not escape Nadya. 'We had an established pattern of holidays,' says Svetlana. 'At weekends we were taken to the dacha – winter or summer, every year until the war. Summers we spent partly near Moscow in the classic Russian setting of Zubalovo, and also a month or so at Sochi on the Black Sea. When I was small my father came too – it was a family holiday.'

Photographs from the Alliluyev family collection taken in the 1920s show Stalin looking relaxed, happy, handsome. 'He had found security, friendship and support in the Alliluyev family,' says his daughter. In a country devastated by a world war and a civil war it was a life of relative luxury and privilege. Svetlana describes her childhood as 'a sheltered existence which gave me an idealistic view of the world.'

She recalls happy childhood days at Zubalovo. 'There were huge lilacs near the dacha, white, violet, and dark purple. There was an alley of white jasmine; inhaling the fragrances – this is my childhood. Going for walks in the woods with Mother, or Aunt Anna and my cousins, finding wild strawberries, wild raspberries, blueberries. In my early memory Mother was very beautiful. She was young and had a natural grace, and a melodious voice which was low and pleasant. One day we were walking in the country through the woods, and I was sent to walk in front. Mother was walking behind with her sister Anna and they were talking, and I remember how their voices were very alike. We would go to gather mushrooms – and the fragrance of those mushrooms! They were brown, orange, yellow, red – Tolstoy describes mushroom-picking in the classic Russian way, and the memory of it stays with you all your life even if you only do it once.

'There were orchards and a kitchen garden with red and white raspberries, red and white currants, cherries, apples, and all variety of vegetables which grew abundantly. Summer time was wonderful at Zubalovo. We had rabbits, chickens, trips to the river, and outings to the forest gathering nuts. We would pick flowers and make herbariums. The beauty of nature around us was all geared to some kind of knowledge and education.'

But the privilege of office worried Nadya right from the beginning: she disliked the position of First Lady. 'She had some friends from her school days,' recalls her daughter, 'but they were not eligible to visit her in the Kremlin. She would see them somewhere else. We didn't even know who they were, and when she died they didn't even come to see the family. But it was known that she had her circle of more understanding friends somewhere out there.' These were the people who kept her in touch with the lives of ordinary people.

Many of these friends didn't even know that she was First Lady – she kept her two lives quite separate when she enrolled at the Industrial Academy to study textiles and synthetic fibres, and insisted on travelling to work on public transport. It was at the Academy that she first met Nikita Krushchev, who was Party Secretary there. Later he attributed his successful political rise, and survival, to the fact that Nadya spoke well of him to Stalin.

Nadya believed passionately in education: for her children, for society, for herself. 'She studied a lot, and took the education of her children very seriously,' recalls Kyra. Stalin dismissed such women as 'herrings with ideas'. But Nadya belonged to a generation of women who were acquiring a taste for emancipation; she never, for example, took her husband's surname, preferring to use her maiden name of Alliluyeva. She and others like her were uncompromising in their idealism, and quite severe in their manner. Tokaev, in his *Betrayal of an Ideal*, writes that she made many friends and no enemies: 'Nadya Alliluyeva was an outstanding personality. Among the Kremlin womenfolk there were many who put on airs, but she was always simple. Her every gesture was unassuming, there was never anything strained or forced about her; she was always the soul of frankness and honesty.'

'She was loved by the people who were close to us,'

continues Svetlana, 'members of the politburo like Voroshilov, Kaganovich, Molotov, Ordzhonikidze,' all of whom were long-standing comrades-in-arms of Stalin. Ordzhonikidze had been a close friend since Georgian days, and a Bolshevik since 1903. From 1921 he served on the Central Committee of the Communist Party and gained notoriety for his high-handed dealings with the nationalities issues. He became one of Stalin's closest associates in the politburo, and a carousing companion at the legendary dinners over which they all met to discuss government business, and which would invariably end with the singing of rowdy songs. In the style of a Georgian chieftain, Ordzhonikidze liked to parade through his capital city on a white stallion presented to him by a mountain tribe, a flamboyance that appalled Lenin.

Ideologically committed to the development of the USSR as a modern industrial power, Ordzhonikidze became, in 1932, Commissar for Heavy Industry. Svetlana remembers him as 'very loud and warm and Georgian. He loved to have me on his lap when I was a girl. They were all very fond of my mother, and I reaped this love.'

Voroshilov, Stalin's favourite general, had met his future boss while commanding the Tenth Army at Tsaritsyn in 1918. He was to play an important part in Stalin's rise to power, and managed to outlive him by many years. Kaganovich, of humble Jewish origin, was a Party organisation man who became one of Stalin's chief henchmen and held high office until the late 1940s. He died in 1991 at the age of ninety-eight. Molotov, a Bolshevik since 1906, ascended the ladder as Stalin's lieutenant until he was effectively his deputy. From 1926 onwards he was a member of the politburo, and purged the Moscow Party Committee of anti-Stalin membership. His reward was to become prime minister through the thirties, and deputy chairman of the Party until 1947, second in power only to his leader. He was best known in the West for his work as foreign minister after World War II, being the major spokesman at international conferences. He also served under Khrushchev until the two men fell out over de-Stalinisation.

There were other frequent, famous visitors to Zubalovo. Abel Yenukidze was one; a close friend of Stalin's from early days, he was a member of the first Georgian Bolshevik Committee formed by his friend, and held high positions in government after the revolution. According to Trotsky, in his biography of Stalin, Yenukidze had his suspicions about Stalin's pretensions even in those early days, which quite possibly sealed his fate: 'I am doing everything he has asked me to do, but it is not enough for him. He wants me to admit that he is a genius.' Nevertheless, as Nadya's godfather, he loved both her and Svetlana dearly. 'These Georgian people were big and fat and loud and sunny. When I see Italians I see the same nature: they love children, love their mothers, love their elderly people, love good food and drink, and there is a lot of noise around.'

During 1922–3 Lenin became ill, suffering a series of strokes which rendered him incapacitated. Stalin was creating for himself a strong position in the Party organisation, building a power base within by promoting those on whom he could rely for support. Lenin became worried: 'He has unlimited authority and I am not convinced that he will use it properly. He is too rude . . . A way should be found to remove him.'

But this was written in 1922, in papers that remained unpublished for long afterwards; his warning was not publicised and Stalin took care that it should not be. He allied himself with Zinoviev and Kamenev against Trotsky, and after Lenin's death in 1924 cleverly out-manoeuvred his chief opponent, Trotsky, who was eventually expelled and finally exiled. His attention then turned to those politburo members whose authority now threatened his power: Zinoviev, Kamenev, Kirov and Bukharin.

Towards the end of the decade Bukharin and Kirov both became regular weekend guests at the dacha, and even visited the family on holiday at the Black Sea. Bukharin was aware of Stalin's machinations, only thinly disguised by friendship. In 1928 he said to Kirov, 'He will strangle us. He is an unprincipled intriguer who subordinates everything to his appetite for power. At any given moment he will change his theories to get rid of someone.' He perceived that Stalin was unhappy at not being able to convince everyone, 'himself included', that he was greater than everyone. But Bukharin was preaching to the converted; Kirov had already described Stalin as 'sly, revengeful and obsessed with vanity and lust for power'.

Bukharin had joined the RSDWP in 1906 as party organiser and propagandist and had worked with Lenin on early editions of *Pravda*, whose editorship he assumed after the October revolution. He made his views known within Party circles, disagreeing with the Treaty of Brest-Litovsk whose terms bought Russia a costly peace in World War I. Bukharin, at that point, wanted to transform the war into a general European revolution, rather than selling out for peace.

After Lenin's death he opposed the policy of rapid industrialisation and collectivisation in agriculture, supporting Lenin's New Economic Policy and thus allying himself with Stalin who at this time was using these issues to undermine Zinoviev, Kamenev and Trotsky. In 1928 Stalin reversed his views, espousing collectivisation and industrialisation, and denounced Bukharin for opposing it. Bukharin was expelled from the politburo in 1929, and although appointed editor of *Izvestia*, the official government newspaper, in 1934, he never regained his previous power or influence – nor his erstwhile close friendship with Stalin.

'All of these people could talk openly with my father, they all had a natural relationship – unlike the later people like Malenkov and Beria. They all stayed with us in our home – it used to be open house. Molotov, Zhdanov, all of them were very nice to me, asking me how school was going – and I was good at school so we had friendly little talks,

*83*

especially the old ones like Kaganovich, Molotov, Voroshilov, who had known my mother well. They had a particular
tenderness towards me and my brother, because of her,
because she was so greatly loved.'

Nadya was indeed the pivot around which all this hinged.
'They adored her, there is no other word for it. Nadya was
adored as a creature who was good-looking, young, who was
good to everyone, a jolly character who had a great sense of
humour. There was something about her which made her
the centre of things. She had exotic features from her gypsy
ancestry, a streak that came from my grandfather Sergei. It
was a look that was not strictly Russian. She had a lovely
profile, a classic look.'

For Svetlana 'childhood was a very happy, warm time.
Everybody loved me – there was an abundance of love.
Childhood was a paradise, like an enchanted island. My
mother *was* my childhood, for the years that she was alive.
Everything in the home was organised by her; it was her
"rule" and Father didn't interfere – he just came home late
in the evening for dinner with his political colleagues. We
had our own life there which was all done by her, very
organised, with Nanny, and cooks, and maids, my governess
and my brother's teacher. She didn't give me her full time,
there were others to do that: to feed me, wash me, dress me.
It was "Victorian", shall I say.

'She was not alone in this – the ladies of her circle, upper
government members, were all working – they were not at
home playing happy housewives, they were doing important
jobs. My mother was studying at the Industrial Academy
and she wanted to become a textile engineer.

'She was very fond of my brother, he was her favourite
and everyone knew that, so I don't remember her being
physically affectionate with me. I was a quiet child, obedi-
ent, I did everything right . . . But she wanted perfection
from me, so she was always telling me that I didn't behave
well. But she certainly loved me; there were those wonderful
days in the country. It was just that she was afraid to be too

Sergei Yakovlevich Alliluyev, 1866-1946. *(Alliluyev Family Collection)*

Olga Eugenievna Alliluyeva *(centre, front)* with *(from left to right)* Pavel, Fyodor, Nadya and Anna in the early 1900s. *(Alliluyev Family Collection)*

Olga Eugenievna Alliluyeva, 1877-1951. *(Alliluyev Family Collection)*

Nadezhda (Nadya) Sergeyevna Alliluyeva in her early teens, taken on a trip to Finland. *(Alliluyev Family Collection)*

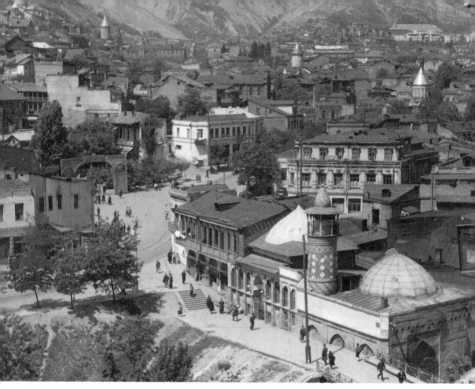

Tiflis, now Tblisi, capital city of Georgia. *(Society for Cooperation in Russian & Soviet Studies)*

The house in Tiflis (Tblisi) where Stalin conducted a Worker's Circle in 1898. *(Society for Cooperation in Russian & Soviet Studies)*

The house in Batumi used by members of the underground movement, including Stalin, in the early 1900s. *(Society for Cooperation in Russian & Soviet Studies)*

Baku in 1919. *(Hulton-Deutsch Collection)*

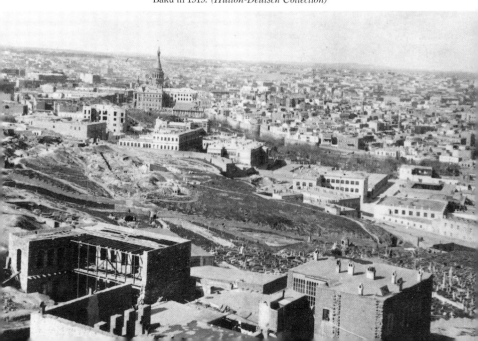

Yekaterina Svanidze, Stalin's first wife, who died in 1908 after their son Yakov was born. *(Alliluyev Family Collection)*

*(Left to right)* Stalin, Lenin and Kalinin at the 8th Party Congress in March 1919. *(David King Collection)*

Vladimir Ilyich Lenin (1870-1924), seen here reading an issue of *Pravda* in 1920. *(David King Collection)*

Lenin addressing revolutionary allies in Moscow, 1920. Leon Trotsky and Lev Kamenev can be seen to the right of the platform. *(Society for Cooperation in Russian & Soviet Studies)*

Lev Borisovich Kamenev, 1883-1936. *(David King Collection)*

Grigory Yevseyevich Zinoviev, 1883-1936. *(David King Collection)*

Kamenev *(left)* and Zinoviev at the Marx-Engels monument in Moscow. *(David King Collection)*

*Above:* Stalin at his desk, *c.*1935. *(David King Collection)*

*Right:* Leon Trotsky, 1879-1940. *(David King Collection)*

Feliks Edmundovich Dzerzhinsky (1877-1926), the first head of Lenin's secret police, the Cheka. *(Society for Cooperation in Russian & Soviet Studies)*

Stalin relaxing at his dacha with Dzerzhinsky. *(David King Collection)*

Kliment Yefremovich Voroshilov (1881-1969), close friend and collaborator of Stalin. *(David King Collection)*

Voroshilov (*right*) and Budenny in 1922. *(David King Collection)*

Stalin with his young wife Nadya, relaxing over a picnic with friends in the early 1920s. *(David King Collection)*

Portrait of Nadya Alliluyeva taken in her mid-twenties. *(Alliluyev Family Collection)*

Nadya with her sister Anna in the mid-1920s. *(David King Collection)*

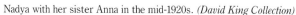

Kaganovich at the wheel, *c*.1930. *(David King Collection)*

Stalin and Voroshilov sharing a joke, 1940. *(Society for Cooperation in Russian & Soviet Studies)*

*Back row, left to right*: Yenukidze, Voroshilov, Kaganovich, Kuibyshev. *Front row, left to right*: Ordzhonikidze, Stalin, Molotov, Kirov. (1934) *(David King Collection)*

Molotov addressing a meeting at the Red October Factory in Moscow, *c*.1929. *(David King Collection)*

Lazar Moiseyevich Kaganovich *(left)* (1893–1991), loyal henchman of Stalin who outlived him the longest, with his brothers, 1925. *(David King Collection)*

Vyacheslav Mikhaylovich Molotov (1890–1986), staunch supporter of Stalin, diplomat, prime minister and foreign minister during World War II. *(David King Collection)*

Abel Yenukidze, one of Lenin's Party workers and a close friend of Nadya Alliluyeva. Godfather to Svetlana, he 'disappeared' in 1936. *(David King Collection)*

Portrait of Nadya Alliluyeva as a young woman. *(Alliluyev Family Collection)*

Nikolai Ivanovich Bukharin (1888–1938), economist and member of the Politburo 1924–9. He was executed in 1938. *(David King Collection)*

Stalin *(right)* relaxing on holiday with Abel Yenukidze by the Black Sea. *c.*1930. *(David King Collection)*

Sergei Mironovich Kirov (1886-1934), member of the Politburo and thought by some to rival Stalin's power. *(David King Collection)*

Kirov addressing the 17th Party Congress, January 1934. *(David King Collection)*

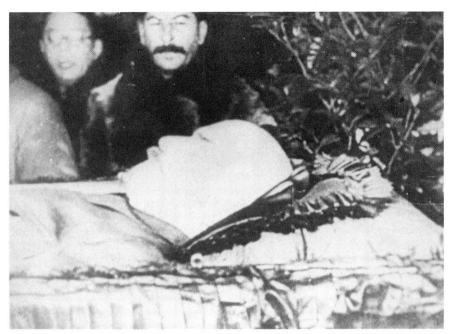

Lenin lying in state in his open coffin in January 1924 (Stalin looks on), before being embalmed and placed on display in the mausoleum in Red Square, Moscow, where he still lies.
*(David King Collection)*

Stalin with Kirov, 1926. A subsequent copy of this photo appears in publications after 1934 with Kirov obliterated. *(Society for Cooperation in Russian & Soviet Studies)*

*(Left to right)* Molotov, Kaganovich, Stalin and Ordzhonikidze bearing the urn containing Gorky's ashes from the House of Trade Unions. *(Society for Cooperation in Russian & Soviet Studies)*

*Above left:* Nadya Alliluyeva in profile, mid-1920s. *(Alliluyev Family Collection)*

*Above right:* Nadya with baby Svetlana, *c*.1927. *(Alliluyev Family Collection)*

Kirov (*left*) with his friend Ordzhonikidze. *(David King Collection)*

soft on me, she didn't like the idea of spoiled children. I was my father's favourite; he was sterner and more demanding with his sons, but I was a little pet to play with – which meant that my mother wouldn't spoil me – I had enough from him!

'She wanted it all to be perfect. She organised beautiful holidays for us children, and birthdays where we all put on a big performance. I remember these gatherings going on until the early thirties – everybody was there and it was cheerful and gay and funny and everyone laughed and brought their news. It was very normal and very human. It was our family milieu and my father loved it.

'We recited poetry in German, in Russian, and did dancing and singing; it was a big show and she was the soul of all this. I know that she wanted to launch me into the arts; we had lessons in music, dance and eurythmy, painting, drawing and modelling. She had high expectations. She believed that art helps people to heal and develop, which is why we were taught these things so early. She was very wise. My father had tremendous respect for her, and there was love between them.'

Yet Kyra remembers her as 'always very serious and reserved. I was shy in front of her, and even frightened because I thought she was annoyed by my gaiety. She liked everything to be quiet and orderly. They say that her character had changed because of her marriage, that she used to be a very cheerful and playful young girl. Perhaps she was preoccupied with her own burdens, she was moody, or just tired perhaps. But she possessed no light-mindedness, she never showed any frivolity. My mother criticised her for studying too much, for working instead of staying at home with the children, for giving them both a governess and a nanny – she brought up her own children.'

Kyra wasn't the only one to be slightly overawed by Nadya's powerful presence. Eugenia Aleksandrovna, Kyra's mother, told Svetlana in later years how 'as soon as Uncle Pavel brought her into the family she got on very easily with her father. But she was afraid of Nadya, because of her discipline.' And she went on to talk about the relationship between Nadya and Joseph. ' "Your mother loved your father with such an obsession that I was afraid to see it. There was something frightful about it. It shouldn't be like that." Nadya idealised him, so he was never, to her, a real man, he was an "exaggeration". She was sensitive and serious, she was also too young to understand him. Stalin for his part was not sensitive – he was simple, a strong man of action who needed the company of his peers. Aunt Eugenia understood his character, and he loved her jokes and anecdotes and mimicry. She was *fun* – a rare commodity in the Kremlin in the 1920s and 30s.

' "Your mother was jealous of him; not only was he very busy with politics, but he said once in passing that he liked a particular singer at the opera. He had a good ear and liked to go regularly. Nadya had a fit of jealousy and everybody knew about it; she couldn't stand it if a word was said about another woman. She had this burning passion, which dated from her childhood, from when she was sixteen and met the hero from Siberian exile. She couldn't cope with it: it was too much for her."

'But,' Svetlana adds, 'my mother was not a fool. She was very young; she fell in love, and they lived together for fourteen years. There were happy moments to remember, and my father was absolutely loyal to her. He was not a ladies' man, he was never chasing women. To say that a singer was good and that he liked her voice was enough to make her jealous. But there was never anything more than that.

'She felt very strongly about things. She argued with him, raising her voice, and he didn't like that. But she was quite independent with her pronouncements about the way she was bringing up the children. She did it her way, guided by anthroposophists from Steiner schools.

'I still have a great admiration for her. My aunts Eugenia and Anna talked to me more and more in the later years, about what a good mother she was, what a wonderful hostess,' says Svetlana. 'Even though she was so much younger than my father, she could entertain all different types of people. She kept everything together. They said what a happy house it was when she was there, the children were happy because they were around her, and this happy family went here, there and everywhere. It was not so closely guarded as it later became – she watched very carefully that bodyguards and security were kept at a distance. "They are not members of the family, and they should not be meddling here!" '

This strong sense of organisation coloured Svetlana's early years, leaving her with clear memories of the most stable period of her life. Central to this stability was the presence in their midst of a simple Russian woman with a heart of gold.

## Chapter Ten

# A GLIMPSE OF CHILDHOOD

Ideology is fiction that doesn't realise it's fiction.

— Mario Vargas Llosa

When Svetlana was four weeks old Nadya employed a nanny, Aleksandra Bychkova, who remained one of the family until her death in 1958 at the age of seventy. Svetlana remembers nothing but good of her. 'All my memories of Nanny are very sweet; how she fed me, and how she gave me my bath when I was tiny. At Zubalovo there was a metal bath, like a big bucket, and I remember sitting in it when I was three years old, while she poured water from the pitcher. She had these nice, fat, kind hands. The water was heated over firewood and you could see the flames heating the copper – it was lovely and warm. It was always Nanny, because Mother was too busy somewhere else. She would wrap me up in a big towel, cut my toenails, dry my hair, clean out my ears.

'One of her jobs was to read to me, which she did very well. There was a story about a little monkey who was brought from her native Africa by a sailor on a boat to a cold northern country, and finally it ended up in a cage in the zoo. She read it over and over again, and I sobbed my heart out every time. She was great at fairy tales, too – she knew Russian ones, and Grimms, off by heart, and she told them beautifully.

'Nanny was my guardian angel. She was with me for thirty years, and she was the one and only stable person who was always there for me. In a way she was a mother-figure – although my mother could never be replaced. She was extraordinary: she had kindness and humour, a childlike nature – and she was always there. I do not know what I would be without her.

'There was one full day I remember being with my mother – it must have been at a weekend because Nanny had gone somewhere and Mother replaced her. It was unusual – and rather disturbing because all she was doing was *cleaning* everything! Cleaning the bathtub, which stood on four legs, reaching underneath it which I had never seen anyone do before. She was possessed by some sort of obsession for making everything clean, so all I saw of her, apart from her feeding me, was cleaning and scrubbing.

'Nanny was the kind of person for whom nothing was hard: she accepted things. My parents were the Law: she was well-trained, and never argued. She had been living with families since she was twelve, as a maid or kitchen help. Later on she got fatter and fatter – she had a big round face with dimples and by the end of her life she looked like a Buddha figure – with a huge belly, full of smiles. She had no enemies, everybody loved her and she occupied her legitimate place; nobody was allowed to replace her. She had an incredible personality; how she didn't lose her mind in our home I don't know!

'When we were children, Grandmother was "out" – she was old, she was not understanding. The children were not being brought up in the right way, she thought, because we had governesses and teachers, and were learning foreign languages like German from the age of four. My mother forced our education, very much so. I think she was right, but Grandmother had never had anything like that in her life, and she thought that all the discipline and being made to read and write and learn languages was a form of torture.

'So my mother just banned her from coming – this is what my nanny told me in later years. Thus Grandma Olga would appear very seldom, and sit there silently, looking on with obvious disapproval. She developed a gesture: she would open her mouth to say something, then put her hand over her lips and say, "Oh, no! I'm saying nothing! I'm saying nothing!" very humbly. And that obviously suited my mother – "Don't tell the children to do this and that – don't *flap*."

'As a child I was kept strictly away from religions. Nanny never uttered a word – she knew that it was not her place to talk about it. She had her faith, and lived her life as a perfect Christian, but she wasn't at all "churchy". Her faith was in her attitude to people: she had no enemies, and she loved everyone.

'Grandma was more independent and she would talk about God. We children would ridicule her and say, "Where is God, then, show us." She would become very angry with us, she thought we were being brought up in a terrible modern way which was not right, and that basic truths were not being explained to us.

'My brother Vasili was five years older than I, and he liked to destroy things. He would take my dolls, or pull up the flowers we had planted. We didn't get on at all; five years difference in age means you are in two different worlds. He despised me, he always tried to dictate to me: "Don't play with dolls, you should read books, you should play *my* game. . ." and he threw them out. But these were the only bad things that happened to me! I had four cousins who were boys too, so I ended up with the electric trains! I was always a tomboy because I had boys around me. Vasili was bossy, and we were not very close; we had different interests and were kept apart so that he had boys around him, with their interests. He was mischievous, whereas I was rather quiet and stayed in the background.

'My mother adored my brother, and he was terrified of Father. She knew that he had delicate nerves, and that he needed a lot of special attention with special teachers. She saw trouble ahead.'

Kyra was the nearest to Vasili in age: 'Vasili and I were always on good terms. For some reason he liked me, although we fought and quarrelled like equals in our childhood. I would answer him back, and that gave him a certain

*90*

respect for me. He was a complicated character; we never knew what he might do next. He had sudden changes of mood, which is true of all the Alliluyevs; a kind of instability – sudden anger, but the next moment total kindness again.' Aleksandr Pavlovich, whom everyone calls Sasha, remembers that 'Vasili was in general given to doing strange things, and he was cruel to animals.'

Kyra continues, 'He was very musical, although he never learned anything properly. I had a good ear too, and sang easily, an ability which attracts people. And he was proud of that and liked to show me off to people, because we were both very sociable.'


Nadya was struggling on with family life in spite of her personal conflict and unhappiness. But by the mid 1920s the marriage was deteriorating visibly. She told friends that she felt like a prisoner being married to Stalin. Just after Svetlana was born in 1926, Nadya had packed her bags and left for Leningrad to live with her father, intending to leave Stalin for good, but he had persuaded her back. However, subsequent angry rows between them were not infrequent, and Nadya would give as good as she got. 'She had a lot to put up with from my father,' says their daughter.

'She was very fond of my half-brother Yakov, who was only six years younger than she was. From his pictures you can see that he was special.' Yakov was Stalin's son by his first marriage to Yekaterina Svanidze, given a biblical name, Jacob, to match his father's Joseph. He was known to the family as Yasha. Yekaterina had died when he was a tiny baby, and, says Svetlana, 'there is a picture of her lying in her coffin which shows how beautiful she was, with a serene beauty which people who knew her testified to. She had a quiet nature, and my father was evidently very fond of her. It is often quoted that he said when she died, "She melted my heart: with her die my last feelings for people." She probably couldn't melt his heart, actually,' adds his daughter knowingly.

'Yasha had her quiet temperament, unlike his father and not at all like Vasili who was volatile. He was very fond of me, and was always fighting with Vasili because he disliked the things my brother said to me – he often used bad language and Yasha would fight him for that. He was not good to Yasha – he was not a kind brother.'

Yasha had been brought up in Tiflis by his dead mother's brother Aleksandr Svanidze and his wife Maria. Aleksandr – Uncle Alyosha as he was known by the family – insisted that they bring Yasha to Moscow to finish his education in the early 1920s, but, in Svetlana's words, 'that was the beginning of his troubles. He was a Georgian boy – he should have been left in Georgia . . . because he belonged there. He was fond of me, and acted the kind protective elder brother. I remember him as very tender and very pleasant.

'But he had trouble learning Russian, and Father took one look at him and said, "Oh, he is not very bright, he doesn't pick things up quickly." ' It was clear to Pavel's son Sasha that 'Stalin, just as much as he liked Svetlana . . . disliked his sons. We all knew this, it was a very obvious fact.'

Svetlana continues: 'Yasha graduated in electrical engineering at the electric power station, a peaceful occupation which didn't quite fit his father's idea of what a man should do.' Yasha disliked his father's dogmatism as much as Stalin disliked his son's lack of obedience.

Sasha remembers how 'their relationship was very strained. I always feel something like pain when I think of Yasha. Somehow he never looked like a part of the family, ever. My parents and grandfather were at their best with him, but one could always feel that his own father disliked him. This coldness would take various forms. He liked to make fun of him, and Vasili was also not kind to him.

'Stalin did have a very difficult relationship with Yasha and it was clearly causing grief to the family. Their characters didn't match at all. But to us children Yasha and Vasili were already adults: Vasili was not an attractive character: he was an unkind man, he was cruel to animals, cruel to the people close to him – and this may be connected to the fact that his father didn't love him enough, that he was never shown any affection.' Svetlana concurs: 'All the love Father had was for me, and he told me that it was because I looked like his mother. My brothers didn't receive any of this lovingness; you weren't supposed to show such things towards boys. Boys have to grow up and become warriors – which Vasili and Yasha did, simply to please him. But they were not really warriors at all, either of them, it didn't fit them. They were brought up very strictly.'

Nadya defended Yasha and took his part, and a bond developed between them that Stalin resented. She also made sure that Uncle Alyosha and Aunt Maroussya were regular visitors to Zubalovo. More trouble arose, however, when at a very young age Yasha embarked on what his father regarded as an unsuitable marriage; he fell in love with Zoya when they were both students. But this first marriage didn't please Stalin, who said that he didn't like Zoya's social behaviour, nor the fact that she was a priest's daughter. His rough interference was enough to undermine the relationship, and he effectively forced Yasha to break up with Zoya because he had married against his father's wishes. To add tragedy to these difficulties, the young couple's baby daughter died. The sequence of events culminated with Yasha attempting suicide in 1929, when he was still in his early twenties. 'He shot himself in our kitchen,' as Svetlana recalls. 'He wounded himself severely and spent many months recovering. My mother was terribly shocked by this, but my father only laughed. "Ha!" he said, "Missed! Couldn't even shoot straight!" I suppose you call this military humour; at any rate it was recorded in the family as one of his jokes.

'Georgians have this attitude towards their sons in particular,' explains Svetlana. 'Sons have to be perfect, they have to be warriors, to be brave, to show a good example. This quiet, shy young man obviously just wanted to live quietly and do his work, but that was not the ideal, that was a disappointment to his father. Yasha knew perfectly well that he was a disappointment and it was hard on him.'

As soon as he was well enough to travel, Yasha went to Leningrad to recover, to be looked after by his step-grandfather Sergei Yakovlevich, and he lived there until the mid-1930s.

The Svanidzes became very much a part of the extended family life of the Alliluyevs during the twenties and early thirties. 'I remember the Svanidzes well,' says Sasha. 'Maria Onissimovna was a singer, a very beautiful woman, and together with my mother they would arrange children's parties with celebrations and performances that were the brightest impressions of our childhood. She and Uncle Alyosha were very Georgian, very lively. He was a short, stocky man, blond and blue-eyed, with a small moustache, very firm, very energetic – not the typical Georgian with a big nose. He walked with a cane, and once he brought us a snake wrapped around it! He was jolly, temperamental, and he could be aggressive. The family was very close-knit and strong. They had two sons, the older one Tolya from her first marriage, who was already adult, and the younger one Johnik, named after John Reed.' Reed was an American communist journalist who went to Russia in 1917 and wrote an eye-witness account of the October revolution – *Ten Days that Shook the World*. He is the only non-Russian to be buried in the Kremlin Wall.

Kyra remembers how 'We used to meet at the dacha, for years, and we were all very friendly. Uncle Alyosha was a cultured man, a bank director. His wife was a beauty, an opera-singer of Spanish-Jewish origins.' Svetlana continues, 'The community of Jews in pre-revolutionary Georgia were artists and merchants of a high class. She was a tall, stunning woman with huge blue eyes and they made a handsome couple. They brought up Johnik in tremendous luxury, they gave him everything and almost over-educated him for those days: he had a teacher and a nanny, and learned many foreign languages.

'Johnik told me once of his initiation into Georgian culture. Although his father was a civilised Party man and international banker, he was a Georgian through and through at home. He would tell stories from Georgian history to his son, roaring with laughter. There were battles where they chopped everybody's heads off and all the heads rolled down the hill. Johnik said, "I was horrified. I said to him, 'Do you mean that the heads, separate from the bodies, were rolling down the hill?' 'Yes, of course, they chopped off heads in the middle ages, ha ha ha!' " Johnik said to me, "I had nightmares, I couldn't sleep, and my mother told my father that he shouldn't talk like this. 'Oh, no! This was just war,' he said, 'ha ha ha!' "

'This was the Georgian way: they have no fear, it is very medieval. When there is love, there is love. When there is hatred, there is hatred.

'I remember practically every visit they made to us; they were loud-speaking, loud-laughing, good-looking people bringing news from Europe and always bearing presents of dresses and books. When they were there in the family dacha everybody was relaxed and talking about whatever they wanted.'

Aleksandr Semyonovich had been the first Soviet finance minister in Georgia, was a great friend of Orzhonidkidze, and both Stalin and Nadya adored him and Maria. There are photographs of them all in those early days, a group of good-looking, relaxed and cheerful people. Aleksandr had spent some time in Geneva in the National Bank of Foreign Trade and people admired the couple for their cosmopolitan attitudes at a time when foreign travel was a privilege and a rarity. They were colourful people, larger than life, full of *joie de vivre*. They evidently contributed not a little to the happy atmosphere of the Stalins' family life in the early days.

*Chapter Eleven*

# PAVEL AND ANNA

Ideals are brutal things.

— Krishnamurti

Perhaps too these lively weekend visitors made up for the regular absences of Nadya's brother and sister. During the 1920s Pavel Sergeyevich and Anna Sergeyevna were occupied on assignments that took them far from Moscow. Pavel was especially fond of Nadya, and Anna Sergeyevna draws a sympathetic portrait of him in her memoirs.

By her account he was, from early childhood, supportive of the revolutionary activity of his parents. When his father was exiled or imprisoned he would take on the mantle of head of the family, and plan with the others how to help the family while the breadwinner was away. 'We can begin by selling newspapers . . . get work packing and delivering parcels' – this was Pavel, aged nine.

'We dreamt of growing up quickly to take part in the people's struggle waged by our older friends. But we had also learned to keep quiet about many things' – Anna, aged seven.

Pavel was a rebel during his schooldays; he mocked his teachers and read adventure stories through lesson-times, detesting 'the spirit of resignation which they tried to inculcate in school. Pavlusha had to be removed from school: he continued to study at home, taught by student friends, as he prepared for final examinations.'

One day Pavel decided to run away, to begin the kind of life that he was reading about in books – travel, danger, struggle and adventure. He was, however, grabbed at the railway station by his mother and taken home, where he decided to work inside revolutionary circles. His father approved: 'Let him take a look at the life of working people and take a dip in that ocean of misery,' said Sergei Yakovlevich. He started work at the cable network and in the evenings studied at a technical institute. 'Of course he was a member of a revolutionary cell; we guessed that much. Although he never said a word, there was an aura of conspiracy around him.'

By the time Pavel was eighteen he was being treated as an equal in his father's repair shop. In 1913, aged nineteen, he led their strike committee, exhorting the men to working-class solidarity. 'He had a capacity for communicating with them and compelling them to speak for themselves,' remembers Anna Sergeyevna. He submitted their demands to the management, and was promptly arrested. He spent a month in solitary confinement, much to Fedya's impatience, who wondered why fourteen-year-olds couldn't be entrusted to do real revolutionary work too, and who longed to be in prison alongside his brother.

'Pavel was questioned a number of times and asked to disclose the names of the strike organisers. The investigator used various tricks, but Pavel played the young simpleton and kept his mouth shut, giving no one away. Finally most of the strikers' demands were met, and Pavel was released from prison.'

This episode weakened his health, and soon afterwards he was diagnosed with 'glandular tuberculosis' and spent three months in hospital. After an unsuccessful operation he was prescribed sun and rest, and spent some time convalescing in the Crimea with his father. 'Pavel was completely transformed. Father, too, was revived by his stay in the Crimea: a holiday after many years of trials, worries and unending work.'

Pavel was mobilised for World War I early in 1915. 'He works as a mechanic in a military car repair works in

Petrograd. When he can wangle leave he comes to Samsoni-evsky and talks irritably about his job. He speaks of the sons of the well-to-do Petrograd families who bribe their way out of the front line and get cushy jobs in the rear. They drive up in hansom cabs just in time for roll-call in the barracks.'

He was soon sent to the front, and when the family saw him off at the station 'He seemed gay, like a man who has burst out of the confines of a prison. But we could not hide our sorrow.

' "Now, now, let's have none of that," Pavel said, smiling. "I'll be writing . . ." '

He was at the front, in the trenches, for two years, with a long spell in military hospital. He kept his promise and sent regular letters home, confirming Olga Eugenievna's impressions of the horror and wastefulness of the war. His regiment was finally transferred to Novgorod, one of Russia's oldest cities. After the war was over, Pavel was elected secretary of the Bolshevik Party Committee there. Lying on the Volkhov river in the north of the country, Novgorod won prosperity by trading furs obtained in the forests of northern Russia. In medieval times the city was self-governing, finally being forced into submission to Moscow by Ivan the Terrible. It became the most prosperous city of the seventeenth century, and in 1611 sent a folk army to rescue the throne for Tsar Michael in Moscow, the first of the Romanovs. Novgorod has, like Moscow, an impressive kremlin or fortress dating from the fourteenth century, and many fine churches. It was here that Pavel met the woman who was to become his wife, Eugenia Aleksandrovna Zemlyanitsyn.

'Aunt Zhenya, as we called her, was quite different to him,' recalls Svetlana. 'She was very cheerful, pug-nosed, blue-eyed, pink-cheeked, a blonde Russian girl who was the daughter of a priest. She had a good-looking face, and her skin was always young. All the Alliluyevs tend to be dark-haired with big brown eyes, but the Zemlyanitsyns were blond and blue-eyed. When Uncle Pavel first brought her home (I am talking here from the memories of others, before I was born) it was the time of civil war and hunger. Everything was rationed and there was very little food. They arrived from Novgorod and she saw their table full of food! She immediately made very tactless jokes about it, and everybody shrank! But my father liked that, and he always liked that quality of hers; she was forever coming out with all kinds of things that no one else would dare to say. She learned that she could say anything and that it would be accepted. Stalin became very fond of her, because she was fearless. She was jolly, and kings and rulers like easy people who play the fool and who are not afraid.'

Eugenia's daughter Kyra enlarges: 'She was less explosive than my father, more balanced; they were a good match. She was tall and blonde, very jolly by character, very witty and very smart. Unfortunately she was *too* smart, she understood too much! She was very straightforward: if she did not like things, she would say so right away, quite clearly. She was never false, and that attracted people to her.'

'She was very artistic,' remembers Svetlana. 'She was a talented actress in Chaliapin's studio, and she could have found her way in the world of art theatre. She was very, very Russian, two hundred per cent so, traditional Russian and cultured with it. When she married Uncle Pavel she went to the front with him in the civil war, and dropped her career to be with him. He was wonderfully good-looking, a very gentle soul – too kind, too soft according to his wife, although she recognised how difficult it was to fight for one's rights in those days. He could not fight for his opinions – he was not macho, not a military type of man. He was in the army because it was the way: men *were* in the Red Army after the revolution. He was like my mother – like all of them – sensitive.'

Pavel's youngest son Sasha says, 'My father was a southerner, shorter in height than my mother – she never wore high-heels around him. He had a very good relationship with Stalin, whom he regarded as an "elder", a senior

partner. Stalin trusted my father and called him a "sheep"
– meaning a harmless one, not one of the wolves.'

'He was appointed military commissar in the Red Army,
and although he had not had any higher education he was a
man of great practical ability. He served with distinction
during the civil war, fighting against the British Expedition-
ary Forces in Archangel and the Bashmaks in Central Asia.
By the end of the decade he held the rank of General of
Tank Forces.

'Stalin often gave Pavel unusual assignments, which even
in those days it was not judicious to refuse. In the early
twenties he sent him to northern Siberia to join an expedition
of the famous geologist Urvantsev. They found coal and
iron ore in the place that was to become the town of Norilsk,
and my father was the manager of this remarkable venture.'
Norilsk, now the largest town inside the Arctic Circle, was
founded in the 1930s using political prisoners to mine, in
addition to coal and iron ore, nickel, cobalt and copper.
This frozen concentration camp of mines was christened by
its desperate inhabitants 'Black Death'. Its smelting complex emits as much sulphur dioxide as the whole of Canada,
and two thousand square miles of taiga around Norilsk has
been ruinously damaged by the pollution.

'Mother went with him. They had baby twins born there,
but they died in infancy due to the severe climate. My
parents were living in deerskin tents, it was before they built
the first house. Then Grandma asked Stalin to have her
favourite son returned, because he was not in great physical
strength or health. That assignment was an extraordinary
one, and Stalin continued to give him all sorts of unusual
posts.'

Kyra, Pavel's daughter, bears this out: 'Stalin loved my
father, he trusted him fully. He had a wonderful character:
he was a great peacemaker, he could alleviate arguments
and smooth out sharp corners. He was an extremely soft-
spoken and delicate person. Everything my father did was
out of kindness – he was not trying to be clever or trying to

please. As a father he was kind, but explosive as well. We are all explosive people! In a moment! There is gypsy blood in our ancestry, fiery, like a match being set off!'

In the late 1920s Stalin sent Pavel and Eugenia to Berlin under the guise of a trade delegation. In fact his brother-in-law was a military attaché negotiating with Hitler in the early days of Nazism. While they were there Nadya paid them a short visit; she was stressed and unwell and had been advised by her doctors to take the waters at Carlsbad. It was on this visit that she asked her brother to send her a pistol.

Two of Pavel and Eugenia's sons were born in Berlin – Sergei in 1928, and Sasha in 1931. The family returned to Moscow in April 1932, reuniting them with the rest of the Alliluyevs: increasingly quarrelsome parents, a disabled brother, Nadya struggling with her marriage to Stalin and, seemingly the most stable of them all, Anna and her husband Redens.

After the 1917 revolution Anna Sergeyevna studied at the Neuro-Psychiatric Institute in Petersburg, but affairs of the heart were to interrupt her aspirations to a career in psychotherapy, although she was remembered by many as a natural 'carer', a listener, someone to turn to in trouble. In 1920 she met and married Stanislav Redens, a key figure in the revolution. 'My father was a Pole, and he worked in the All-Russian Emergency Committee set up in 1918,' says Volodya, his younger son. 'In 1922 he had an interview with Dzerzhinsky who employed him as his secretary at the Lubyanka' – headquarters of the NKVD and infamous jail in the centre of Moscow. When Lenin appointed Dzerzhinsky head of the newly-founded Cheka in 1922, Redens worked under him and made his career in the secret police, eventually being sent to Odessa in the Crimea, Russia's third city and second port after St Petersburg, and scene of the mutiny on the *Potemkin*.

'Dzerzhinsky died in 1926,' (one of the few to do so of

natural causes in those days) 'in my father's flat – more or less in his arms. Stalin was a pall-bearer at his funeral. After Dzerzhinsky's death my father worked with Ordzhonikidze, first in the Working Class and Peasants' Inspectorate, then assigned, in December 1928, to Georgia.'

Volodya tells a story about his father at work which demonstrates that he was a man of high principle. 'When Redens went to take the post of chief of the Cheka in the Crimea, some sailors who had been involved in the requisition of valuables kept some for themselves. My father was informed of this and gave an order to hide five gold pieces in the flat of one of their colleagues. Then he sent the two sailors to search the flat and to make requisitions. They handed in only three gold pieces. Redens had the flat checked for the other two pieces, but when they were cross-examined the soldiers immediately said that they had taken the rest of the money for themselves and that they didn't see anything wrong in that. My father gave orders that they should be shot. And so they were. My father said that Chekists could not be this sort of man. Because of this, the authority of the Cheka in the Crimea rose a good deal.

'My father gained great respect in Georgia, where Beria's career in the GPU [the Georgian secret police] was in its formative stages.' Twenty years younger than Stalin, Lavrenti Beria's aspirations to power knew no bounds. From all accounts he was an extremely unpleasant little man whose skills, learned in the secret police, eventually earned him a degree of indispensability to Stalin. 'But in Georgia Redens was his boss and wouldn't let him put forward his own line.'

'During the civil war,' Svetlana reminds us, 'Beria fought first with the Reds and then with the Whites – as the situation changed so did his allegiance. At one time, fighting for the Whites, he was taken prisoner by Kirov and Ordzhonikidze who were then leading the Red Army there, and they ordered his execution. But this order was overlooked: he was a little Mr Nobody and the army had to move on and there were other matters to consider. So they forgot to shoot him.'

'By the year 1930 Beria realised that it would be imposs-ible for the two of them, he and Redens, to work together,' Volodya continues. 'They came into conflict because my father didn't give Beria scope to develop and he stood in his way to power. Father had a direct line to Stalin in Moscow, which was certainly not to Beria's liking. This man, who stood so close to Stalin, was a very great nuisance to him.

'Beria got rid of my father by getting him transferred to the Ukraine: from then on the two had little sympathy for each other. Meanwhile Beria, delighted to have Redens out of the way, climbed up in Georgia to the post of general secretary of the Georgian Communist Party, and was later transferred to Moscow, looking for more power. Nobody in our family liked him, though at the beginning my father regarded him as a very good worker. Yes, he committed this sin.'

From Leonid's description of his father as extrovert and fun-loving, it would seem that there was also a personality clash between Redens and Beria. The only thing that mattered to Beria was power, even in those early days. He was both immoral and apolitical: his only creed was that the ends justify the means.

'He only got to Moscow,' Volodya goes on, 'after Kirov had been murdered and Ordzhonikidze was dead. The latter had known Beria from his early days in Georgia, and it was believed that Beria used this liaison to further his rise to power. All the family circle, who knew the Georgian situ-ation well, knew for certain that he was not a man to be close to Stalin. So as far as Beria was concerned the family had to be removed.

'Everyone in our family knew that he was a scoundrel. Nadya spoke out against him quite openly, so did my mother Anna Sergeyevna. He was quite obviously a villain. He wanted to isolate Stalin from his relatives, to close every

*103*

possible uncontrolled channel through which reality might reach Stalin.'

'He hated all of our family,' adds Kyra. Svetlana describes him as 'very clever, and very manipulative. He got everything he wanted. And he was a horrible man with a horrible face. According to my mother too he was horrible! She wouldn't have him around. She was outspoken enough to tell father that he shouldn't invite him to the house. Every time they went on vacation to the Black Sea Beria would visit them, because Georgia was where he was stationed – he was boss of the KGB at the time. She loathed him, couldn't stand him, couldn't sit near him. She called him a "dirty old man" and without doubt he noticed her antipathy.

'There were quarrels over him with father; he would arrive and my mother would scream at Father, "Don't let him come here! Don't let him in!" My father would reprimand her and say, "You with your funny ideas. You women always have something to say. It is none of your business, he is one of my comrades, he will always be here, I need him." So her opinion was disregarded. But she had this feeling inside, an intuition about him.'

Stalin's association with Beria was to influence Redens' fate in the late 1930s, and indeed the destiny of the Alliluyev family. The few photographs of Redens in the family collection show a man of thickset build, a pleasant face with a heavy jawline that matches a wide neck. He has straight eyebrows and a longish nose, and a crop of short, wavy hair. A dogged expression appears to be characteristic of him.

Says Svetlana, 'Redens was quite a charming person if we can forget that he was, after all, a close associate of Dzerzhinsky working in the secret police. What his work was I never really knew; although he is known for being one of the victims of the purges, how many people were *his* victims we shall never know.

'As a person he was very pleasant, attractive-looking,' she continues, 'a handsome man who loved his wife and children and was loved by everybody around: a pleasant image remains in the memory.'

His son Leonid has childhood memories of Redens as a family man. 'He was cheerful – and he liked football. Family life wasn't that simple, though. We children lived with our nanny Tatyana more than with our parents who were away a good deal. Father was at work, and rarely there. When he was there, he was very good with us. I remember lots of music in our childhood, and how he loved doing photography – developing and printing.

'Tatyana was a remarkable woman – you don't see her sort any more. She came from a simple family, and first of all went into domestic service with a family of lawyers. She then joined our family when I was one year old.

'Tatyana Ivanovna Moskaleva was a good friend of Aleksandra Bychkova, Svetlana's nanny,' continues Volodya. 'These two women were absolutely amazing, outstanding in their devotion to the families they worked for. Amazing kindness, hard-working. Our nanny Tanya was a spinster, very pretty in her youth, and quite remarkable-looking even in old age. She came from a village in Ryazan area and worked for other people all her life. She was of exceptional honesty, decency and diligence, completely truthful, hardworking, loyal.

'I have no words to describe her and all that she has done for us. She was very religious and pious and was often visited at home by her companions, old women of the same sort. But she never did any "converting" among us, and never even liked to talk about it. She stayed in her own world in this matter, and we in ours. She would even be quite stern in stopping us before that sacred door. Nowadays that breed of devoted servant is gone, they belonged to a different era. She was closer to us than our own mother.'

One of Lenin's confident pronouncements was that 'every idea of God is unutterable vileness'. To him, and therefore to his followers, their ideology was their religion. Svetlana remembers that 'in the early thirties you couldn't pronounce the name of God. When my nanny was hired in 1926 my mother asked her if she was religious. Nanny had been coached into what to say, and said, "Oh, no, no, no,' thinking it would make her life easier. But Tatyana was far more honest; from the beginning she said, "I am religious and want to go to church", and it was accepted. She was the one who prayed for all of us, for the living and for the dead. Maybe her prayers protected my cousins in later years, to help them emerge as undamaged as they are, healthy mentally and emotionally, from what they had to go through.'

Leonid continues: 'Tatyana died on Easter night 1948, and my great-aunt Zemlyanitsyn, who was religious too, used to say that if you die on Easter night you go straight to heaven!

'We saw more of our parents in the summer at the dacha than at any other time of the year. I remember my father as relaxed and easy-going, very sociable and enjoying life.' Kyra also remembers how 'he was very friendly with me – both Anna and Stanislav loved me so much! He was a Pole, very handsome, very pleasant. They often used to take me to the theatre – although they had two sons they enjoyed me because I was a girl. They would take me on holiday to Kharkov or to Sochi, as if I were their daughter. I could sing or whistle lots of tunes from the opera and Redens loved that! I have very, very warm memories of him.

'He adored Svetlana and Vasili too – all of us children. Aunt Anna was the kindest person in the world. She presented me with a piano for my music studies! I was rumbustious and quite a tomboy; I was always fighting or jumping around, but she never minded that!'

Anna Sergeyevna had been thoughtful and sensitive ever since she was a child. She showed early signs of a social conscience, tempered with the revolutionary zeal of her parents. She was inquisitive with her religious instructor at school, asking him, 'Why doesn't God allow sinners into paradise even for a little while? After all, God is all merciful?'

Came the reply, 'Because a sinner in heaven would feel as much out of place as a beggar at a rich person's ball.'

'Here, too,' muses the young Anna, 'the poor and ragged were excluded from paradise. How were they to blame, those for whom life on earth was a hell? I thought to myself with pride: let Him make promises about paradise in heaven, while Father, Mother and all our friends fight to create paradise on earth – for everyone without exception.'

Svetlana remembers Anna as 'a living saint, a real humanitarian. She helped many people in unbelievable ways, working hard to use her connections to push for what she wanted. Many people came unofficially to her funeral, to show their gratitude to her. Yet she was not strong – she had been very ill with TB as a young woman, and had only one lung – the other one collapsed. But she lived for others.'

'My mother Anna Sergeyevna,' says Leonid, 'was a forceful person, but very kind. She was very sociable, and loved people.' Her younger son Volodya describes her as 'a very kind soul, she had a very soft character. She was extremely sensitive to the needs of others, forever involved in helping other people. Our home was always full of people coming to see her, and she would feed them all, listen to them all, and offer every help she was capable of.'

But in 1932, when her sister Nadya desperately needed help, Anna Sergeyevna and her family were in Kharkov, an old walled city in the western Ukraine. Redens had been posted there, and Anna was unavailable to help Nadya through a crisis that ended in tragedy and which marked a turning point in the family fortunes.

# PART TWO

*Chapter Twelve*

# 'THE GOOD YEARS'

T here is a photograph in the Alliluyev family collection of Sergei Yakovlevich on holiday, standing with his arms folded over a long, belted shirt, peasant-style. Going by the exotic plants and a lush vine that are also in the picture, it was taken one summer at the Black Sea. For their annual summer vacation the family went to Sochi, a fashionable resort set against picturesque mountains. Its mineral springs and warm climate have attracted visitors ever since the city was established in 1896, to enjoy its gardens of subtropical shrubs and trees. Sergei looks relaxed and at peace with himself; Svetlana, as she turned the pages of the album, paused over this one and said, 'That was in the late twenties, early thirties – the good years.'

Sergei Pavlovich reminisces: 'There were two dachas near Moscow: we used to visit Zubalovo One, Stalin's place, up to 1934; after that we moved to Zubalovo Two. I remember Grandpa taking us there to help us move in.' Svetlana remembers how 'the boys lived at Zubalovo Two, where Mikoyan had his dacha, and we lived two miles away – a lovely walk through the woods. We used to go to the river together, on outings and childhood expeditions. The Svanidzes lived at Zubalovo Two, and other families as well, including Jan Gamarnik.' Gamarnik was a Bolshevik military leader who headed the political administration of the Red Army. He committed suicide in 1937, apparently to avoid arrest and trial for treason. 'There were lots of photos from that period,' Sasha Pavlovich recalls, 'which were all seized by the KGB in the forties. They still have them.'

'We were close to the Mikoyan children,' continues

Sergei, 'the "Mikoyanchiks" as we used to call his five sons.' Mikoyan, an Armenian and Old Bolshevik, was, like Stalin, educated at an ecclesiastical seminary in Tiflis, but abandoned his vocation to take up revolutionary activities in the Caucasus, leading the underground movement in Baku. Mikoyan supported Stalin in the power struggle of the early 1920s, and was appointed People's Commissar for external and internal trade in 1926. In 1935 he was elected to the politburo; in 1946 he became deputy premier with responsibility for directing the country's trade, a post which he managed to hold on to until Krushchev's time.

Kyra remembers how 'We were all friends, and close in accordance with our age: Leonid and Sergei, me and Vasili – on that basis. And we were close to Svetlana, too.' But, as Sergei points out, 'When Svetlana grew up, then we all got friendly and age meant less. The Mikoyans' place was a much more democratic one than Stalin's – there were more people around, more families living together and lots of activity. At Stalin's dacha I saw no one besides members of the family, and sometimes members of the politburo.'

'Grandpa was more a part of all this than my own father,' says Svetlana; 'he was a parent-like figure. Father was never there, except for appearances now and then. Mother was always at her work, so she was substituted by Nanny and by teachers.

'Vasili had his own teachers in charge of him, because Mother was so fearful for him – she knew that he was a very highly-strung boy and needed special attention. So with his teachers he would read and write essays and collect plants from the woods to make herbariums. He always had friends of his own age staying with him in the summer, and his teacher would take them for a trip on the river, or on bicycles, and they would make camp, spend the night there, and cook the fish they caught. And all this was put into motion by Mother.

'Vasili was rather aggressive, and Yasha would protect me from him like a kind older brother, and the two boys would fight each other.' Kyra remembers Yasha as 'very kind, and very handsome too'. Sergei's description of him is 'very soft', although there was twenty years in age between them. Their younger brother Sasha has a specific recollection of Yasha in the 1930s. 'He seemed to me, as a small boy, a very gloomy man, dark and clumsy, and he was a bit deaf. He liked to shoot fish in the river with a short military rifle – a game they all played in the army. You walked along the shore, shot into the water, and the fish were shell-shocked and turned over, paralysed. Then you dived into the river and caught it by hand. Once when I was seven or eight, I asked him if he would let me hold the fish. He gave it to me, and I let it back into the water where it revived and swam away. He was terribly cross with me, he was mad as hell, and I was frightened out of my wits.'

The cousins all have childhood memories of Grandpa Sergei Yakovlevich. Svetlana says, 'We loved him because he spent time with us: he took us into the woods to collect mushrooms, and I remember picking hazelnuts with him, sitting up on his shoulders when I was about four or five. I was tired from the long walk in the country so he was carrying me, and I could pick the nuts from the branches as we walked. We had white rabbits as pets, and we helped him to feed the ducks and geese, the chickens and guinea-fowl.

'The boys loved him because he taught them to work with tools, metal, nails and wire – and they all grew up to be good handymen!' Sasha admired his skills: 'He was a highly-qualified locksmith, working in metal, and a highly-qualified fitter.' Svetlana continues, 'My grandparents had suddenly become part of the aristocracy, because my mother was First Lady. They could leave off working, and live off their very comfortable pensions as old founder-members of the Party.

'Grandpa found ways to participate in it all – as handy-man, electrician, plumber, whatever. His last job had been in the Electric Society, and then on one of the large electric stations, so he was qualified in many ways – but without any formal education. He was completely loving, charming with everybody, helping the household, and in the garden, pruning trees and cutting back in the woods. He was always on good terms with the cooks and maids and gardeners, the people in charge of the cows, the chickens and geese. It was the life of a big country household – a bit like a farm although we didn't own the land; it belonged to the state, of course. There were orchards and he would help apple-picking, and he would work in the vegetable garden. He was on good terms with everyone and everyone adored him. In his later years he had a grey-white beard and moustache, old-fashioned, a Byzantine face.'

Volodya's impressions as a young boy were 'that there was nothing he could not do – he was a jack of all trades. He loved us all very much but he was also quite strict with us. He hated to see us idle. He was severe, uncompromising, firm in his views, very demanding on us and on everyone around him. A man of integrity and honesty, who disliked idleness and was forever involved in something.'

Sasha's memories are that 'he looked a lot like a latter-day Ivan the Terrible. I believe his roots were perfectly Russian ones, although he did indeed have an exotic gypsy look. He treated me well, although he was often severe and hot-tempered. One time when Volodya was fidgeting at the table, Grandpa poured his soup down his front! That was how he was.

'While we lived at Stalin's dacha, up until the war, Grandpa was our main man, bossing us all. He liked to organise elaborate games with the grandchildren – he would set out treasure hunts in the woods, or a paperchase for all the kids to join in.'

Kyra has 'especially good memories of Grandfather. He used to say to me proudly, "You are my first grandchild!" and so I was his favourite. He walked very fast, and I had to follow him at a run! As a result of that I developed, for the rest of my life, a very quick walk, like running away from a fire, which has irritated many people!

'Grandpa was wonderful. He adored children, and when we all lived in Zubalovo during summertime, he would often go secretly to the woods to hang sweets on the branches of the trees. Then he would take us children there and say, "Look, kids! There is a candy tree here!" That was Grandpa. In winter he would take me on typically Russian sleigh rides with a horse – except it was not a troika, but just one village horse!

'Grandfather loved to give joy to children, to everybody. He was, however, a very despotic man in his youth, a revolutionary, a rebel. But after the revolution he somehow became reconciled with himself, and began to enjoy life quietly. He was very sweet with me – I used to amuse him and put him in a good mood. He had an especially soft spot for me. Probably it was my openness and accessibility that he liked. Vasili and Svetlana, whom he loved too, were often away from their dacha, but I was right there, near to him.'

Svetlana remembers how 'Everybody adored Grandpa, but found Grandma very difficult.' Yet Volodya, the youngest, found the reverse: 'It was easier to be with Grandma – she was kinder and milder.' But it was true, says Kyra, that 'it was Grandpa who played with us more. Besides, later on Grandma lived in her flat in the Kremlin and it was a nuisance to go there – to get a pass and all that. But Grandpa lived with us for quite a few years.' The relationship between Sergei and Olga had succumbed to the stresses and strains of three decades of marriage. By the mid-twenties they were living separate lives, although both were closely involved with their family. For a while Sergei lived in St Petersburg, but after Pavel's death and Redens' arrest in 1938, he moved into the House on the Embankment to live close to his children and grandchildren.

Olga Eugenievna chose to keep an apartment in the Kremlin and live alone. 'She was an independent character – she had been the wife of a revolutionary, had experienced prison and exile, she had worked very hard, and travelled wherever the Party wanted him to go. Finally she returned to Moscow with Nadya and the others, and Grandfather remained in Leningrad for a while, visiting Moscow only occasionally. She wanted to live alone and have her old age in peace: for that she needed a lot of independence; it was not done very much in her generation – people stayed together.'

Svetlana describes her: 'She was very tiny, but always had her nose in the air so she looked taller. She kept her belongings in a trunk and she would take out two or three old dresses and make them into a new one. She wore gloves and hats when nobody else was wearing them, funny hats which sat low on the forehead, twenties-style. She wore black quite a lot. She had good taste when she was young – my cousin has photos which show her looking charming in a Chekhovian, early twentieth-century way, wearing a hat tied with voile. There was some kind of finesse on her side; we don't know who her German ancestors were, but I picture some romantic person!

'She would take her promenade around the estate, up to the birch grove and back, or sit in the shade under a parasol – she couldn't take the sunshine. She took to the role of Grand Lady with some pleasure, and not without natural style. Yet my mother hated her high position and tried to avoid it – and my other uncles and aunts remained simple, too. But Grandma separated herself from the world once she had climbed a little higher up the social ladder. She had ingrained in her a contempt for people who were not "quite right", she was very critical, and she was a little bit of a snob – this developed with her old age. She sat in her room complaining that the cooks and maids employed by the state did not do their jobs right – which was probably true because she was a better cook and better at everything domestic, as people who have worked all their life usually are. She could see that things were not right; she had this gesture of putting her hand up to her mouth and saying, "Well, I am not going to say anything, I had better not talk, I will not get into trouble."

'Grandma and Grandpa had their conflicts, which we as children did not understand. They lived separately for the last twenty years of their marriage.' Kyra remembers how 'Grandmother stayed in her small flat in the Kremlin, but Grandfather then lived with us.' 'When we were all at Zubalovo,' Svetlana continues, 'his room was at one end of the dacha, hers at the other. They would meet at table, and we watched the conflict! They would exchange prickly remarks – Grandpa in a jovial tone, laughing and making a joke of it. Grandma was very easily offended and would get in a temper or a mood, and sometimes even leave the table.

'She had wanted to break out several times. She had had other men in her life – she was attractive, a real beauty in her youth with grey-green eyes and blonde hair. She was a little bit ahead of her time in deciding to live alone, without her husband. I remember one of her mottos: "It is much better to be lonely alone than lonely with someone." But she was never a miserable, pitiable little old woman. She was always neat and tidy, there was always an air of great independence about her.'

Kyra remembers her as 'a more complicated character. She was very, very German. She liked *Ordnung* – order. As a child I was always put off by that, by her extreme orderliness. In her kitchen there were separate cloths for washing this or that, and I was petrified by these demands! But Grandma could sing well, she knew Italian songs and she had a good voice and ear.' Svetlana too recalls that 'She could sing nicely to the guitar, although it was difficult to get her to do so – she said we wouldn't understand anyway because it was in German. Grandma was quite literate – I always wondered how. She always read newspapers, and wanted to know what was going on in the world.

'She retained her faith but she couldn't go to church because of her revolutionary background – whereas my other grandmother in Tblisi, Stalin's mother, went to church all

*117*

the time. But Grandma Olga was cut off from that. She was German Lutheran by upbringing, yet she always held an old rosary made of amber beads which had belonged to her mother and grandmother. They were melting away – they became smaller and smaller with wear. Denomination didn't matter to her: there was God, there was soul, and she would be offended when we children asked her, "Grandma, where is your soul, then? Show us where it is. Show us your soul." She got very annoyed with us for talking like that. "You will know when it aches," she said. Another great remark of hers.'

Svetlana still holds these memories as precious: 'When my cousins and I start talking about our childhood, we can't stop talking about how wonderful it was, how beautiful at Zubalovo. All those woods are still there, more or less, although the land has been built up around them. Life gave us a feeling of motherland and a beautiful and productive, educational childhood.'

## Chapter Thirteen

# A DEATH IN THE FAMILY

One death is a tragedy, a million just statistics.

— Stalin

The private apartments in the Kremlin where Nadya and Joseph Stalin now lived with their children were in the old Poteshny Palace, a picturesque, rare late-seventeenth-century building with a fourth-storey bay window. It was originally used for court amusements, and housed the first tsarist theatre. 'The apartment had two rooms for the children,' says Svetlana, 'and I shared mine with Nanny. There was one for the governess, and a dining room large enough to have a grand piano in it. There was no room for pictures on the walls – they were lined with books. In addition there was a library, Nadya's room, and Stalin's tiny bedroom in which stood a table of telephones. My parents slept separately. There were two bathrooms, a kitchen, and a housekeeper's room which had an ultra-violet lamp in it for the children's good health. It was homely, with bourgeois furniture. The staff – cook and housekeeper – were very nice, and it was kept snug with wood stoves kept stoked up by a man who also delivered the firewood.'

Among Nadya's friends at the Industrial Academy were students returning from the Ukraine where they had observed the horrors of the forced collectivisation taking place in the countryside. Nadya became less and less able to resolve the dichotomy of living on the one hand as First Lady, and hearing from her peers on the other about the human effects of policy dictated from the ivory tower in which she lived, the Kremlin. The strain was affecting a

*119*

marriage which was already in trouble, and the relationship between Nadya and Joseph became increasingly unstable.

Collectivisation, the process of forcing the peasantry to give up their individual farms and join large collective ones, had started in 1929, the year which had also seen lavish celebrations of Stalin's fiftieth birthday, and which marked the true beginning of his long 'reign'. For the first time the press was describing him as Our Great Genius Leader, and his grip on power was strengthening rapidly.

But the re-writing of history that also took place at this time could not escape the facts of widespread famine. Stalin's solution was to find a scapegoat: he decided to liquidate the kulaks, the relatively wealthy peasant farmers whose business was providing the nation's food but who had little interest in socialism. Eighty per cent of the population were peasants farming privately owned or tenanted land, but a Party that did not believe in private property was faced with an ideological problem. Forced collectivisation was Stalin's answer, which he saw as providing the economic foundation on which to build industry. He stressed the imperative need for rapid industrialisation: 'We are fifty or a hundred years behind the advanced countries,' he said. 'We must make good this distance in ten years. Either we do it, or we will be crushed.'

He accused the kulaks, as a class, of living off the fat of the land, and of hoarding grain for themselves at the expense of the nation. Five million of them were dispossessed; the kulaks' vengeful response was to slaughter their livestock. Mass deportation to Siberia ensued as punishment, and any active resistance was met with the same sentence. The carnage included the slaughter of fourteen million cattle, one third of the nation's pigs, and a quarter of its sheep and goats. Everyday life was a spectacle of horror in villages all over Russia. People were starving, and as the famine became more desperate there were recorded cases of cannibalism. Agricultural workers were accused of sabotage and wrecking, and of keeping back their harvest from the towns and the capital.

The Party was divided over these measures. Bukharin and his wing believed that there was no need to interfere with the private economy of the kulaks, that it was possible for socialism to progress without so doing. Stalin disagreed, following the old maxim that in the name of revolution everything was permissible, including the sacrifice of human beings.

Show trials began, often with children accusing their parents, and in 1932 Stalin forbade collective farmers to leave their villages. By 1932 two million people were doing time in the gulag, although this was concealed from the general public by the verbal camouflage of communism that was fast becoming the norm. It is estimated that in all ten million perished as a result of collectivisation.

Nadya's inability to tolerate her husband's policies was taking its toll; the couple grew further and further apart. 'By 1931 Nadya was talking of leaving my father for good,' says Svetlana. 'She was intending to divorce him; after fourteen years of living with him she definitely wanted out. She was going to wait until she graduated as a textile engineer in six months' time. She was then going to take a job, take either one or both of the children with her, go to Leningrad to live with her father, or possibly to the Ukraine to live with Anna Sergeyevna. It was all planned: she was leaving him. But I don't know how much my father knew of it. Aunt Anna told me all this years later.'

Volodya takes up the tale, telling what he learned from his mother Anna Sergeyevna about Nadya. 'She suffered from extremely serious headaches which affected her periodically, and the gaps between these periods were becoming smaller and smaller. She was in a state of depression. Besides that, Nadya was a great deal younger than Stalin and she needed attention which Stalin could not, for obvious reasons, give her. Also, marriages between nationalities are not always happy because the people involved have different ideas about what marriage should be. In the end, all these things brought about the tragic climax.'

After one argument with Nadya about the morality of collectivisation, Stalin ordered the arrest of all those students at the Industrial Academy who had been in the Ukraine, and commanded his wife to stay away from the Academy for two months. A photograph of Nadya taken at this time shows her pale, anguished, evidently deeply anxious and disturbed. She was telling her friends that she had lost her love for life. She was deeply opposed to collectivisation; the moral ravages of these policies distressed the young idealist deeply. Yet she was completely powerless to affect Stalin's thinking.

'I remember what proved to be my last day with her; it was only a few days later that she died,' recollects Svetlana. 'I loved her room; there was something about it. I went there whenever I could. There was a thick, pinkish, raspberry-coloured rug, oriental, thick and soft, and I liked to sit on it. She had her bed in there, her desk, a drawing table for her studies, and some books. There was a huge old-fashioned divan with cushions on it and a long bolster, and I loved to sit there too. I remember her scent, a Chanel perfume which still reminds me of her.

'On this day she was admonishing me, telling me what I should and shouldn't do, and blaming me for drinking wine. Father had this Caucasian habit of giving wine to children, and she thought it was bad for us, she was frightened that the habit would develop. She didn't drink because it didn't agree with her. "Don't drink wine if your father gives you a sip. Don't take it." I remember that very well. These moments with her were so very few, that I can remember clearly her talk with me.'

The last time Nadya was seen in public was during the anniversary parade in Red Square on 7 November 1932. According to a Soviet official called Aleksandr Barmine, who spotted her with her brother Pavel, 'She looked pale and worn, little interested in the proceedings around her.

I could see that her brother was deeply concerned.' The following evening, 8 November, Nadya and Joseph were invited to a party at the Voroshilovs' Kremlin apartment, as part of the celebrations of the fifteenth anniversary of the October revolution. There are various versions of what exactly happened, but apparently Stalin openly insulted his wife – 'Oy you, have a drink!' and she screamed back at him, 'Don't you dare talk to me like that,' got up from the table, and rushed out.

Her friend Polina Molotov followed her, and walked around the Kremlin palace with her until she calmed down. When they parted Nadya appeared to be in full possession of herself.

The following morning the housekeeper, Karolina Til, went in to the bedroom to wake her mistress, and found her lying in a pool of blood. Lying by her side was the lady's Walther pistol that Pavel had sent her from Berlin. The shot had passed through her heart.

On instructions the newspapers reported her 'sudden and premature death' as due to appendicitis. All the children were told this story too. Six-and-a-half-year-old Svetlana remembers only that 'It had all been very strange; suddenly everyone was crying and we were sent away to the dacha, to Zubalovo.' It wasn't until nearly ten years later, when she was fifteen, that she discovered, in an English magazine, the story that her mother had committed suicide.

Nadya's simple furniture, her knicknacks and papers were put under lock and key. The key was given to the commander of the KGB. 'She left a little iron box which could not be burned, which was always kept in my father's room. Not long before he died I went in there and opened it. Inside were the personal belongings which had been gathered up from her dressing table. There were a few notebooks, and some plans she had written out. She had very neat, fine handwriting – not neurotic, but well-organised. She had written out her plans for the next day in the Academy where she was studying – all her designs for the future.

'Obviously something just overcame her; a blackness. She wrote a dreadful letter. In it she poured out everything that she didn't like, in a final valedictory gesture. My aunts told me that it was destroyed immediately so that it would not get into the public arena and be exploited politically. She said that she was opposed to Stalin's policies, to the purges and everything that was going on. She really spoke out.

'My father thought that she was probably on the side of the opposition, with Bukharin, supporting them against him. She had no doubt talked about these things many times with him. But she produced this sincere letter and left it for him to read: "Now you have the truth: and I am killing myself." '

Doctors were not permitted to examine the body and there was no medical verdict. Foreign correspondents in Moscow were censored if their reports dwelt on the suddenness of Nadya's death because this might be seen as a 'reflection on the efficiency of Soviet medicine'. The news of her 'unexpected death' immediately aroused rumours of murder, which were widespread around Moscow. Yet those close to Stalin at the time describe him as a drained and broken man. However, it was his wife's political defection that affected him as much as her death: the public revelation that her views, more liberal and democratic than his own, were closer to Bukharin's wing of the Party, stung him.

'But that is only part of the story,' continues Svetlana. 'She had her opinions, it is true, but it was not just a political issue. Eugenia Aleksandrovna told me later, in the forties, about the depression she used to suffer from; that mother could probably have been helped but that it just wasn't done in those days. She told me what a terrible shock it had been, because everybody loved her, and nobody believed that she, of all people, would do that. That she was a very responsible wife and mother. But she also felt that the contradictory passion that she had for my father was probably one of the contributing factors to her suicide.

'She had this depression which would grab her – the curse of heredity. It was a form of incipient schizophrenia that had plagued Olga Eugenievna's family. It was well known in the family that she had these terrible depressions when she couldn't cope with life. When things were normal she worked, she studied, she had her family life – but once in a while she would get into a state of melancholy when she didn't want anything and nothing was good enough and she wasn't interested in anything. Sometimes she was almost deranged. This very strong depression would last for a while, maybe a couple of weeks. Nanny knew all about it of course, because Nadya went to her for help. Some of her friends knew, too. But none of them could do anything to help. And finally she couldn't cope.

'It had some physiological connection with feminine problems – she had had a couple of abortions – which were never attended to. She was frail – she was not a formidable, big, fat Russian woman; she was pale and sensitive. She was very young and she wasn't helped enough; nobody paid attention to the real problem. It was at a time when, especially in Russia, psychology was not in vogue. To spend too much time with doctors was considered bourgeois. It wasn't done; you coped on your own. So she was overlooked. It just happened that no one was available to help her so she was brewing away inside, and she couldn't get it out of her system.'

Nadya's youngest nephew Volodya, who was born after Nadya died, nevertheless gathered some theories from his mother Anna in later years. 'She and Stalin were very different people, both with a harsh character, and of different ages, different outlooks, different nationalities. Nadya's health underwent a progressive deterioration, and she suffered from increasingly regular headaches. At one point it became impossible for her to work, and she was examined by doctors who categorically ordered her to rest. As I see it, it is an ordinary everyday human tragedy. Stalin is supposed to have got offended with Nadya because she said *vi*, the polite form of "you", whereas he spoke to her using the pronoun *ti*. Well, perhaps, but what does that add up to?

'Rumours that Stalin had killed her started up immediately after her death, but it was all nonsense. A story goes around that Kameneva, the wife of Kamenev, who had an old score to settle with the Alliluyevs from pre-revolution days, said that Nadya had been shot in the left temple, and pointed out that she was right-handed. Naturally the conclusion to draw from this is that Stalin shot her, or gave instructions to kill her. But Nadya shot herself in the heart, not in the temple. Anna talked to Stalin about this many times, and he would say to her, "Well, what's to be done about it now? It's no use crying over spilt milk."

'He knew that Pavel had bought the pistol for her – she had asked him to do so, presumably for self-defence. He asked Pavel, "Was it you who bought her the pistol?"

' "Yes."

'Stalin's comment was, "You found her a present all right, didn't you. Could you not have bought her some other gift?" '

Kyra comes to her father's defence. 'My father was a military man, and he thought a pistol was simply a necessity.'

'At the leave-taking,' says Svetlana, 'he rejected the coffin saying, "She went away as an enemy" and walked away from it. He didn't go to the funeral and never visited the cemetery.' Says Volodya, 'One of the reasons that Stalin didn't even go to the funeral was that he was very offended by her action.' 'She was very beautiful in her coffin,' recalls Kyra, who was an impressionable twelve-year-old when it happened. 'Very young, and her face was clear and lovely. She was pure and beautiful.'

Volodya continues, 'People are people. Within the family no one ever blamed Stalin. Neither my mother, Anna, nor Grandmother Olga approved of what she had done to herself. They were on Stalin's side in this conflict. They never accused him of causing Nadya's death. They thought she was the only one to blame. Mother and Grandmother had a better understanding of Stalin's position: the enormous work that he shouldered. He was unable to give attention to his family, it was simply impossible while he was the leader of such an enormous country. Nadya was much younger than he, and she didn't understand.

'I emphasise that it was a personal drama; it had nothing to do with political factors. It was the drama of two people with very complicated characters, who obviously loved each other in their own way, and unfortunately came to a tragic end.' But, adds Leonid, 'Although she was a very delicate person, she saw beyond the idol to the reality. She understood his true nature.'

Svetlana remembers that 'There were many photographs taken when she died, in her open coffin. She was beautiful even then, with a magical quality about her. I was frightened though, and crying, and I remember my mother's godfather Yenukidze holding me on his lap to protect and console me. It was the last time I saw him.

'I was only six and a half. I didn't like this thing called death. I was terrified. It was my first taste of death, and it was then that I developed a fear of dark places – to me it was associated with something deathly. I still have that fear of dark rooms today: I can't sleep in a totally dark room, I have to have a little light somewhere. I associate darkness with annihilation, darkness and death.'

## Chapter Fourteen

# TRUST BETRAYED

The movement was without scruples; she rolled towards her goal unconcernedly and deposited the corpses of the drowned in the windings of her course. Her course had many twists and windings; such was the law of her being. And whosoever could not follow her crooked course was washed on to the bank, for such was her law. The motives of the individual did not matter to her, neither did she care what went on in his head and his heart. The Party knew only one crime: to swerve from the course laid out; and only one punishment: death . . . the logical solution to political divergences.

— Arthur Koestler, *Darkness at Noon*

'My mother's death was a turning point in all of our lives – in family life, and in my father's life. Family ceased to exist; she had been the one who kept it going. She was the cement of our family life, and when she died it all fell apart. We moved from our apartment in the Kremlin where we had all lived together, and the ten years after my mother's death passed in monotonous isolation. I lived in the Kremlin, in a smaller apartment, as in a fortress, in which the only kind being near me was Nanny. Father went to live in a dacha of his own which was nearer town – Blizhny, at Kuntsevo – so that he could easily get to his office and back, and continue his own way of life with his crowds of politicians around him. We were left alone with teachers and governesses.

'We continued to go for weekends to Zubalovo where Grandma and Grandpa still lived and where things continued more or less in Mother's way. But without her it was not the same. She had been the soul of it; when she died, it faded. Even the playground had been dismantled.

'I remember Bukharin still being around and coming to see my father in the early thirties. Both he and Ordzhonikidze stayed at Zubalovo, still in simple company, as friends with children all living together, although it happened less and less after Mother died. Probably they were quite shocked by it too, and didn't want to come.

'It was a terrible shock to everybody. Everyone had to cope with it separately and get over it in their own way. Eugenia Aleksandrovna said to me, "I'm quite sure that my husband Pavel died sooner because of Nadya. He went to pieces – she was his youngest sister." ' Eugenia's younger son Sasha concurs: 'Nadya was the favourite, the youngest in the family, much loved by everyone. My father was the oldest and he felt that he had not done enough for her. He suffered very much over that.

'It caused a profound complication in his relationship with Stalin, because of the pistol he had bought her. He always felt some guilt about her death. This matter came between the two men, who before had been very close.' Svetlana was told by Eugenia Aleksandrovna that 'Pavel and Anna constantly blamed themselves for not being available when she needed them. "How could we have missed it? Why didn't we see it coming?" The amount of pain that it caused was staggering. Starting with the children, our lives were turned upside down.

'It was a terrible shock to my father. He said to his sisters-in-law, "I can't go on living after this," and became deeply depressed. That frightened my two aunts, Anna and Eugenia, who stayed on for two weeks in our apartment because they were afraid to leave him alone. They tried to make things easier for him, not holding him responsible, trying to console and support him – "We all feel terrible about it." Eugenia Aleksandrovna would take his side against Nadya. He was in a shambles, he was knocked sideways. Saying that he didn't want to live any more was something they had not heard before. They were shaken by that.

'He wanted to resign from the General Secretaryship, he felt he could not continue. But the politburo said, "Oh no no no, you have to stay!" Molotov and others near to him saw to it that he carried on working and that he wouldn't resign. They convinced him that he would be all right.

'For my father it was a matter of trust betrayed. For this very strong, unsentimental man, trust was extremely important. When somebody betrayed trust, be it a colleague in business, or in the family, it really hit him. He had trusted her, and what did he get? A stab in the back, that was how he saw it. He couldn't get over that. He felt deceived and betrayed.

'It was then that he hardened. He believed that if he couldn't trust her, he couldn't trust anybody. For the revolutionary in him, it was shattering. We saw him becoming colder and colder, and turning his back on his family.' Kyra thinks 'He was offended and hurt by the way she left him. If he had any traits of suspiciousness and bitterness in him at all, all that became accentuated as a result of her suicide. He stopped trusting others; even she had betrayed him. If he had these qualities in embryo, after her suicide they developed fully.'

Stalin was not the only one to be deeply affected. Svetlana, who still bears the scars sixty years later, goes on: 'My brother Vasili was completely destroyed by her death. My mother had paid extra attention to him because he was a difficult and sensitive boy. She knew that he was terribly afraid of Father because he was not the kind of boy that Father wanted him to be. Father had hit him a couple of times, to which Mother objected, and so with Mother gone he was on his own. His teacher stayed on for a little while, but then he was fired. Then Vasili went to airforce school at the Military Academy and that started his drinking, and with it the effort to become a macho man, which he was not. He was only eleven when she died, and he was ruined by it. Her absence from his life was perfectly awful. She had been his everything.' A photograph of Vasili taken in his mid-teens illustrates her point: a waif, he sits on horseback looking orphaned, a lost expression in his eyes; thin, wistful, and desolate. The rest of his life was spent in a search for what could not be found, through drink or with women, to ease a pain that could not be salved.

'Olga Eugenievna had always predicted that things would end badly,' recalls Svetlana. 'Everything went not as she thought it should. Her daughter had married Stalin and she was against that. "Your mother was a fool," she used to say to me. She knew him well, and she thought that he was not for her. She was right, but nobody listened to her. So her reaction was, "Ha-ha! I was right!" But Grandmother never really understood Mother.

'In 1933 we moved immediately to another apartment: my father felt that he couldn't live where my mother had lived, so we did a swop with Bukharin, to an office building under Stalin's official office. It was not like home, it was very formal, with a large dining room where Stalin entertained Churchill in 1942. Nanny stayed with me, so did our exceptionally sweet housekeeper Karolina Til, so that we could continue as before. He would come to the apartment to have supper every day, so we were supposed to be there, meet him and talk over our day at school. He tried to stay in touch, although I didn't see much of him after she died. But he tried to be closer, to see me every day when I came home from school; he would check my copy books and look at my marks. During my school years he tried to be a parent who was interested in my progress, which was all that mattered to him. This was the regime that was religiously followed from 1932 until the war, in 1941. Every weekend we went to Zubalovo, and in the summer to the Black Sea.

'At seven I was sent to school, which was a terrible shock at the beginning. I couldn't quite make the transition from studies at home with a governess to regular school. It seemed very dull in comparison! School took all day, for one thing;

but I adjusted to the pattern of school life. I learned German and French, and then started English at eleven. I took it very seriously. Father said to me, "Who needs German, who needs French?" So I had an English teacher at home, even on vacations. I found it easy and I enjoyed it.

'I loved my years of school and I was a good student. I had a tremendous respect for my teachers – it never crossed my mind to disobey them. What teacher said was law. Ten years in the same school gave me a very good and secure feeling of continuity.

'I was my father's favourite. He was sterner and more demanding with his sons, but I was a little pet to play with. He was very affectionate with me, in a typical Caucasian way – the Georgians and Armenians overflow with affection for their children. Not so much the boys – they had to grow up and be men; but a girl was a plaything – until she grows up and becomes something else. When I was sixteen there was a complete break when I met someone and fell in love.

'I didn't adore my father, though. I had this great question which really disturbed Nanny: why, out of Mummy and Daddy, do I love Mummy more? But out of Grandfather and Grandmother, I love Grandfather more? I couldn't understand why. Nanny told me that I must love everybody. "How come you don't love Daddy, you don't love Grandma? You must love everybody!"

'I appreciated him more as a father and a parent when I grew up. I do appreciate now that he was a very loving father. I couldn't grasp it at the time. He always had this tobacco smell, puffing clouds of smoke with his pipe. He was always kissing me and smooching and I didn't like his moustache on my face. He would squeeze me and hold me in his hands. I saw the figure of my mother as more beautiful. I had great affection for her, but not for her mother Olga Eugenievna.

'Father created a secret friend for me, a girl called Lelka. He was always telling me how good Lelka is, and how well she does everything. He did it to tease me. He used to draw pictures of Lelka doing this or that, Lelka on a horse, Lelka in a boat. Then I started drawing Lelka. Finally I hated Lelka! She was a model child who did everything perfectly. It always ended in him laughing at me, and I was not fond of this girl.

'Father felt betrayed by Mother's suicide: he kept asking Eugenia Aleksandrovna what was missing in him: he could not understand it. They told me that it was very difficult to explain to him. She was so young, a different generation – from a generation of women who grew up with the revolution and wanted to have their own lives and their own jobs. He could not understand that: he was an Asian man. She was pushing something and meeting with a wall. Obviously she did not understand him, either!

'There was a rumour that he remarried, to Rosa Kaganovich. But he couldn't; twice his marriages had ended in tragedy, and that was enough. He would not try again. He was fifty-three when my mother died, so he simply took to his bachelor home at Kuntsevo which he rebuilt for his purposes.

'My mother was lucky to have died at this time. If she had lived she simply would not have been able to take all the accusations against old friends like Bukharin and many others. She would have been on their side and then things would have got even worse for her. God knows what would have happened. I don't like to think. She was not like Olga Eugenievna who sat there silently with her hand over her mouth – "I will not say anything, I am not supposed to talk." No, Mother spoke her mind.

'It was not long afterwards that the purges started. But I think they would have happened anyway, because this is a part of the process of revolution – there is a historical pattern which was followed by the French revolution too. People turn against each other. No matter how idealistic it looks at some point, when it comes down to it, revolution is blood-shed. When people smell blood they go for each other, until they all kill each other. Revolution invariably ends up being a travesty of its ideals.

'My theory is that my mother would have been a victim too. I don't think she could have escaped it. She was a very strong woman and she would have stood by her friends. So her suicide saved her at least from becoming a victim of that.'

Between 1934 and 1938 Stalin moved to discredit and eliminate his major rivals both real and potential. He also saw fit to wipe out the Old Bolsheviks, those died-in-the-wool revolutionaries who had been behind the 1917 revolution and who knew all there was to know about him, who would never become subservient to him because they well knew that Stalin was no Lenin. Between 1937 and 1938 members of almost the entire Party hierarchy below polit-buro level and over thirty-five years old were secretly arrested and executed. Three widely publicised 'purge trials' in Moscow found many of them guilty of treason (plotting to murder their leader, usually) and executed. Subsequently it was established that the accused were innocent of all charges, that they had signed confessions under intensive torture and interrogation. Zinoviev and Kamenev were among his first victims, accused of joining Trotsky in a terrorist organisation to remove Stalin from power. Bukharin and Rykov, the leaders of the right-wing opposition to Stalin, were tried in 1938, accused of acts of sabotage and espionage with intent to destroy the Soviet regime and restore capitalism. They were sentenced to death and shot.

These trials highlighted a nationwide purge that sent millions of alleged 'enemies of the people' to prison camps, or to an early grave, during the 1930s. Arguments have raged ever since as to whether such purges are necessarily inherent in the totalitarian control of one person over a bureaucracy, or whether the secret police got out of hand, or whether this was an example of Stalin's psychotic paranoia. These speculations remain unanswered.

Sasha often wonders 'what would have happened if Nadya

had not shot herself. Would Stalin's character have changed under her influence? I ask myself if he became more embittered and more cruel after her death – and because of it? I do not know the answer: but I do know that her death had a big negative impact on his character; a character which had been a hard one even before it happened.'

*Chapter Fifteen*

# TERROR AT HOME

A prince must possess the nature of both beast and man.
— Machiavelli

According to most historians it was the assassination of Sergei Kirov in Leningrad in 1934 that signalled the start of the Great Terror. Sergei Mironovich Kirov was known as a staunch supporter and friend of Stalin, who had appointed him chief of the Leningrad Party organisation in succession to Zinoviev. He was elected as a candidate member of the politburo in 1926 and supported Stalin against Bukharin and Rykov. In the early 1930s, however, he showed increasing independence in the conducting of affairs in Leningrad, became associated with protests against collectivisation, and it is probable that he was leading a group in opposition to the Party purges. At the 17th Party Congress in February 1934 Kirov was elected to the Central Committee's secretariat, making him Stalin's most powerful and indeed popular rival. On 1 December he was shot at the Communist Party headquarters by one Leonid Nikolayev.

Within months, over 30,000 people were arrested in Leningrad alone. Stalin immediately introduced the death penalty for Party members who transgressed – transgressions whose definition became increasingly inclusive. 'An enemy of the people' could be apprehended on the slightest pretext, which often amounted to nothing at all. It was enough to be a 'son of an enemy of the people'. Being a 'Trotskyite', or even mentioning the arch-enemy's name, could mean the end of freedom. Sentences of twenty-five years' hard labour in the Siberian camps were not uncommon, and were carried out without trial or conviction. From 1936 to 1938 between seven and eight million people were arrested, a figure now confirmed by the KGB authorities. At the end of the decade, 23,000 NKVD men perished, accused of trying to slow down the purges, where in fact they simply had not been able to fulfil their quotas of daily executions.

It was obvious to everyone that there was political gain for Stalin in Kirov's death. Khrushchev, in his 1956 speech at the 20th Party Congress, hinted at Stalin's direct participation in Kirov's murder, but was never afterwards permitted to refer to it. Volodya is aware that 'There is a great deal written about how Stalin was involved in the murder of Kirov. In fact he had nothing to do with it. My mother, Anna Sergeyevna, was with Stalin when they phoned him and informed him that Kirov had been murdered. My mother said to me that neither before or after had she ever seen Stalin in the state he was reduced to after that phone call.

'Moreover Stalin knew that the murder would be linked with his name, saying that he made use of it to unleash the Terror. But it was also used by the other side; it was just that Stalin turned out to be on the stronger side. He had nothing to do with the murder.'

The infamous Moscow show trials began in 1936, the year that Stalin's mother died. Sergo Ordzhonikidze suggested to Stalin that it was time to stop the arrests and slow down the repressions. Stalin sent his old friend three NKVD men, a doctor and a revolver. Offered the choice of suicide or execution, Ordzhonikidze said goodbye to his wife, went into his bedroom and shot himself. 'People were always shooting themselves in those days,' says Svetlana. The official version was that he had died of a heart attack.

In 1937 Stalin had his chief of staff, Marshal Tukachevsky, arrested along with seven other Red Army commanders. They were tried on charges of conspiring with the Germans, and shot. During that same year 40,000 officers of the Red Army were purged, one-third of whom were executed. Seven hundred monasteries in Mongolia were 'purged' and recent evidence shows that up to 100,000 Buddhists died at the hands of the NKVD in a province of eastern Russia.

The next victim close to home, Abel Yenukidze, was arrested in 1936 and never heard of again. Svetlana says, 'My father had known Abel Yenukidze for ages; he was my mother's godfather. Although he was not a big shot, he was well-known, he had worked for Lenin, was quite high in the Party hierarchy – and yet he was a victim. The cruelty is that members of the family could not be spared.'

Volodya takes up the point. 'But Stalin was the kind of person to whom it was a matter of complete indifference whether it was a relative or not a relative. It was all the same to him, who the enemy was – his brother, his son, his daughter, his niece. He didn't look at such matters. That was his most negative quality in my view. Yet there was no alteration within the family in our attitude to Stalin at this time.'

The first of Stalin's immediate family circle to succumb to the horror of these years were the Svanidzes. Abel Yenukidze's secretary of ten years' standing, Mariko Svanidze, sister of Stalin's first wife Yekaterina, was arrested in 1937 and died in prison. Stalin's brother-in-law by his first marriage, and his wife, Uncle Alyosha and Aunt Maroussya, were also arrested, charged with espionage and imprisoned. 'The fact that they spent half their time abroad was very bad for them, because they could be accused of spying,' says Svetlana.

Kyra Pavlovna takes up the story: 'The Svanidzes had just been to our housewarming party in the House on the Embankment. I remember her putting her coat on as she was leaving. Then, a few hours later, we were told that they had been arrested. We were horrified. Their son Tolya told us the news – he himself had not been arrested. But we had just seen them and it was such a shock. In general, life presented us with many surprises in those days!' She laughs as she says this.

Her younger brother Sasha tries to explain how it felt. 'It was a particularly Russian, Soviet thing to happen and it is very hard for other people to understand the feelings involved. Yet even at this young age – I was only six – we understood that the Svanidzes had been arrested and jailed. The supposition was that they had done something wrong, that they must have been guilty of something. All this was based on our total faith in the guiltlessness and sinlessness of Stalin. We all believed in him as we would believe in God. Everything was based on that faith. Everything that we know now was not known then, especially to us children. Our mother became a very strong protective buffer, our guiding force.

'A story was circulated about how Svanidze refused to confess anything, and thus he had chosen prison and death. He was a proud man, and said – according to this legend – that he had no guilt whatever and would not seek a pardon.

'It was all so complicated to understand at a psychological level. Maria Onissimovna was friends with my mother, and she managed somehow to pass a letter to her, asking her to pass it on to Stalin. She described the horrible conditions in prison and was begging for help from her close relative. Eugenia Aleksandrovna passed on the letter, which infuriated Stalin, and after that Mother believed that letters asking for help made things worse.'

Sasha's elder brother Sergei Pavlovich thinks that 'our mother Eugenia Aleksandrovna understood from that experience that the best thing is not to meddle. Shortly afterwards Aunt Maroussya was moved to a very severe labour camp, and there was no mercy for her husband either.'

In 1942 Alyosha was shot. Maroussya, sentenced to ten years in a remote labour camp, died of a heart attack on hearing the news. Sasha Pavlovich comments, 'I simply cannot believe in her being able to survive in prison. She was a beautiful woman, of noble bearing, very well-dressed, who always attracted attention. She looked like a statue, she had tremendous dignity. I simply cannot imagine her in prison. She could indeed have died on hearing such shocking news.'

The Svanidzes' elder son Tolya was killed in the war against the Germans in 1941, fighting as a volunteer in the defence of Moscow. Their younger son Johnik was arrested, aged ten, as a 'son of the enemy of the people' and sent to a dreadful orphanage for the children of arrested parents. He returned from exile in 1956 with permanent psychological damage. Kyra remembers how 'he used to visit my mother, but after she died he stopped visiting us, so the connections were severed. He managed to become a specialist in African studies in spite of his instability of character, and did a PhD in economics. He died recently and we read the notices in the newspapers. None of us went to the funeral – it was a pity we did not know about it.'

In the November of 1938 Pavel Sergeyevich, returning to his office after a vacation at the Black Sea, found his department purged, and most of his colleagues arrested. He had a heart attack and died within hours. Two weeks later his brother-in-law Redens was arrested, and later shot. NKVD records show that 350,000 people were shot during that year, although acknowledged experts now put this figure at nearer 1.5 million.

The oldest residents still in the House on the Embankment remember the fear that paralysed them during the days of terror. They knew they were constantly watched and listened to; some of them were put under house arrest. The doors of neighbours were sealed shut after they were taken away, or NKVD men moved in to take the place of their victims. Chekists stood on every floor; fear became instinctive to the children who grew up there.

Between 1936–8 between seven and eight million people

had died. in the camps. On one day in 1937 Stalin and Molotov signed 3,167 death sentences, after which they went off together to watch a film in the Kremlin movie theatre, one of Stalin's favourite forms of relaxation. By the end of the 1930s around ten million people inhabited the gulag, only 10 to 15 per cent of whom had any hope of survival. Svetlana, talking about these terrible years, asked herself at the time the rhetorical question: 'I wondered, "Is it some kind of a game?" It was all so easy, playing with lives . . . Now it is like looking into a deep well, and seeing what you don't want to see.'

Yet in a certain respect Svetlana agrees with her cousin Volodya that 'Although we lost relatives and are victims ourselves, we saw so many reasons for the purges. The caricature way to present it is that one man wanted something, and in order to get it he killed and killed and killed. This is how they present it nowadays. But it was much more complicated than that. It was the Party struggle. At the time, the politburo supported him in all he was doing, he could not do these things without politburo support. Their line was that they were fighting the opposition, that was what the Party struggle was about. To put it into caricature instead of historical objectivity is something that none of us can stomach.'

Volodya continues, 'The country was approaching war, and an opposition party had been formed with an underground regional committee, printing press and so on. It had a relatively large army which was ready to act at any moment. All this forced Stalin to take certain measures to liquidate what we call the fifth column.

'There was also his theory that the class war, as we made our progress towards socialism, would be aggravated. For all that, he should have realised that such a theory might lead to the most undesirable consequences. Nobody made any secret of the fact that hundreds of thousands were exiled with no appeal. But I do not consider it correct that all these people were wrongly repressed. The question is, what percentage were incorrectly suppressed.

'Article 131 of the constitution stated that every citizen of the Soviet union was obliged in every way to protect and increase socialism, and that people who made any attack on socialist public property were enemies of the people. That is to say, any thief. The situation in the country was such that these measures were demanded.'

Sasha's temperament inclines him towards counting the blessings, showing a remarkable lack of anger in his acceptance of these terrible events. 'We did not suffer total annihilation: our flats were reserved for us. We got some pension money. We could live in Moscow, and later on, when we were older, enter colleges – and the same for Leonid and Volodya. So some kind of special treatment was given to all four of us in this respect.'

Volodya remains doggedly loyal. 'Our relationship with Stalin lasted as it had been from the very beginning. It carried on right to the end of his life in our family.' His loyalty illustrates the insidious effects of the culture imposed upon his generation. The experience of his own impotence in the face of indescribable fear and pain appears to have effected a low evaluation of human freedom. His ongoing respect for Stalin in spite of the deaths in the family – whom clearly he loves deeply – is a measure of the slavery in which Stalin held them. It is a mirror of the mass hypnosis of Stalin's personal power which seduced an entire nation into submitting to his whims.

Kyra, however, retains the human perspective with this understatement: 'It is nevertheless difficult to understand that people in his own family suffered from the repressions.'

Not every minute of Stalin's life was spent purging his country during the thirties, although the games of politics were reflected in leisure times at home. Sasha has a memory of an incident from family life just before the Great Terror started. 'There was a game of billiards at Stalin's dacha, not long before the arrest of the Svanidzes. Pavel Sergeyevich and Stalin were playing against Svanidze and Redens. One year later, please note, the only one left alive was Stalin; the others were dead or arrested . . . Anyway, the traditional rules of the game are that the losers must undergo the humiliation of crawling under the table. Stalin and Pavel Sergeyevich lost the game, but instead of crawling under the table my father, thinking quickly and diplomatically, asked me and Sergei to crawl instead of them. We did so with pleasure. However, Kyra objected and said, "This is against the rules! They have lost, let them crawl under!" My father got very cross with her and hit her with a billiard cue. I was very angry with him and we had a quarrel, but in the end he forgave her and was kind to her.'

Volodya says: 'Pavel was very close to Stalin who gave him important personal assignments. Even the fact that Pavel bought Nadya the very pistol with which she shot herself – even this did not stop them from seeing each other later.' Kyra remembers how Stalin 'sent my father to Paris as Commissar with the Red Army ensemble and choir to perform there, a very important – and first – demonstration of that kind. There was a World Exhibition there, and the USSR was represented. He also sent him to Prague.' Sasha adds that 'he permitted Eugenia Aleksandrovna to accompany my father to Paris, if only for one week, and she kept memories about that all the rest of her life. And that was because she personally asked him to permit her this trip.' There is a large collection of photographs in the Alliluyev collection showing Pavel and Eugenia on this trip, looking carefree and happy, really enjoying themselves; 'young and gay' in the days of art deco.

Volodya feels that 'It was a large and close-knit family – they all saw each other very often in those days.' Svetlana says, 'Everyone was very loyal in the family, they were very close-knit. For all of them, my father and my mother were central figures and it revolved around them.'

The sudden death of Pavel was deeply shocking for the family. His niece Svetlana recounts it in outline. 'Uncle

*143*

Pavel Sergeyevich died when I was twelve. I remember him as a wonderfully good-looking man, I remember always being hugged and kissed and played with, especially after my mother died. My brother and I were very much loved and caressed by him. It was such a shock, because he had a sudden heart attack at his work, terribly upset by the sight of an empty department when he returned from his vacation at the Black Sea. Almost everybody had been arrested while he was away – all his Red Army colleagues had gone. He attempted to save certain people, trying to get hold of my father and talk to him, but it was no use, and he had a heart attack.'

Kyra was deeply affected. She was eighteen when her father died. 'My father was so young, only in his forties, and such a handsome man he was. He had such long dark eyelashes – even when he was dead we could see those long lashes.

'There was a puzzle about his death. He had just returned from his vacation in Sochi, had given up smoking, was suntanned and looked marvellous. The next day he went to his office. They rang us from there and asked, "What did he eat?" – because he had had an attack of nausea. "Well, just the usual breakfast – coffee and so on." As always he walked down from the eighth floor, not using the lift, for exercise. Suddenly at 2 pm they telephoned us: he had had a heart attack and they took him to the hospital. He was calling for my mother. But for some reason they did not send for her in time, and she only got to see him when he was dead. We children saw him later laid out in his coffin.'

Sasha was only seven when he lost his father. 'Father had not spent too much time with me. I saw him for the last time a day before he died; he called me from the dacha, he had just returned from his holidays and I remember him forever as he was that day. We saw him in the evening, had breakfast with him the next morning. He was only forty-three. Next day he died suddenly.

'It was the most severe shock for Sergei Yakovlevich. This

was when Grandfather was really broken. It was the second great blow for him – his younger daughter had died just a few years before.' His family appeared to be disintegrating around him. The repercussions on the family were far-reaching: Pavel's wife Eugenia Aleksandrovna was outlawed from visiting her relatives in the Kremlin, and soon after-wards, after Redens' arrest, Anna Sergeyevna suffered the same indignity. Family life was – here as elsewhere – frag-menting under the effects of the revolution.

In all, the Great Terror claimed, between 1929 and 1940, six million workers, fourteen million peasants and three million intelligentsia. Their fates were various: some per-ished in camps, some died from starvation, some were executed by shooting. These twenty-three million people were 'repressed', or 'finished off', in the terminology of the time; 'liquidated' was another favourite. This 'bloodbath of absolute dictatorship' as Svetlana describes it, was per-petrated for the sake of one man's need to hang on to power, in the name of an ideology that could never work. It was a medieval tyranny sanctioned by the sacrifice – and by implication, the complicity – of the people who participated in the game of building a utopia. The parts were being sacrificed for the whole, as in Peter the Great's time, for a matter of principle.

At Yale University in the 1970s an experiment was carried out with a view to testing the limits of the average man's obedience to authority, and showing the power of a figure-head over ordinary people. Dr Stanley Milgram's results clearly showed 'the capacity for man to abandon his humanity, indeed the inevitability that he does so, as he merges his unique personality into larger institutional struc-tures.

'It is ironic that the virtues of loyalty, discipline and self-sacrifice that we value so highly in the individual are the very properties that create destructive organisational engines of war and bind men to malevolent systems of authority.'

Dostoevski, in *Notes from the House of the Dead*, describes the addiction of this authority: 'Whoever has experienced the power, the complete ability to humiliate another human being . . . with the most extreme humiliation, willy-nilly loses power over his own sensations. Tyranny is a habit, it has a capacity for development, it develops finally into a disease . . . The human being and the citizen die within the tyrant for ever; return to humanity, to repentance, to regeneration becomes almost impossible.'

And another power, the power of the collective, was moving inexorably on its course. A Leviathan was on the move, bringing indiscriminate destruction in its wake. This imaginary Satanic monster of legend, whose definition includes 'a man of vast power', came to have its name applied to the organic whole of a commonwealth; a monstrous creature whose untrammelled power sweeps all before it as it rolls on towards its destiny.

## Chapter Sixteen

# LEVIATHAN

> In those years only the dead smiled,
> Glad to be at rest.
> — Anna Akhmatova, 'Requiem'

Pavel Sergeyevich's tombstone stands slightly apart from the other family graves in the Novedevichy cemetery in Moscow, next to Molotov's. It is noticeably larger than the headstones of Fyodor, Anna and his parents, which stand next to each other in the adjacent bed. Pavel's memorial befits a man who reached the rank of General of Tank Forces of the Red Army: the great slab of polished dark-grey marble has his portrait embossed on it, his personal details engraved, and at the base is carved a bas-relief of a large tank in action.

The family plot lies in a corner of this quiet cemetery, under the gleaming gold towers of the medieval Novedevichy Convent. Birch trees in autumn match the gilt domes, their burnished leaves rustling in light rain. Olga and Sergei, Fyodor and Anna lie buried under granite-coloured marble headstones, which simply tell their names, dates of birth and death, and the date that they became Party members. Medallion portraits in low relief are engraved into the dark stone of the parents' headstones; the rain runs over their faces like tears. At the opposite end to Pavel's grave stands a tall, square pillar of white marble with a graceful head sculpted from the top. This is Nadya's memorial, erected by her husband and which, Svetlana emphatically maintains, he never visited. The elegant monument is now protected by thick perspex to guard against not infrequent attempts to vandalise it.

'Anna Sergeyevna was in Kazakhstan with my father on 2 November when she heard the news of Uncle Pavel's death. She left immediately for Moscow,' says her son Volodya, 'but arrived late for her brother's funeral. She was still there in Moscow in the House on the Embankment when, on 19 November, my father was recalled from Alma Ata to the capital.' Alma Ata, capital of the Kazakh republic in central Asia, is named after the many apple trees that grow there. It is considered one of the most beautiful cities of the CIS with its tree-lined streets, parks and orchards, surrounded by a mountain landscape. 'Redens had been sent to Kazakhstan as People's Commissar for Internal Affairs early in 1938. He was arrested on his return to the capital.' His colleages in the NKVD tried to compel him into confessing that he had been spying for Latvia, but to no avail. As with so many other failed forced confessions, Stalin grew restless. He arranged for Anna to be brought to her husband in Lefortovo prison with a promise of freedom for him, and safety for all the family, if he would admit to being a counterrevolutionary. Redens tried to persuade his wife that Stalin could not be trusted in anything, and asked the duty officer to take her away.

When Stanislav Frantzevich Redens was arrested, says Sergei Pavlovich, 'the NKVD came to search their place in Moscow. Grandfather Sergei was there, and they would not let him go. Now he was Stalin's father-in-law, after all, and he suffered very deeply from this insult. It was the first time he was forced to be present during a police search.'

'I never knew of any accusation against my father,' continues Volodya, 'although he was incriminated by an alleged link with the Polish intelligence service. He was in a very senior position in the NKVD so evidently he must have taken a part in the purges. But he was rehabilitated in 1961 after new evidence came to light.'

Kyra remembers the day when they heard the news. 'It

Karolina Til (*left*), housekeeper to the Stalins in the 1920s and early 1930s, and Aleksandra Bychkova, Svetlana's nanny from 1926 until her retirement in the 1940s. *(Alliluyev Family Collection)*

Svetlana, aged five, with her brother Vasili, aged ten, in 1931. This picture was taken by their mother Nadya not long before her death. *(Alliluyev Family Collection)*

Svetlana, aged eight, with papa Stalin, on vacation at their Black Sea dacha in 1934. *(Alliluyev Family Collection)*

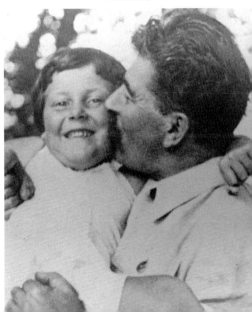

*Above:* (*Left to right*) Anna Sergeyevna Alliluyeva with her niece Kyra Pavlovna and her brother Pavel Sergeyevich, Kyra's father, in Berlin in the late 1920s or early 1930s. (*Alliluyev Family Collection*)

*Left:* An official Military Academy portrait of Yakov Iosevich Djugashvili (1908-43), Stalin's elder son by his first marriage. (*Alliluyev Family Collection*)

*Below:* (*Left to right*) Vasili, Yakov, Svetlana (*in front*) with their grandmother 'Keke', Stalin's mother Yekaterina Djugashvili, in 1935. (*David King Collection*)

*Back, standing left to right:* Mariko Svanidze, Maria Svanidze ('Aunt Maroussya'), Sergei Yakovlevich Alliluyev. *Centre, seated left to right:* nanny Aleksandra Bychkova, governess Nathalie Konstantinova, Anna Sergeyevna Redens. *Front, left to right:* Svetlana, Vasili with Bukharin's daughter on his knee. *c.*1930. *(Alliluyev Family Collection)*

(*Left to right*) Sasha, Sergei and Kyra Alliluyev, children of Pavel and Eugenia, *c.*1932. They still live in Moscow today. *(Alliluyev Family Collection)*

Stalin (*right*) with Vasili and Svetlana. *(David King Collection)*

*Left:* Pavel Sergeyevich Alliluyev, Nadya's elder brother (1894–1938). *(Alliluyev Family Collection)*

Eugenia Aleksandrovna Alliluyeva (1898–1974), wife of Pavel and sister-in-law to Stalin, 1932. *(Alliluyev Family Collection)*

*Right:* Anna Sergeyevna Alliluyeva, Nadya's elder sister (1896–1964). *(Alliluyev Family Collection)*

Family group, 1937. *Left to right:* Pavel Sergeyevich, nanny Tatyana Moskaleva, Stanislav Redens holding baby Volodya, his wife Anna Sergeyevna. *Front:* Sergei Pavlovich *(left)* and Leonid Stanislavich. *(Alliluyev Family Collection)*

Stanislav Franzevich Redens (1892-1941) of the Cheka. He was husband to Anna Sergeyevna Alliluyeva and father of Leonid and Volodya. *(Author's collection)*

Anna Sergeyevna Alliluyeva, 1947. *(David King Collection)*

Mikoyan *(left)* with Voroshilov. *(David King Collection)*

Beria *(right)* with a Civil War veteran in the Trans-Caucasus, mid-1930s. *(David King Collection)*

Ladies of the Kremlin at a tennis party in the 1920s: Nadya Alliluyeva (*left*), Mme Voroshilov (*centre*) and Mme Mikoyan (*right*). *(Alliluyev Family Collection)*

Sergei Yakovlevich Alliluyev on holiday by the Black Sea, late 1920s – 'the good years'. *(Alliluyev Family Collection)*

Anastas Ivanovich Mikoyan (1895-1978), Peoples' Commissar for Internal and External Trade, *c.*1938. *(Hulton-Deutsch Collection)*

*Top:* Stalin (*centre*), Ordzhonikidze and Kaganovich inspecting a new model caterpillar tractor at the Auto-Tractor Institute, 16 July 1935. *(Society for Cooperation in Russian & Soviet Studies)*

*Above:* Svetlana (*left*) with brother Vasili and their cousin Sasha Pavlovich, 1934. *(Alliluyev Family Collection)*

*Below:* Stalin, Molotov, Voroshilov, Kalinin, Kaganovich, Mikoyan and Dmitrov on Lenin's Mausoleum, 1935. *(Society for Cooperation in Russian & Soviet Studies)*

Stalin with his daughter Svetlana in the 1930s. *(David King Collection)*

Nadya Alliluyeva, 1930/31. *(Alliluyev Family Collection)*

Nadya in 1932 at Zubalovo, the family's dacha near Moscow, not long before her suicide. *(Alliluyev Family Collection)*

Nadya in her open coffin, November 1932. *(David King Collection)*

White marble memorial to Nadya Alliluyeva in the Novedevichy cemetery in Moscow, erected to her memory by Stalin. *(Alliluyev Family Collection)*

Nadya's monument is now covered in thick perspex to guard against attempts to vandalise the family graves. *(Author's collection)*

Vasili Stalin, on horseback aged about sixteen, a
young boy devastated by his mother's death.
*(Alliluyev Family Collection)*

A 1937 USSR montage proclaiming the Stalin
Constitution. *(David King Collection)*

Banner depicting Stalin at a Physkult parade in
Moscow, 1939. *(David King Collection)*

Svetlana, aged eight, with her brother Vasili, aged thirteen, in 1934. *(Alliluyev Family Collection)*

Svetlana, aged ten, with her father at the height of the purges, 1936. *(Alliluyev Family Collection)*

Svetlana in 1937 or 1938, aged about eleven. *(Alliluyev Family Collection)*

Svetlana sent this picture to Stalin for his birthday in 1937. 'Your expression is not suitable for someone your age', he scribbled over it before sending it back. *(Alliluyev Family Collection)*

Sergei Mironovich Kirov. *(David King Collection)*

A mourning public file past Kirov's body as it lies in state, December 1934. *(David King Collection)*

Kirov lying in his bier, 1934. *(David King Collection)*

Stalin colluding with Kaganovich, 1937. *(David King Collection)*

Lavrenti Pavlovich Beria (1899-1953), supervisor of Soviet internal security and member of the Politburo. *(David King Collection)*

The tombstone of Pavel Sergeyevich Alliluyev, which stands slightly apart from the other family graves in the Novedevichy cemetery, Moscow. His wife Eugenia's stone is to the left. *(Author's collection)*

Volodya (*left*) and Leonid, sons of Anna Alliluyeva and Stanislav Redens, a photo taken before their father's arrest in 1938. *(Alliluyev Family Collection)*

Molotov signing the Russo-German Pact, October 1939. Stalin can be seen in the background. *(David King Collection)*

Generalissimo Stalin.
*(Hulton-Deutsch Collection)*

A view of the port at
Odessa, 1940. *(Society for
Cooperation in Russian &
Soviet Studies)*

Molotov greets Churchill, August 1942. *(David King Collection)*

Voroshilov addressing a meeting. *(David King Collection)*

was terrible. I do not know how Aunt Anna remained alive. They were such a happy couple, he was such a lovely man, and her husband of twenty years. I don't know how she lived through that.'

Leonid remembers 'the feelings that my mother had – how terrible it was for her after already losing her sister Nadya. Volodya and I stayed on in Alma Ata with Nanny Tatyana until we were sent for in Moscow. My brother was only three or four when it happened, so his memory of his father is very sketchy. I was ten. It was only much later that my mother explained to me what had happened.'

Volodya's view is that 'Uncle Pavel's death created something of a chance for Beria to get rid of Redens. My father had been an obstacle to Beria in Georgia, and in his capacity as inspector he had had a direct line to Stalin. This was not to Beria's liking.

'Whether he organised that himself or whether he was lucky that Pavel died, I don't know. If Pavel, the peacemaker, had been alive, my father's arrest would never have happened. He was a key factor. Uncle Pavel was very close to Stalin.

'As soon as Mother came to herself she rang Stalin, who told her to "come and have a talk". He said that Molotov would be present too, and that Redens "would be brought" to the meeting, and "we shall make an enquiry about all this. And bring Grandfather Sergei Yakovlevich with you." But at the last moment Grandfather, for some unknown reason, refused to go. To this day I do not know why. So Mother went with Grandmother Olga Eugenievna and as a result a quarrel occurred, and that was the end of it.'

Leonid's version goes like this: 'Anna and Olga went to see him, and Stalin said to Olga, "Why have you come? No one called you." Anna, who was a forceful personality, shouted at Stalin, and he threw her out. Not only did this meeting achieve nothing, it may have made things worse. In any case it proved that Stalin wasn't going to do anything about the situation.'

Volodya continues: 'God knows what happened: maybe

*149*

Stalin was enraged by Sergei Yakovlevich's refusal to participate, thinking that he did not want to contaminate himself with all this. Or possibly there was a threat of some kind from Beria's direction to harm someone else in the family. Or maybe there was something that Sergei Yakovlevich didn't trust Redens about, maybe that's it.'

Leonid makes another point, concerning the personal relationship between Sergei Yakovlevich and Redens. 'It was a complex story. Redens came from the revolutionary elite, high up in the Party, whereas Grandfather was a simple, original revolutionary. There was a difference of character between them – Sergei was very stern and serious; Redens came from a different background, he was easygoing, relaxed, not so fervent, and I saw that there was conflict there. Maybe he thought that to go with his daughter to plead with Stalin for this man would be like throwing pearls before swine.'

'If Uncle Pavel had been alive,' according to Volodya, 'something could have been achieved, he would have been able to stop him. Pavel and Grandpa would have stood up to Stalin. But only the women were left, and the women on their own failed.'

But Sasha argues that 'It was an individual trait of Stalin that he made all the decisions by himself, alone. Yet the women in the family, my mother Eugenia Aleksandrovna, and Olga Eugenievna, could speak to him as equals and ask things from him without fear. Anna Sergeyevna, too, could and did. Sometimes he would change his decisions because of them and do what they wanted. But men avoided asking him about anything. Men would not go to him for favours.'

'Belonging to the family was rather dangerous,' remarks Svetlana wryly. 'Although Redens was removed by Beria in an internal struggle of the NKVD, my father would not protect him.' Leonid agrees that 'It is possible that Beria was responsible for his death, but he could not have done it without the acquiescence and knowledge of Stalin.'

*150*

Volodya continues, 'We didn't know at the time whether my father had been sentenced – there was no court procedure. For a long time we believed that he was still alive. Mother remained devoted.' Indeed Anna Sergeyevna, according to Svetlana, refused to believe in his death – she fondly imagined right up to the end of her life that her husband had been exiled to the far north and had raised another family. Even his sons do not know the details of Redens' death; the assumption is that he was shot in 1941, three years after his arrest.

Why Sergei Yakovlevich did not intervene to save his daughter's husband remains a mystery. The man was quite likely crippled with grief after the loss of his eldest son, following Nadya's suicide. Perhaps he also knew too much about Redens and the part he had played in the repressions. But 'Grandfather was no weakling,' says Volodya, 'he was not afraid of anybody, neither Stalin nor Beria. He said that Beria was "an enemy of the people" – in the presence of Stalin! I can only surmise that pressure was put on him *not* to go to the meeting. He was the last man left in the family – there were no others after him. Grandfather was held in tremendous respect and therefore he could change things. But he said at Pavel's funeral, less than three weeks before, that there is nothing more terrible in the world than to bury your own children.'


The arrests, trials, and executions of the late 1930s in Russia still evoke horror that such inhumanity can exist. Deserted camps in Siberia pay silent witness to the hundreds of thousands of human beings whose lot was undeserved slave labour in freezing conditions, in thin clothing and on minimal food rations. Shallow pits reveal their bodies, thrown carelessly into piles without the decency of burial; heaps of bones define banks of corpses used as windbreaks around living quarters. Survivors have described the execution missions of squads of NKVD men who would call at the camps regularly. These visiting parties called the mass shootings 'cleansing actions'. More sophisticated methods were advocated in the KGB handbook which makes chilling reading in its understatements: 'To incline the accused to confession is a difficult matter and demands great agility and skill from the person conducting the inquiry.' A telegram from Stalin to party officials set the seal on this diabolical period: 'The Central Committee of the All-Union Communist Party explains that the application of methods of physical pressure in NKVD practice is permissible from 1937 onwards.'

Svetlana the historian – she graduated in history at Moscow University – looks at the purges in this context: 'This is the course of revolution, which turns on her own, and devours them. These people were devoured by the Leviathan. It is the ideology that is the monster. These people had no influence over events, they were the victims. But at the same time they were also accountable. Everything in Russia at that time was collective: the purges, the gulags, all relied on the complicity and collusion of the people. One person alone couldn't have done all this – not even Lenin. All the people who surrounded my father in the Central Committee went along with it as well. They didn't object openly, so it was their heritage too. It became a phenomenon of the collective, supported by everyone, not only around Stalin but in the country as a whole. It is a great disservice to the public to put history into caricature, because we never learn anything from this. We are all responsible for everything that happened.

'But,' she admits, 'we didn't see the tragedy. "Power corrupts, and absolute power corrupts absolutely." There is a cycle that is typical to revolution – revolution is circular, as the word implies. As one of Dostoevski's characters in *The Possessed* prophetically puts it, "I am afraid I got rather muddled up in my own data, and my conclusion is in direct contradiction to the original idea with which I started. Starting from unlimited freedom, I arrived at unlimited despotism." '

*152*

## Chapter Seventeen

# EVIL GENIUS

The most monstrous epoch in human history.
— Joseph Brodsky

By the end of 1938 Beria had made it to Moscow and succeeded Yezhov as chief of the NKVD. Yezhov had held the post for two years, following on from the infamous Yagoda, and had administered the most severe stage of the great purges which were named the 'Yezhovshchina' after him. He 'disappeared' in 1939. Beria, on taking over, gave orders to reduce the numbers of inmates in the camps; but not in any humanitarian way by letting the innocent go free. In the Kolyma camps for example the sick and weak were, after a hot bath, driven out into minus 50 degree centigrade frosts, where they immediately froze to death. They were then put into cages fixed to tractor sledges, rigid and upright, and carried to the marshes. Here their corpses were unloaded with steel hooks. Thus were the number of inmates reduced.

It would appear from all accounts that Beria's life was dedicated to torture and execution. He was also a pervert, choosing to have sex with children and virgins. He selected victims himself from the streets. Yevtushenko, in his autobiography of 1966, has a memory of this man: 'I saw the predatory hawk-like face of Beria muffled in a scarf, when he pressed himself against the window of a car creeping along the pavement in search of the next female. After this the same man addressed the people speaking with pathos about communism.'

But Beria was essential to Stalin's purposes; Stalin needed

to attribute his mistakes to others and fix the blame on the 'enemies of the revolution' who had committed the sin of offending his personal pride – even by omission. Beria was his agent, and ideally suited to the job; his obnoxiousness was evident to everyone except, apparently, Stalin. 'It was difficult,' says Svetlana, 'for a little local KGB man from Georgia to make his career in Moscow. The family circle, who all knew the Georgian situation very well, knew that he was not the man to be close to my father. They had their opinions, they were outspoken, they were not at all intimidated. So as far as Beria was concerned they had to be removed. Each one dead was another step up the ladder for him.'

Sasha remains mystified about Beria's ascent. 'All our family was completely baffled as to why Stalin made Beria – a provincial KGB man – so close to himself and to the government in Moscow. Our Georgian relatives, our friends, many people around knew well what a scoundrel Beria was. He was a cruel, immoral man, who loved intrigue, who was a pervert in many ways – and none of us could understand why suddenly Stalin put such trust in this man.

'My mother Eugenia Aleksandrovna took a great personal dislike to him. He was well-known as a womaniser, and once he tried very clumsily to court her – while Stalin and my father Pavel Sergeyevich sat nearby. So Mother walked up to Stalin and said, "If this bastard does not leave me alone, I shall smash his pince-nez." Everybody laughed, but we all feared that Beria never forgot this humiliation. That was before 1938, while Beria was still gradually acquiring a position close to Stalin in Moscow.'

Svetlana embroiders on the theme of Beria's attitude to women. 'I became friendly with his wife, who was a beautiful woman. She was a figurehead wife, since it was well-known that he had a harem of mistresses. She lived in her half of the apartment – the civilised half. She would come out of her sanctuary for official occasions, but she suffered very much over the other women.

'She told me how she met Beria. She went to him to plead for the freedom of her brother who had been arrested, in Georgia, when Beria was head of the secret police there. She was about sixteen. He saw her, she was pretty, so he locked her up in the special carriage of his special KGB train and she became his wife. She said to me, "When I hear the word *love*, my blood curdles!" Beria was following primitive Caucasian habits of stealing pretty women.'

Sasha goes on, 'Beria was the executor, a direct participator in the events of those days. He implemented "the crimes", he accused the victims, named the "participators" in "espionage", in "plots" and so on. Beria supplied Stalin with information, true or false, and Stalin could act accordingly.'

Svetlana looks at the currency that bought Beria his high position: 'Kirov and Ordzhonikidze were the other two people who knew what Beria was like, having witnessed his early days in the Caucasus, and they had to be eliminated too. They would never have permitted his rise to power.

'Beria got to work on my father. He was influential in removing any feminine influence from around Stalin: aunts, Mother, the Svanidzes. Perhaps he saw that Stalin could possibly have been influenced by the women and he didn't like to see that. After the purges, from 1938–41, my aunts were forbidden to visit. Then our old housekeeper, Karolina Til, was sacked because she came from Riga, and the new one was Beria's sister-in-law, a stupid Georgian woman. New rules were set for the household by my father, and my aunts couldn't come there.'

The isolation around Stalin proved fertile ground for Beria: he swiftly established a power base, making Stalin more and more dependent on him, fending others off, maintaining control of the area immediately around his precious leader, and thereby nourishing his paranoia.

'Beria wanted to eliminate this big circle of independent people around my father,' declares Svetlana. 'He wanted to have my father to himself, as his patron, to listen to him and follow his advice: so he had to eliminate them all. But they would stand there like a wall and not let him close. So he had to go to extreme lengths – and he did. My aunts and cousins believe that this is what happened, that it was a plan carried out at their expense and at the loss of their lives. Beria succeeded: the family were dispersed, they disappeared, and after the war my father was completely isolated. Beria was there every minute he could be. He had made his career, and his opinions were listened to.

'When the purges started Eugenia Aleksandrovna tried to protect people, and she clashed with Beria like dynamite, especially because she was good-looking, and he was a great womaniser. One time he tried to touch her knee under the table and she immediately said, "Joseph! he's trying to squeeze my knee!" and the whole table looked at Beria. He practically disappeared! She said later, "I think he never forgot." He was furious that she could get away with it.

'Another time she was dressed up for a party in an outfit with a frilly jabot, and spent a lot of time close to my father laughing and making jokes. Beria got annoyed, came over and joggled her jabot saying, "What is this you have here?" She got really angry and grabbed him by the turtle-neck sweater he was wearing under his jacket. It was not the fashion to wear turtle-necks, and she pulled him hard towards her and said, "How dare you come to dinner in this?"

'There was a telephone table in the apartment in the Kremlin,' recalls Svetlana, 'with various telephones – long-distance and special government lines which were not open to the city. But father kept one city telephone, and once in a while he would call Aunt Eugenia and talk to her – he liked to do that.'

But the warm friendship between Eugenia Aleksandrovna and Stalin was to be one of the casualties in family relationships that beleaguer this story. Her remarriage had the effect of cooling it considerably on Stalin's side. For Eugenia Aleksandrovna was not a widow long, as her daughter Kyra tells. 'She remarried pretty soon, in 1939 or 1940; she felt very lonely and scarred in those years with three children. Her new husband, an engineer, had two children as well, and was a widower. They had known each other for a long time. His wife had been arrested as an enemy of the people – she was Polish. So they decided to join together, there was a lot of similarity in their situations. She felt that this way the boys would have a father, the girls a mother.'

'She married,' says Svetlana, 'Nikolai Vladimovich, an old flame and classmate. His son and daughter joined her three children, and the new family worked well for several years.' Kyra continues, 'But their marriage infuriated everyone, including Stalin. He sympathised with the Georgian tradition of lengthy mourning, and that was the way he felt. So gradually, after that, he ceased seeing my mother. It was the first break in their friendship. Georgians, traditionally, can mourn for decades, so it is shocking to them to remarry so soon.'

Eugenia's second husband also happened to be a Jew, which more than probably coloured Stalin's attitude to his sister-in-law. Beria tried to get his own back on Eugenia Aleksandrovna by circulating a rumour that she had poisoned Pavel Sergeyevich. She had a motive in that she had wished to remarry, he alleged, and Kyra Pavlovna saw how Beria sowed his poisonous seed. 'It was suggested that Eugenia wanted to remarry and that she got rid of her husband. It was nonsense, of course! But it gave Stalin that small wound which later grew larger and larger, and which poisoned his thinking about her. He became very reserved with her, yet they had always been such good friends.'

Svetlana agrees with Sasha that 'Beria was a professional executor. He enjoyed interrogating people – sitting there and receiving his pleasure. The persistent idea among the Alliluyevs is that Beria was an evil genius in the family. That he influenced Father, got his trust, and wanted to get rid of a certain number of people to further his own career. Sovietologists jump on me and say, "Oh, she is putting all the blame on Beria." Not so. I simply point out the things they did together. He was very clever, a cunning politician.

'Children have instincts about people like this. There was something unpleasant about him. The others – Molotov, Voroshilov, Kaganovich – had a certain dignity, they talked to my father as equals, calling him Joseph, and *ti*, the familiar form of "you". Beria could not handle these older statesmen who remembered and loved Nadya, and who had been close to the family for a long time. They never flattered my father. Beria was always flattering him. Father would say something, and Beria would immediately say, "Oh yes, you are *so* right, absolutely true, how true!" in an obsequious way. None of the others, even if they did agree with him, were flapping their wings like this and being 'yes men'. He was a creep.

'He was always emphasising that he was devoted to my father, and it got through to Stalin that whatever he said, this man supported him. Others might disagree and argue with him, because they had their own opinions. But Beria was his man.'

'I was a small boy while all this was going on,' says Leonid. 'I was taken to Stalin's home at Kuntsevo in the thirties, but then after 1941 I didn't visit it at all. I liked being at the dacha, among the adults – I was, if I may say so, a nice, well-behaved child! I remember two or three times being in the Kremlin apartment with the others – but not the conversations or the politics. I remember all the books in the apartment, and running around it as a child.

'I liked stuffing tobacco into Stalin's pipe. Although I was very young, I had the impression of Stalin being a complicated man, of being "alone in company".

'One summer at Kuntsevo, which had large grounds, I got lost. I happened upon a large group of adults, including Stalin. They all laughed at me except Stalin, who was nice to me and said, "Have you got lost? Come with me, I'll show you the way." He was all right with children, but I wouldn't say particularly affectionate with them – it was no big deal.

'I do remember one time being with my mother Anna Sergeyevna and Stalin in a big room, sitting at a table. It was in 1937. We were eating hard-boiled eggs and knocking the tops together. I remember Uncle Joseph saying to me, "Look, you've beaten me!"

'But Anna Sergeyevna said what she liked in front of Stalin – she was not shy or reserved. He was the husband of her beloved sister and they had known each other for a very long time, so she was on very familiar terms with him. But after my father Redens was arrested, I had the feeling that Stalin was avoiding her.'

Sasha, of all the cousins, was singled out for special attention by Uncle Joseph. 'I was one of few children with whom Stalin communicated at all. Before the arrests began, the whole big family would gather together at holidays and celebrations. There would be a dinner – or more like a supper, looking something like a typical Georgian banquet. Uncle Joseph would sit at the head of the table, in the middle of one side, with everyone around, and we children were always part of the picture. My first memories of him are of a host at the sumptuous table. He would always carve the chicken himself, and would offer it to everyone – he knew how to take care of his guests. He would serve the wine. Food was always good and he saw to it that everyone would be pleased – he was attentive to their needs.

'It was much later – probably only during wartime – that I understood who he was and what he was about. But at those dinners he was very kind and generous, and everyone behaved with respect to him. I was also the smallest, and going by photos an attractive-looking child, and Stalin had some kind of preference towards me. I am not bragging about this, simply saying that he liked me best.

'Of course, we didn't see him that often; Stalin seldom visited Zubalovo after 1937. The last time was in 1941, just before war broke out. We were at the Mikoyans' dacha.

Leonid, Volodya and Aunt Anna were staying there, although Redens was already in prison.'

It seems that Stalin chose this moment to visit Anna Sergeyevna to try to persuade her to get her husband to confess to counter-revolutionary activities. Volodya was there too. 'I saw my uncle only once. He came to Zubalovo after the argument with my mother about my father, and I saw him after this. I was very sweet then – you can see from the photo that I had curly blond hair! I met him with my mother; he got out of the car and said, "With a son like that I can forgive you anything." He spent quite some time with us that day – it was a relaxed family atmosphere. Sure, he was a busy man with no time, but on that day he was in a most friendly mood and I retain very pleasant memories of him. He was nice to me. I cannot say anything bad! That was the only meeting I had with him.'

Sasha recalls the idiosyncratic behaviour of his uncle on that occasion. 'Suddenly Leonid came to fetch me and brought me to Zubalovo. Stalin and Molotov were already there having supper, and he had requested that I be brought right away. Then he asked me about Sergei, who was then fetched too, in a second car! And what about Kyra? Well, she had to be there too, and a third car was sent to fetch her. We could not just all gather together on our own – the initiative had to be his alone.

'That was the last time I saw him. I was about nine or ten years old. He wanted to take me on his lap, and because I was so big I had to "help" him with that. Being very close I saw that he was pock-marked, and that the colour of his face was not healthy – yellowish, and his moustache stained with tobacco. I was so close to it I could see that it was dyed. Molotov sat next to him and he was as pale as a corpse. They both looked very bad; I even thought to myself that Molotov is going to die soon! Yet he lived for at least another forty-five years!

'There was one funny episode in 1936–7. That year there had been a famous expedition to the North Pole from Russia, which included a dog, Skolya, who had become very famous worldwide. The dog, a black Siberian husky, was later presented to Stalin and lived at Zubalovo. Yet I, knowing about this dog as everybody did, could not figure out why it had been presented to this family and why I suddenly met him one day, when on vacation visiting my grandfather.

'Later in life I found it curious that he singled me out as a special child, whereas he was very dismissive of his own sons Yakov and Vasili. But then, I absolutely did not understand what Stalin was about.'

In Germany, Hitler was preparing for war. When Britain and France signed the Munich agreement with the Nazis in 1939, Stalin saw this as giving a free hand to Hitler on his eastern front. He immediately appointed Molotov as minister for foreign affairs and began to explore the possibility of accommodation with the Germans. For Russia was not ready for war. The army had been greatly weakened by Stalin's purges of 1937 which had robbed it of 40,000 officers, most of them of high rank. Nor was Russian equipment comparable with that of the Nazis. Guessing that Hitler would not want war on two fronts, Stalin negotiated with him and they signed the German–Soviet non-aggression pact on 23 August 1939.

By April 1940 Europe appeared to be at Hitler's feet. Stalin, although publicly trusting Hitler's word and forbidding anti-German propaganda, nonetheless accelerated his arms industry, placated Hitler with trade concessions, and strengthened his frontiers. He also concluded a non-aggression pact with Japan, as his nephew remembers from a visit Stalin made to their dacha in 1941.

The visit evidently made an impression on all of the children, and Sergei describes it with his own eye for detail. 'I remember Stalin vividly from those years. We all saw him *en famille* for the last time in 1941. The Japanese minister for foreign affairs visited Moscow and Stalin went to see him off – even to the very carriage of his train! A most unusual event, he never did that for anybody else. I presume it was because the agreement had been made that Japan would not enter the war on Germany's side. Both Stalin and Molotov were happy; so happy that they came straight to Zubalovo from the railway station. Then we were all invited over from our dacha. He was in a very good, cheerful mood. It was not particularly a party, a celebration, but he was in a good mood and my mother explained why, although I was still only twelve. Leonid and Volodya were invited, Svetlana was there, Grandfather and Grandmother, and my mother explained to me how important it was that the neutrality of Japan had been secured, even if for a few years. This was April or May 1941 – the war with the Germans had not started. We knew nothing of what was coming upon us.'

## Chapter Eighteen

# WAR

By late spring 1941 Hitler's plans to attack the Soviet Union were obvious to all but Stalin. German troops were massing on the Russian borders; German aircraft were flying daily over Soviet territory; intelligence reports testified to Nazi intentions. Yet Stalin refused to believe them, insisting that Hitler would keep to the non-aggression pact, and took no preparatory defensive measures.

In the early dawn of 22 June 1941 Hitler invaded Russia, launching a 4-million-man *Blitzkrieg* along a 1500-mile front. In the first day the Germans shot down two thousand Soviet planes, and killed hundreds of thousands of Russian soldiers. The same number were taken prisoner. There was silence from Stalin: for ten days he neither said nor did anything. Molotov addressed the nation over the radio in his place, and not until 3 July did Stalin rally himself. Then, over the radio, he called on the peoples of Russia to fight the Great Patriotic War, the National War of Liberation, fusing the cult of Stalinism with a new element of patriotism. This nationalist revival, and Stalin's strong leadership, were extremely significant in the eventual victory of Russia over Germany.

World War II was a major turning point in Svetlana's personal life. 'I was fifteen when the war started in Russia in 1941. My brothers immediately joined the army and went to the front, and I had to leave Moscow with the rest of the family. Adult life started for me then. I still had three years of school ahead, but everything was different. My childhood was over.'

*163*

Svetlana describes the extraordinary reaction of her father to Hitler's invasion and the breaking of the pact. 'To him it was a failure of all his politics. He had believed that the Germans would never attack: "You can trust the Germans, you can trust Hitler. We have a pact. They will attack everybody else, but they will never attack us." He just sat there, completely depressed, for quite a while. He just couldn't get himself together. It was 22 June when they attacked, and not until 3 July did he speak to the nation. It was a very strong speech raising the country to war; by then he had pulled himself together.

'He was sixty-two, and for the next four years he worked twenty-four hours a day.' The economy was immediately geared to supply the needs of the front, much of the labour for the arms industry coming from the camps. The threat from the invading Germans was very real; by November they had made spectacular advances into Soviet territory, advancing to Leningrad, Kiev, Kharkov and much of the Crimean Peninsula. They were fast advancing on Moscow; in 1941 Stalin ordered the House on the Embankment to be wired for demolition should Hitler succeed in taking Moscow, refusing to allow his foe the pleasure of capturing it. The house was evacuated for the duration of the war, and lost fifty-two of its inmates to the Nazis.

Svetlana was told that she must get out of the city, and flee eastwards. 'By the middle of August the Germans were quite deep into the country. My father had phoned Aunt Eugenia in June and told her, "Things are very bad, you should leave Moscow and go to the Urals because the situation is so grave." She almost fainted because she couldn't believe that things were so serious. He trusted her, he could tell her things in a very simple way which he wouldn't do for others.'

Kyra takes up the story: 'In spite of the rift in their friendship, when my mother telephoned him he did talk to her. He told her then that all her family should leave Moscow together with Svetlana but she said, "No, we shall go separately, to the Urals." '

Sasha elaborates: 'Stalin called Eugenia Aleksandrovna at the very beginning of the war and asked her to accompany his children, and us, and Yakov's daughter Gulia, and grandparents, to the Caucasus to one of his dachas there – to be a sort of elder in the group, a responsible person. But by then my mother had her own family – ourselves and her step-children and her second husband, and her little nephew lived with us, and her mother – so she apologised and excused herself. It was very unusual for anyone to turn down a direct request from Stalin. She wanted to take her own family to Sverdlovsk. He was hurt by her refusal, and she understood that he was hurt.

'But there is also another reason: all our family disliked Beria tremendously, and Eugenia Aleksandrovna simply hated him. Mother believed that she would rather stay away and as far as possible from this involvement. She did an unacceptable thing: she refused this assignment, turned him down.'

Stalin then turned to his other sister-in-law for help, the all-forgiving Anna Sergeyevna whose husband had recently been shot. Her son says, 'In the week that the war began, Stalin called my mother, Anna Sergeyevna, and said that the war would be very long and very hard. He asked her to take the rest of the family to the east, to safety.

'So Aunt Anna went with them all – her sons Leonid and Volodya, Svetlana and Galya – Vasili's wife, Gulia – Yakov's daughter, Grandpa and Grandma, and they all went to Kuibyshev where the capital had been moved to – the ministries, the diplomatic corps, and all the children from the top families as well.' Yakov, before going to the front himself, had asked Galya to make sure that his wife Yulia and their child Gulia were looked after by the family. He knew it was no use asking Stalin to take care of them. Galya herself was pregnant, and gave birth to her first child that autumn.

In Sasha's opinion, 'in 1941 Stalin certainly had too many

things on his mind to remember about us. I know, however, that Mother did telephone Stalin during the war years maybe once or twice, by the special lines. Those were very brief conversations and he was not very outgoing. Obviously he retained some hurt against her. By 1947, when my mother was arrested, I believe he was experiencing the beginnings of his illness – possibly sclerosis, and vascular insufficiency, which contributed to his irritability.'

Both Stalin's sons went into active service in 1941. Yakov's unhappy life entered its last phase. Svetlana's memories of her step-brother are tender ones. 'For the couple of years before the war started, Yasha and I studied together in spring. I was preparing for my school exams and he had finals for the Military Academy. We would sit together and do our studies – he was the wonderful older brother that one can dream of.

'He was already married, his little girl Gulia was born in 1939, but he was very fond of me. I got along very well with Yulia, who was Jewish. He protected her like a knight from Father, who had no time for her. He stood by her. He was about thirty-three when he left for the war, and I was fifteen.

'He had met Yulia, his second wife, through Aunt Anna. Yulia was a Jewish Ukrainian, and her first husband had been a top KGB man. He was arrested, and she ran to Aunt Anna for help; they had something in common – arrested husbands, both of whom had worked in the KGB in the Ukraine. Through her, Yulia met Yakov.

'He was a wonderful father, gentle, not a military person at all. It was an evil twist of fate that he had just graduated from Military Academy when war broke out, and his whole class became officers armed with heavy howitzers. They were loaded into trains and shipped to Byelorussia which was surrounded by the Germans. Whole detachments of the army were taken prisoner. He was not alone. It was sending them to certain death.

'Officers were supposed to shoot themselves if they were taken prisoner: that was the rule. A Soviet officer does not give himself up. It is beneath him to be captured: if he is taken, he is a traitor. Yakov was slow-witted, he was also wounded, and he had his own ideas. His philosophy was that this was war, and he was a prisoner, and so what? He would go through it. He was not fanatic enough to shoot himself. He was interrogated by the Germans many times, up to the highest echelons, because he was who he was. They were delighted to have their catch – such propaganda! He behaved in a quiet and dignified way and they all noticed that. He didn't know the Grand Plans of his father because he wasn't closely involved with him. He behaved like a perfect officer in the circumstances, and he endured being treated worse than the others because he was constantly being taken to be on show to the German Army. He was a prisoner of war for three years.'

A cell mate described him as 'independent and proud'. Apparently Yakov refused to stand up when German officers walked past, and he was put into solitary for this. He was convinced of Soviet victory. What he didn't know was that back at home his father, on hearing the news of Yakov's capture, ordered the arrest of Yulia and of her mother, and ordered that little Gulia, his granddaughter, be sent to a state orphanage for children of arrested parents. He accused the women in the family of persuading Yakov to go to the front in order to surrender and blacken his father's name.

Svetlana went to her father; according to the family it was the first time she had spoken so firmly to him. Gulia was his very own granddaughter; she implored him to give back the child. Svetlana herself was not much more than a child, in her mid-teens. At first Stalin was unmoved, but she managed to persuade him, and Beria received an order to hand Gulia over to her relatives. She was returned to Kuibyshev to the older Alliluyevs, until her mother was released eighteen months later.

In her thirtieth year Gulia married an Arab communist student, Hosin-ben-Saad, and they had a son Selim in 1970.

He was born handicapped, and has lived his life retarded and deaf. He is the end of one branch of the Stalin tree.

News of Yakov's capture reached the Western countries, but nobody in Russia knew anything of his fate until after the war, although it is certain that Stalin did. In 1943 General Zhukov encircled the German Sixth Army at Stalingrad, killing 200,000 of their soldiers. The remaining 90,000 surrendered after General von Paulus and twenty-three other generals had been taken prisoner. The German high command approached Stalin and offered him the return of Yakov for the exchange of von Paulus. 'I have no son called Yakov,' came the reply.

The Alliluyev family photographs include two press cuttings of Yasha when he was a prisoner of war. 'In the press pictures I can see his face becoming absolutely drawn, my God it was a suffering face. In later years I talked to Gulia about it all, and she said, "We are all born under some kind of unhappy, unlucky star. Everything that we ever did goes badly for us: for Papa, for me, for my son. It was like a curse. Like being drawn into a dark circle in which we couldn't survive."

'Yakov didn't even have a good childhood. His father wanted his sons to be military, so he influenced Yakov to abandon his chosen career and go to military academy – it was a sign of the times that every patriot should. Had he remained in his profession his life would probably have been saved.

'I believe that he was told, as he was paraded in front of the Germans, that his own father would not exchange him for General von Paulus. The Germans would not have missed the chance to tell him. And it was true. Father's refusal was not a surprise; it was part of military honour, that mentality. "We don't talk to these people. We don't show our weaknesses." "As if I would trade with the Germans," he said to his daughter. "No. War is war."

'The official version of his death says that Yakov was shot while attempting to escape. But,' continues Svetlana, 'I don't think there was an attempt to escape. They were told, these prisoners, not to approach the high-voltage barbed wire. You couldn't escape through it because the whole surrounding field was covered with it. The fact is that he made for the fence, knowing it to be very high voltage, and was shot by a guard who had orders to shoot anyone who approached it. I deduce from that that he simply wanted to die. He had reached the end of his tether.

'It was spring 1943. Nobody knew how long the war would go on. Then at the end of the war there would be no disgrace. He had had enough.'

The battle of Stalingrad had proved the turning point of the war. Hitler lost his nerve, his armies gradually retreated and by April 1945 Berlin was surrounded by Zhukov's armies. On 8 May 1945 Germany surrendered: the war was over. Peace treaties were signed, but returning Russian POWs were rewarded for their courage and suffering by being sent to prison camps. Stalin refused to sign the Geneva convention and one-and-a-half million POWs died as a result. His fear was that they might no longer accept his dictatorship, having seen Russia from abroad, and he did not want people at home to have any contact with those who had been to other countries.

But to this day the Russian people feel gratitude and admiration for Stalin for having won the war against the Germans. To many of them it is the justification of his long dictatorship. As Voltaire said, 'In the eyes of the people, the general who wins a battle has made no mistakes.' This particular battle was won, however, at high cost. The official figure of war dead in Russia between 1941 and 1945 was put at seven million. It is now known that it was over twenty million – and this does not include uncountable millions of cripples. Every occupied city was left half-gutted, and Jewish populations were annihilated. Villages suspected of supporting partisans were wiped out. Twenty-five million people were left homeless after 1700 towns and 70,000 villages were destroyed by the bombardments.

'The only really military man in the family was my father,' says Svetlana. 'He really had this talent. He really liked it, and the best performance he gave in his life was as organiser of the Red Army during the Second World War. He did what he was born for.'

The youngest of the cousins, Volodya, gives this verdict: 'He won the war, although it was very, very tough for the people. 1941 was not a year of defeat, it was a year of victory. Day after day our army totally destroyed the German plans. Hitler, despite the very latest of technology in his troops, arrived near Moscow towards the end of November. He put all his strength into this war. He was armed for imperialism. The fact that our country managed to get through the war was to Stalin's huge merit. And then the economy was restored, and atomic weaponry was created, which to this day has maintained the peace.

'It is no secret that the Germans could not break through the power of the peasantry and it was well-known that the kolkhozes [the collective farms] were very strong. We also created weapons just before the war – in spite of not having enough time to develop our technology – which would not give way to the German weaponry. I do not believe that a frightened people could have created such technology. Today they say that our people functioned in fear, but I do not believe that there was any fear in the pre-war years. It was the strength and power of our country that went into the repressions. But of the preparedness of the people, of the sacrifices and of the achievements of our victory there is no doubt.'

Svetlana tells of how, 'When the war was over, he fell apart and became very ill. They thought he would die. But it was kept a state secret – they didn't even tell me at the time. I had no idea what was wrong; I couldn't even get through on the telephone. "No, you can't telephone him," was the order. I was told this later by my second husband Yuri Zhdanov, because his father was waiting in the wings for the announcement that he would be next in succession.

My father survived, but he was never the same again. He was quite sick after that, which probably affected the course of the Cold War.'

Stalin's victories, however, were confined to the military and political spheres of life. His success in the domestic aspect, home life and parenting, left much to be desired, not least by his own children, whose inner lives were deeply affected by the character and actions of their father.

## Chapter Nineteen

# VASILI'S STORY

All is confused eternally –
  So much, I can't say who's
Man, who's beast any more . . .
  — Anna Akhmatova, 'Requiem'

After Yakov's suicide Vasili was protected at the front; everything was done to ensure that he was not taken prisoner, or put at risk of being killed. Kept under strict supervision, he was not allowed even to fly. He survived the war unwounded, with one enemy plane to his credit, shot down before he was grounded.

His sister Svetlana tells the outline of Vasili's sad life in her book *20 Letters to a Friend*. How this hot-headed, excitable boy who lacked self-control ruined his life through his chronic inability to take responsibility. How power, the legacy of his birthright, corrupted him. How, when the war started, he was appointed captain in the airforce at the age of twenty, and by the end of the war had risen to the rank of lieutenant-general aged only twenty-four, his superior officers eager to win favour with Stalin. How, having then been appointed chief of aviation of the Moscow Division after the war, he became surrounded by shady characters doing shady deals; how he exploited his name and position and privileges, spending government money on playboy pursuits. How the alcohol problem he had always had became worse and worse until, on May Day 1952, he ordered a fly-past over Red Square in unthinkable weather conditions, and planes and pilots were destroyed. This incident cost him his post, and on refusing any other he was stripped of his honours and sat at home, alone and drinking, having thrown out his third wife, whom he had married bigamously.

When his father died in 1953 he went to pieces and acted the megalomaniac crown prince, blaming anyone and everyone for murdering Stalin, putting it about that political rivals had plotted against his father. Six weeks after the funeral he was arrested after a heavy drinking bout and sentenced to eight years in prison. He appealed, and was sent to a military hospital for eighteen months, then sent home to rehabilitate. But the old corrupt ways soon took hold again, he was surrounded by the acolytes of yore, and was returned to prison to serve out his sentence.

In 1960 Khrushchev took pity on him, and they had an emotional meeting. The General Secretary gave the disgraced General Stalin a good apartment in Moscow, a dacha and a car, and restored his stars and his pension, in return for his promise to live quietly. Within no time, however, Vasili was surrounded by his dubious friends and had started drinking heavily. So finally he had to return to jail to finish his term. But not for long; by now his health was so bad that he was released and moved out of the capital to Kazan. He lived in a one-roomed apartment with a nurse he had met in the prison hospital, at a comfortable distance from Moscow as far as the authorities were concerned. But Vasili was by now mentally and physically destroyed, and he died in March 1962 aged forty-one.

Svetlana reminisces about Vasili: 'We were not close, because he was five years older, and always very bossy, so I never loved him. At first I was afraid of him, later I was angry with him. We had different interests, and never agreed, and I came to love him only after he died. Oh my God, I thought, this was my brother, what a terrible life he had, how awful.

'It's only now I feel I had a brother; I never felt it before, because he was quite a menace. He was a very highly-strung child, hysterically afraid of Father. When he was a grown-up man, a general of the army with decorations on his epaulettes, he would tiptoe into the room where we were all sitting at dinner, tiptoe to the table and tiptoe back. I would look at him and think, What is up with my brother? He is meant to be a courageous man, what is wrong with him? Father would suddenly turn to him with some question and he wouldn't even hear it straight. He would say, "Oh pardon me, what did you say?" in panic. Or, "I'm sorry I didn't hear you!"

'Mother knew how he was; she hired special teachers to deal with his nerves. When mother died he was devastated. She was his love and his protection: she was his everything. When she was gone he was only eleven, and he was left with nothing. He didn't like his teachers, so very soon they were gone. Then the entourage, led by Vlasik, father's bodyguard, took care of him. He was a teenager, and they taught him about smoking and drinking and women. He was led by them to his destruction. Mother would not have allowed that.

'My brother, unfortunately for me, provided me with an early sex education of the dirtiest sort, which remained in my subconscious and ruined my ongoing years. He was very outspoken and loved foul language and dirty stories, so I knew all the dirty words from a very young age. In his teens he was constantly using foul language and indulging his inclination to sing dirty songs. His colleagues tried to stop him. "Please stop, women are here! Your sister, she is a young girl!" But it didn't stop him. I would leave the table and go. He couldn't stop himself.'

Volodya, although fifteen years younger than his cousin, remembers wild exploits from their young days. 'I knew him very well! He was a person of extremes; he would give away his last shirt, or he could smash your face up. He drank. All the brothers loved him and he loved us very much too. He was an excellent, outrageous driver and pilot. I was frightened to be in the car with him, especially when he was drunk. I was once with him on a motorcycle and that was scary!

'Aunt Eugenia did not like to go with him in the car, it was too much for her, she was always scared. Vasili was destroyed by vodka, but even more by all the flatterers and sycophants and courtiers around him, who concealed the fact that he was drinking so heavily and hid all his escapades. Stalin found out about this through my mother and Grandmother. Vasili loved my mother, Anna Sergeyevna, but she could easily throw him out of the house. Stalin would be very severe with him, too, throw him out – and then Vasili would come to Anna and beg her forgiveness. She was kind to him, yet he would shout at her and throw her out of his dacha – such things happened too! That was how he was.

'He lived with us during his difficult times, and I used to stay at his dacha for quite a while, and I stayed with his first two children a lot. I knew his first wife Galina (Galya), and we always had a very good relationship with her. My mother Anna loved her very much and pitied her for what she had to go through.'

Kyra recalls that 'in general he was loved by everyone. He had a lot of charm, and he was loved not for his name but simply because he was charming in his own way. He was rather small, thin, short, pale-looking. He liked to court women, to give them presents and he did all this in a lovely way. He possessed a kind of chivalry.'

Svetlana again: 'We were in the same school for a while but he dropped out and went to airforce school to become a pilot. That put him amongst heavy drinkers and older people. He was precocious, ambitious, and he wanted to be strong. He married very early, his first wife when he was twenty, during the war. Galya was a sweet soul. She thought she was very lucky with her catch and her mother thought it was a great stroke of luck!'

Their story has been told in a Soviet newspaper, *Soviet Secrets*, written by 'sources close to Galya Bourdonskaya'. This is part of the outline:

Vasili met Galya Bourdonskaya in the summer of 1940. He

had a way with women and knew how to seduce with flowers, dinner, dancing in the best restaurants. There was no elaborate wedding – it was not in the style of the time. On 30 December Galya visited Vasili at his base. Travelling back to Moscow he asked her, 'Have you got your passport?' He stopped the car at the registry office, where lots of friends were waiting, and they got married.

Vasili didn't tell Stalin of his marriage to start with. The couple lived in the ordinary conditions, in a hostel on the base, eating in the canteen or at home. These were happy days: they kept lively company and were often together. Vasili proved to be an attentive and tender husband.

One day Vasili was handed a letter from Stalin. It was a note in red pencil: 'Why didn't you ask my permission to get married? Well, the devil take you. I pity her: she married an idiot.'

Stalin told Vasili to bring his wife to live in the Kremlin. His apartment was divided into two halves. In Vasili's and Galya's half were bedrooms, a dining room, and a library, and beyond that were a flat where the adjutant lived, and the servants' quarters. In Stalin's bedroom Galya saw an ordinary tough military bed: and not much else besides.

Once Vasili was married the asceticism changed as the young couple made themselves a home and spent money on it. A bed was put in, for their return, of pear wood. For Galya this was luxury on the tsarist scale – although most of the furniture was bought from ordinary furniture shops. Stalin came to look it over. He ordered that in the window should be put a pretty and expensive vase of his choice.

After the war they moved from town to town, but always in reasonable comfort. Their son Sasha had been born in 1941, and Vasili had no doubt of his future: his son and heir would become a great military man – that was his destiny.

Svetlana interjects, 'She was basically a funny, nice girl without much in her head. She produced two children, Sasha and Nadya. But Vasili was still young and ambitious; he started an affair with the wife of a theatre director. Galya was discarded.'

When Stalin came to know of this he took Galya's part – 'he knew his son well enough'. She was provided with a large four-bedroomed apartment in the House on the Embankment. Stalin paid for her privileges out of his own pocket, and gave her access to every advantage. It was not long before Vasili returned, repentant. When Stalin discovered this he said, 'What an idiot. I did everything so that she could live happily with her children. All you women are such fools.'

Vasili did not behave for long, he took to drinking and flirting and the marriage was in trouble again. One day Galya answered the doorbell of their apartment: it was Vasili, who said, 'Come down and talk to me in my car.' He told her that the marriage was over, that she would return to live with her mother, and he handed her a month's wages, drove her to the Arbat where her mother lived and kissed her goodbye on the cheek. She was an hour away from her flat on the embankment. She had been deserted; Vasili took the children with him. They lived deprived of their mother's love with a stepmother who loathed them: they were neglected and hungry, kept locked in an attic room.

Svetlana says, 'How Sasha, her eldest boy, who went on to become a theatre designer, got a sense of beauty and harmony I don't know. It was not from his childhood! He and his sister were left in a dirty room on a dirty bed and nobody looked after them. Their stepmother didn't want anything to do with them, and Vasili didn't want to give them back to their mother. They had a horrid time.'

Galya lived in despair, wrecked by the emotional pain of separation from her children, until after Stalin's death in 1953 when she obtained their return.

Sergei Pavlovich remembers what brought Galya and the Alliluyev family close. 'There is a Russian proverb, "You find friends in misfortune". Good friendships are often forged with common grief or bad luck. We kept in contact with Galya through this difficult time, giving her moral support, and also after 1953, when she told us about the steps she wanted to take to get her children returned to her.

They had been neglected, left to themselves, nobody wanted them. She was scared to come up with such a demand to get them returned to her while Stalin was alive.'

'Vasili's second wife,' continues Svetlana, 'was the daughter of Marshal Timoshenko and he liked that! He dropped the first one for this very beautiful woman. He treated her with a certain respect which he had never shown to his first wife. He didn't even divorce Galya. He just sent her away, didn't send her any money, and kept the children to himself. That was against every law in the country. His status as a military man, as a general, was so protected by everybody that only when he was in prison did his poor first wife, still with the marriage certificate in her hand, appeal to the President of the Soviet Union, Voroshilov, and say, "Here I am, I am still the widow. I have nothing to live on." Then everybody jumped up and thought "Oh how terrible" and returned the children to her, and the children had a pension as grandchildren of Stalin, and so she was given the help to which she was entitled. Only then.

'Until then she was afraid even to open her mouth because she knew very well how that society operated. Her father had been a driver in the KGB, as a girl she had been in KGB school, and they all knew how things worked. If she raised her voice she probably would be obliterated. She was afraid to claim her rightful pension as a widow of a general of the Second World War. This fear is deeply ingrained.

'Vasili went off the rails after Stalin died. He didn't realise that his time was over, that things couldn't be the same. He was offered all kinds of jobs in high positions, but out of Moscow; one was to command a huge section of the airforce in the eastern part of the country. But he said, "No, only in Moscow". When they insisted, he disobeyed, and so the minister of defence said, "Take your epaulettes off, you are no longer allowed to be in the armed forces if you don't obey orders. You are discharged."

' "Fine," he said, "I'm discharged," and went home and sat there drinking.

*178*

'Everything that Mother could predict and foresee came true. She had felt that he had to be handled very gently and that certainly he was not material for the army. Neither was Yakov. They were not army types.

'He experienced a terrible inner devastation when my mother died, that nothing could repair. He kept blaming people for not looking after her. His childhood had gone, and nobody could replace her. In his wives he tried to find a woman who looked like Mother; he was always looking for her – he married one woman after another in his search for her. The second and third had the same style as Nadya – long dark hair and dark eyes, and the parting in the middle, and he liked them to wear it back in a bun like her. His third "wife", Capitolina, was the best of them all – a motherly type who could cope with him, and he called her Mother. It was "mother, mother, mother". She mothered him and she tried to save him. She was a very healthy sportswoman, a champion swimmer. She really loved him: she was two or three years older and she really wanted to help get him away from drinking. She was quite forceful, and didn't last long because he didn't like people who tried to boss him.

'His story is sad, it is terrifying, it is tragic. The acolytes promoted him, they pulled him up through his career and then they dropped him. When Father died they didn't support him – they let him go to prison. Finally they helped him to die. His medical nurse Masha was set up by the KGB. The local KGB registered their marriage without any reference to prior records, about two months before he died. He was obviously ill and dying. He was there under the name Djugashvili, and immediately after she buried him she went to Georgia with his name and collected a great number of admirers, enjoying great benefits. Her two daughters, by I don't know who, accepted my brother's name, and enjoyed great luxury. These kind of women knew what to go for and how to get it and how to enjoy it. It was all tragic and awful and terrifying.

'Capitolina was the one who found that there had been no

autopsy on Vasili, no medical records kept. She wanted to get rid of this illegitimate widow, the nurse who keeps vulgarising him and who will not allow us to open the grave to find out the reason for his death. She started asking and everybody was telling her conflicting things. They couldn't even agree over what to say. A huge crowd came to the funeral, and Masha said to Capitolina, "Who are you?" and she said, "I am here with his children, this is his son Sasha and his daughter Nadya." Masha grabbed her two girls and said, "*You* are his children!" They were frightened to death.

'But Capitolina pushed her way in and tried to find out at least something. It was obvious that it was all done by the KGB. They were protecting Masha: the woman was an informer. It was known at her previous place of work, the Institute of Surgery where my brother was for a while, and where he found her. The professor there said, "We know that she is an informer. You had better tell him about that." I said, "Why the hell didn't you tell him?" and he said, "We did tell him but it was no use."

'Khrushchev let him out of prison. He was very ill, he had no pulse in his legs, and they even thought that they might have to amputate, but they decided not to. The doctors said that this was not the right woman for him, but she went with him to Kazan, and there she was constantly giving him injections of tranquillizers, and sleeping pills.

'Masha said that he was very unruly, and she did it to put him to sleep, to keep him quiet. I had awful photographs of him, looking terrible. Even when he came out of prison he looked better than he looked then; in the seven months that he was in Kazan with Masha he went right down, degraded into death. After years in prison he was still himself – although ill, he was still surviving. At least in prison there was normal food and normal drink. It was definitely her doing. They protected her every minute.

'Vasili didn't have much property; there were his orders, his regalia, his personal arms which were very well-made in silver and gold, rifles and sabres, all presented to him when he was a general. But she got all these. She is the keeper of everything, and the KGB protect her. We tried to get this all to the court and to expose her as an illegitimate heiress. Illegitimately she keeps his grave; nobody can come close. We can't, even his children can't, because the widow has these rights. She is a bigamous widow, but we have to prove that in law; we could do so, because we have the evidence, but Galina was afraid to go anywhere, trembling with fear. We have a big crowd of people who would rally and support her case. Maybe nowadays with more democracy it will finally get to court. We want to bring Vasili's poor suffering body from there to be buried near Mother, because somehow that seems the right place. He was always the *enfant terrible*, but he suffered a lot.'

Galya died in summer 1990, in hospital. She had been seriously ill for many months, unable to leave the house. She was proud of her son Sasha and she was like a mother hen with him. The mother-son link had become stronger than a simple blood-link or friendship. They had become part of each other. This was her last happiness.

Sergei Pavlovich went to her funeral with his sister Kyra: 'She was cremated, although I don't know where the urn is with her ashes. There was an idea that she should be buried at the Novedevichy, at our family plot. But there have been all kinds of happenings on my parents' grave there, next to Molotov's, so some complications arose regarding Galya's burial. There was quite a commotion; they had even wanted to remove everyone from there. One more relative to bury made for more complications. Already Katya Timoshenko is buried there, with her son Vasili Vasilievich who died of a drugs overdose as a young man. So their attitude is, "Another wife? Come now!" A collision occurred for the bureaucrats . . . !

'It is still a very special spot, where all Stalin's relatives are buried. But the issue has still not been resolved; there have been nasty articles in the newspaper – "Why are Stalin's relatives buried there?" ' It would seem unlikely that Svetlana's dream of re-interring Vasili's body near to their mother's grave will come true. The austere gravestones beside Nadya's white marble memorial remain her immutable companions in a cemetery that now reviles the memory of Stalin.

Vasili's line of the family tree has not flourished. Of his two sons and two daughters, two are dead. The younger son died a heroin addict in his early twenties, the younger daughter after lifelong schizophrenia. His other daughter has contracted the family failing for drink, and the only healthy member of the family, the eldest son, is unmarried and without offspring. There is no young Stalin to take his great-grandfather's name into the twenty-first century.

*Chapter Twenty*

# THE GRANDPARENTS' LAST DAYS

The mountains bow before this anguish,
The great river does not flow . . .
Stars of death stood
Above us, and innocent Russia
Writhed under bloodstained boots, and
Under the tyres of Black Marias.
— Anna Akhmatova, 'Requiem'

'Stalin saw less and less of Grandpa and Grandma Alliluyev after Nadya died,' says Svetlana. 'They were all reminded of what had happened, of the past, and in any case it was a huge effort to catch him; he was always busy, particularly in the war years. Later still he simply didn't see them at all. When Grandpa died in 1945 he hadn't seen Stalin for quite a while. The Alliluyev family had had all these misfortunes in the purges and this made him want to see Father less and less: he didn't want to listen to him.'

In Sergei Pavlovich's photograph album there is a portrait of his grandfather Sergei Yakovlevich taken a year or two before his death. The difference to earlier pictures is striking. His head has shrunk into his now stooping, hunched shoulders and he looks like a man carrying a heavy burden. The eyes are hollow, beyond sadness, all emotion spent. His grandson Sergei Pavlovich says, 'He was not the only one to be disenchanted. Grandfather loved freedom deeply. He felt that he could do nothing about the atrocities that were taking place. He became very, very upset. He knew perfectly well what was going on, but he never spoke about it to anyone.

'He was a fighter for justice, an Old Bolshevik, a founder member of the Social Democratic party, when it was not yet the Communist Party. Kalinin had said of him, "Sergei is one of the oldest of the Old Bolsheviks and a born rebel." He was not disappointed in the ideology itself, but in its realisation, the way it was put into practice. To him, for almost twenty years, until 1918, the party was a Social Democratic one, but its implementation after the revolution was not as it should have been. Many others felt the way he did.' They saw quite clearly that Stalin was exploiting the tradition of absolutism in Russia, and could see the irony that the 1917 revolution, the ultimate reaction to tsarism, was evolving into its own brand of absolutism.

Svetlana goes on: 'There was a large group of Old Bolsheviks, veterans who were very much at odds with the new government and Party and young people, because from their point of view things were not as they should be. He was a great Marxist idealist from the rank and file, not one of the educated professional revolutionaries who, according to him, "got it all wrong. We knew what we were fighting for," he would say. The system was not democratic enough, although they might not have said so. But what was happening was all wrong, it was not in accord with their ideas. The result of their humble opposition was that in the 1930s the Society of Old Bolsheviks was banned and disbanded. But they still had their pensions.'

In *Darkness at Noon* Arthur Koestler, writing in the early 1930s, observes this 'old guard':

> They were all tired men. The higher you got in the hierarchy, the more tired they were. I have nowhere seen such exhausted men among the higher strata of Soviet politicians, as among the Old Bolshevik guard. It was not only the effect of overwork, nervous strain and apprehension. It was the past that was telling on them, and sticking to the rules of a game that demanded that at every moment a man's whole life should be at stake. Nothing could frighten them any more. Nothing surprised them. They had given all they had.

'My grandfather,' continues Svetlana, 'was shattered by the fate of his children. How, as their father, did he feel about the revolution as time went on? Well, he suffered deeply over the fate of his children, and finally he died from cancer of the stomach, in 1945. That is the other side of the Glorious Revolution!'

Sergei Yakovlevich did not live to see the final appalling episode of the family saga. In March 1948 his surviving daughter Anna Sergeyevna was the victim of the knock at the door: she was arrested and sentenced to ten years in solitary confinement.

'Olga Eugenievna too was losing her children to the revolution,' says Svetlana. 'It was like the Leviathan, devouring her family. First Fyodor, then Nadya, then Pavel, and finally Aunt Anna was imprisoned and put into solitary for ten years. I think she was completely shocked. It was bugging her all the time: what had she done? Why? She would write letters to Stalin, give them to me, saying, "Here is a letter I wrote to your father", and then she would say, "Oh, no, I won't send it." Time and time again. So her end was not quiet, and she never smiled. She finally died of a heart attack in her seventies. There were many of these revolutionary wives, but they couldn't take it. This is what I call the other side of the story.'

In her *20 Letters to a Friend*, Svetlana remembers how Olga Eugenievna used to complain that Sergei Yakovlevich had ruined her life and caused her 'nothing but suffering'. How she used to go on about freedom a lot – and it was obviously a dig at him. She was often quarrelling and finding fault, especially with the household and the way things were run. Things had not, for her either, turned out as she had hoped.

The youngest of their grandchildren, Volodya, saw her this way: 'Grandma had been arrested and imprisoned too, so she had tasted all that goes with the life of a revolutionary. But all the blows of fate notwithstanding Grandma was an optimist until the end. She enjoyed life.'

Svetlana continues, 'Grandma died without seeing her daughter again, and never knew whether she came back. It bothered her terribly. She couldn't decide if she should send a letter to Stalin or not. There was some kind of pride: pride not to go to him, not to complain and not to beg for anything from my father.' But Sergei Pavlovich interprets this differently: 'It was understood among us all that writing to Stalin might bring something even worse. The Svanidze example was never forgotten. Yet Olga Eugenievna tried through Svetlana to reach Stalin somehow, to do something to help.'

'When Kyra was arrested too,' continued Svetlana, 'everyone in the family suggested that they all write a petition and complain to her uncle. Olga Eugenievna said, "No! He certainly knows what has happened, it is impossible that he does not know, and he lets it be. We are not going to write and beg, oh, no."

'I don't think my grandfather tried to influence Stalin during the thirties,' recalls Svetlana. 'I remember him sitting at the table with my father; once in a while he would come to dinner with the politburo. Grandpa would be very quiet and shy and just listen, perhaps tell the odd joke. He had already lost Pavel; Fyodor was ill; his daughter had committed suicide. They were knocked out by their tragedies, shocked and horrified. Yet they never showed it much: they were always cheerful with us children. They did not fall to pieces, but in the long term they were shocked out of their health.

'I don't actually remember what they talked about around the table, but there was no question of influencing Father. Everybody knew that Grandfather was writing his memoirs, *The Path of my Life*, and sometimes Stalin would joke, "This is our writer" and everyone would go "ha ha ha". It was published and taken quite seriously as a piece of history, and belongs to the Marxist–Leninist Institute in Moscow. But he never saw it in print because it didn't come out until 1946, and then in a miserably chopped and censored form.'

Leonid, Anna Sergeyevna's elder son, perceived that 'Olga Eugenievna suffered greatly. She had a particular relationship with Stalin, a lot of contact, partly because she lived in the Kremlin and could go to him at any time in his apartment, although not to his office. He worked all night, so to see him you had to lie on his sofa until he came out of his office.'

Sergei Pavlovich remembers seeing 'a lot of Grandma because my father Pavel was her favourite son. And we saw a great deal of her after the arrests of first Redens and then Anna Sergeyevna. She suffered a great deal over Nadya's suicide, the fact that she did not die a natural death. And the death of my father hit her very hard. They both died so young. When we were small we could not understand this: but now I realise how young my father was.

'Her Kremlin apartment was very small, just two rooms. The windows looked over the Aleksandr Park into the Kremlin wall. It was on the second floor, very low, because you could see nothing outside but that wall.'

Sergei's younger brother Sasha tells his version: 'Grandmother Olga always enjoyed special treatment from Stalin, and she knew this. She lived not far from him in the Kremlin, and also stayed frequently in a very privileged government sanatorium called The Pines near Moscow, to which she would travel in a state car called up from the government garage. All this was sanctioned by Stalin, while at the same time government cars were coming to arrest members of the family . . . We stayed in our half-sealed flats, penniless, and she would help us whenever she could. It was really a grotesque situation for the Alliluyev family. And some of them in prison . . .

'But she was also very temperamental, and would allow herself to blame Stalin loudly, while knowing that everything around her was bugged and listened to. She called him an "Asiatic"! That worried us, but nothing would stop her. Yet somehow nothing happened to her, and she died of a heart attack in March 1951.'

Volodya again: 'Olga Eugenievna buried two of her children: she suffered greatly in her lifetime. As long as I remember we saw each other almost all the time. She didn't become quieter, not as Svetlana says.' The implication here is that Olga stopped saying much to Svetlana for fear of the consequences: if anything should reach Stalin, who knew what would happen? 'She changed very little. But old age is old age and illnesses occur. She liked to talk and tell us all about her life. We were all very close to her, closer than Svetlana was, because she was around our family most days.'

Pavel's eldest child and only daughter Kyra remembers: 'Olga Eugenievna later withdrew into herself, suffering enormously from the loss of her children. But I would not say that she became silent. With Stalin she always talked as an equal and never felt inhibited in his presence. She was quite happy to say to him what was on her mind.

'Sergei Yakovlevich finally withdrew completely into himself. In the end he died of stomach cancer, from the grief that he kept inside. He never talked about it, and this is what cancer thrives on. He very often stayed in his study at Zubalovo for long periods, and then he would appear looking very unhappy. Children were a great relief to him, he would cheer up with them; with the children around he would forget about his troubles.'

Sergei Pavlovich remembers the last days of his grandfather. 'The last time I saw him was in hospital; I was there for a minor operation in June 1945 and spent some time with him in the old Kremlin Hospital opposite the Lenin Library in Moscow. Grandpa was very ill during the war and died soon after, so he didn't live to see the 1947–8 arrests, thank God.' His grandfather's sorrow made a lasting impression on Sasha. 'When he said at my father's funeral, "There is no lot more sorrowful than to outlive your children and to bury them", it was a phrase I could never forget.'

Sasha had cause to recall these words many years later. The shadow that had fallen on the Alliluyev family did not diminish with the death of the man whose friendship and collaboration had brought Stalin into their midst. It reaches down the generations and touches them still; what kind of a man was Stalin, to bequeath such a legacy?

# PART THREE

## Chapter Twenty-One

# STALIN THE MAN

[People's] fascination with 'types' like myself plagues them with the mystery of why and how a living person can actually do things which may be only those dark images and acts secretly within themselves. I believe they can identify with these 'dark images and acts' and loathe anything which reminds them of this dark side of themselves.

— The words of Dennis Nilsen, from *Killing for Company*
by Brian Masters

In the 1930s and 40s the 'Stalin cult' took on the proportion of a national religion. He was likened to Genghis Khan, Pharaoh, and Moses leading the nation to the promised land – a biblical reference curiously at odds with state atheism. Official propaganda compared him to Peter the Great and Ivan the Terrible ('awesome' is closer to the meaning of the Russian word). Stalin, a keen student of history, was familiar with the lives of these powerful rulers. His interest in historical literature was lifelong, and he had a passion for the biographies of emperors and kings, using them as a yardstick to his own power. And he won his own game; finally no tsar in Russian history had ever ruled such a large empire as that of the USSR after World War II. Stalin had a serious sense of the importance of his historical role; he lived out a hero-identity, which followed a pattern in his life. The theme was 'socialism in one country', pitted against the enemy-oppressor of imperialism essential to this scenario.

Yet Stalin was a man, he was flesh and blood. A little boy, a son, a teenager, a husband – twice, a father, uncle, grandfather. He had limbs, kidneys and liver, lungs and spleen, heart and the rest; he was a human being like anyone. Yet more than almost anyone else in history he has been endowed with archetypally monstrous qualities. Milovan Djilas, deputy prime minister of Yugoslavia who had many direct dealings with Stalin, has called him 'dark, cunning and cruel, a brutal and cynical despot'. But this is caricature: it cannot be the whole story. Djilas himself was originally a great admirer of Stalin's more positive qualities.

Joseph Brodsky has remarked, 'Stalin is very much inside each one of us.' Not a popular thing to say. But Stalin has attracted more projections to him than almost any other ruler in history, perhaps because, in Jung's words, 'The real existence of an enemy upon whom one can foist off everything evil is an enormous relief to one's conscience. You can then at least say, without hesitation, who the devil is; you are quite certain that the cause of your misfortune is outside, and not in your own attitude.' He also comments, 'A man's hatred is always concentrated on the things that make him conscious of his bad qualities.' Jung goes on to draw a parallel between the East/West divisions in politics and our own individual dividedness: 'Our world is, so to speak, dissociated like a neurotic, with the Iron Curtain marking the symbolic line of division. Western man, becoming aware of the aggressive will to power of the East, sees himself forced to take extraordinary measures of defence, at the same time as he prides himself on his virtue and good intentions.

'What he fails to see is that it is his own vices, which he has covered up by good international manners, that are thrown back in his face by the communist world, shamelessly and methodically . . . It is the face of his own evil shadow that grins at Western man from the other side of the Iron Curtain.'

A person who attracts such powerful projections to himself is one who projects powerfully himself, and herein lies one of the keys to Stalin's magnetism. The man's psychological make-up is not black and white; it is as subtle and complicated as his life experience. The boy, and later the man, learned denial, he learned to hide things, to repress them, to keep silent as long as it suited his purposes, and then to perfect the art of projection. A look at the intimate details of his family life gives the lie to generalisations so commonly expressed about Stalin.

Stalin was a battered child. His father was a drunkard, a peasant turned cobbler who spent his meagre earnings on vodka and beat his only son savagely, for no reason other than to relieve the tedium of his impoverished existence. It is possible that the effect of one such beating, when the boy was seven, caused the infection in his left elbow from which he nearly died. The hand never regained its full movement and the arm remained stunted, three inches shorter than the right, causing him pain throughout his life. Fractured left arms are frequently seen in battered children, who are usually attacked by a right-handed assailant. Small wonder that the boy hated his father. Hunger for revenge was instilled early: in a story told years later by Serebryakov, 'When a group of comrades was discussing everyone's idea of a perfect day, Stalin said, "Mine is to plan an artistic revenge upon an enemy, carry it out to perfection and then go home peacefully to bed." '

A schoolfriend, Iremashvili, left memoirs which give some insight into Stalin's childhood treatment. 'Undeserved and severe beatings made the boy as hard and heartless as the father was. Since all people in authority over others seemed to him to be like his father, there soon rose in him a vengeful feeling against all people standing above him. From childhood on, the realisation of his thoughts of revenge became the aim to which everything was subordinated.' Bukharin was later to say of him, 'He is unhappy at not being able to convince everyone, himself included, that he is greater than everyone, and this unhappiness may be his most human trait, perhaps the only human trait in him. But what is not human, but rather devilish, is that because of this unhappiness, he cannot help taking revenge on people, on all people, but especially those who are in any way higher or better than he. If someone speaks better than he does, that man is doomed! Stalin will not let him live, because that man is a perpetual reminder that he, Stalin, is not the first and the best.'

Joseph's mother adored her son: she had lost three babies in infancy before he was born and she lavished on him an intense and possessive love. A devout Christian, she wished to show her thanks to God by giving her son a church education with a view to his becoming a priest. She scraped and saved, and through personal sacrifice found the means to pay his fees at a Jesuit seminary in the capital, Tiflis. His mother's ambitions for him did much to mould the child, and provide a clue to his subsequent development. Stalin, according to his daughter, adored his mother, and their close attachment was important to him throughout his life. His first wife – his mother's choice – was similar to her in name and in nature, as well as in devotion to religion and indifference to politics. Iremashvili corroborates: 'He was devoted to only one person – his mother.'

It is a truism that a man who is the undisputed favourite of his mother believes he is a hero: he can conquer anything, and the means whereby are immaterial since approval will never be withdrawn for long. This was the case with the young Stalin. Self-idealisation, encouraged by his mother, became the mirror of his hero-worship: first Koba, then Lenin, and finally the roles of Generalissimo and Stalin the Genius which he played on the world stage. His sense of himself as a very great man was central to him; the reverse was too painful to contemplate and he developed an extreme intolerance to anything short of perfection.

It also became imperative for the disempowered child to survive his father's attacks. He hated his father and rebelled against the paternal in all guises for the rest of his life. At all costs, he must remain top dog. As a child, he was physically too small to protect himself so his strategy was to wear an armour of indifference and scorn. Iremashvili says, 'I never saw him crying.' In order to survive he must become as strong as his father, at the expense of his softer feelings. Never in adult life did he sympathise with the underdog. To quote Iremashvili again, 'to gain a victory and be feared was to triumph.'

Yet the boy never learned what it felt like to be safe. A deep insecurity was rooted in the inevitable disparity between his ideal and reality. Thus all his life he sought affirmation; his dependence on the attitudes of others does much to explain his relationship with Beria. He always felt alone in the world, yet he was seldom alone. His painful sensitivity to slights or aspersions was the ground of his pathological suspicion. He suspected everyone of wearing a mask: a classic projection.

The boy never experienced unpossessive love from either of his parents. His father died in a drunken brawl when the boy was eleven. His childhood taught him the seeming inevitability of sentence without trial, it accustomed him to meaningless torture. His mother, his arch-protector who loved him so much, also beat him. When he was in power, Stalin spoke of beating as the form of punishment merited by the worst of offenders. The combination of love and brutality was an added confusion to the child. Nobody taught him that the whole world was not like his father, a potential enemy, or like his mother, equivocal. Later in his life the Party was a kind of political family for whom he was the father-figure. He had hardly known a father or a family; this was his compensation. So long as he made sure it was safe.

Stalin's paranoia increased steadily and never, even at the height of his power, did he feel secure. His own despised shortcomings were turned into accusations against others. He learned the art of rationalisation to justify his own discrepancies. But his most powerful weapon was projection, endowing his enemies with the qualities he rejected in himself, in a cathartic disposal which left him blameless. The villain-image of the enemy came to represent everything that Stalin, subconsciously, most condemned in himself.

The child never knew why he was being punished: neither did the grown man's victims. The child, as Wordsworth has said, is father of the man. This man reached a pinnacle of power which distanced him from people and from reality. He was small, only 5'4'', and never escaped from a massive inferiority complex which was observed by Churchill's interpreter, who also spotted that he wore built-up heels, well-hidden by wide and sharply-creased trousers. Nor did he ever escape from the terror of the vulnerability of his position. He lived in constant fear of assassination, travelling in armoured cars, making plans at the eleventh hour, changing houses and even bedrooms.

The fear that he spread among the Soviet peoples had its roots in his own fear. As Marx said to Engels during the Paris Commune, 'We think of terror as the reign of those who inspire terror; on the contrary it is the reign of people who are themselves terrified. Terror consists of useless cruelties perpetrated by frightened people in order to reassure themselves.'

Bertoldt Brecht has a theory that 'The ruling classes of a modern society are in the habit of enlisting rather mediocre people for their enterprises. Such men create the illusion of their grandeur solely by the magnitude of their enterprises – they need not even possess ability. They will always be served by vast hordes of intelligent people.'

Stalin was born in Gori in 1879, then a small town of around 9000 people forty-five miles north-west of Tiflis. Gorky describes the 'apartness and wild originality' of this part of Georgia. The family were very poor. They rented what was virtually a hovel, a single all-purpose room with a table and four stools, a bed, sideboard, mirror, and a trunk containing the family belongings. A little unpainted stool and a cradle were the child's furniture. Today that hovel is hidden under an incongruously grandiose marble façade reminiscent of a temple, a shrine for devout pilgrims.

Svetlana describes her father's childhood. 'His mother Yekaterina, or Keke as she was called, was very simple and uneducated, but with tremendous force of character. Poor and hard-working, she earned her pennies doing laundry so that her son could go to church school and then to college. She had a hard life; her husband beat her, too. On one occasion her son tried to protect her from his father by throwing a knife at him. He had to run away and shelter with neighbours to protect his own life, his father was so angry. She had three babies who died in infancy, but Joseph Vissarionovich survived, and she wanted to make a priest of him to show her thanks to God.

'My father talked about his mother a lot, and always with great love. People today portray him as a caricature; that he neglected and hated his mother. He was a very complicated man. He was made out to be completely black, but there was a great deal else in him. Because of his love for his mother, there was tenderness, there was love, love towards me. He used to say to me, "You look like my mother, it's ridiculous how much! It's unbelievable." I remember my father now as being loving and tremendously tender towards me; had he had no love in him at all, I would not have received that. I got all the warmth and hugs and kisses.

'Grandmother Keke was red-haired and freckled like I am. He always talked about her with love. It has to be understood that he was an Asian man; the culture around Georgia is Asian, and part of that is a mother-cult. He would say, "Oh! How she used to beat me! My God!" But in the next breath, "But she loved me too!" ' In a speech made in the 1930s Stalin used the word 'beat' fifteen times in one paragraph, speaking of beating the enemy. 'Yet there was a precious part of him that went back to his childhood, something which even people who are considered to be coarse have, that little place in their heart for some warmth, a soft spot.

*199*

'In her later years Keke lived like a prisoner in a little room in the governor's palace in Tblisi, a nineteenth-century palace with many rooms, part of which was a public building. She didn't have her own home, nor could she see everybody she wanted to. She didn't want to come to Moscow, with its cold climate, where she had no friends. Nadya tried to get her to come and live with us as part of the family, but she refused, she wouldn't go outside Georgia. Nadya did what she could to persuade her, but even the gift of a warm, soft wool Caucasian blanket did not work.

'I was eight when I visited her in 1935 and I was horrified at her room. I never saw such poverty. It was very simple, with a black iron bed and bundles of dried herbs everywhere. She was sitting on the bed, tears streaming down her face at the sight of her grandchildren. She had a very pale freckled face, knotty old hands with knotty veins, covered with freckles. She patted us and gave us candy on a little plate. I was frightened, because she was in a dark kerchief and all the women in her entourage wore them too. And she didn't speak my language. In my childish way I wanted to ask, "Why is she living in such poverty?" We lived in a different way, and there was Grandmother living so poor. This stuck in my head. But of course she didn't want it any other way.

'Recent biographies of my father say that he didn't go to his mother's funeral, he didn't put a cross on her grave. I have to deny these stories. He visited her when she was ill and close to death, in 1935. It was a big effort for him to drive all the way from Moscow to Tblisi with his whole entourage, a thousand miles, but he did it because he wanted to see her.

'There is a photograph of that visit, taken by Vlasik, and it is extraordinary: they were sitting at the table in her little room, next to each other, he with his hand on her shoulder. Both are looking into the camera and there is *bliss* on these two faces. She was happy beyond her dreams; he had come to visit her. And the expression on his face was one that I have very seldom seen: like a happy cat that had got the cream.

'I have never seen him look like that – he was never like that with anyone else. With others he was tense, he was in a hurry. It was on that occasion that she told him, "What a pity that you did not become a priest!" All that he had achieved was nothing to her, it was just a pity that he had not taken orders! He loved that! He told me this story over and over again. He felt that she had remained true to herself, she hadn't changed and that was what she wanted of him. He used to smile at that story.

'He didn't have a cross put on her grave simply because that was not done in those times. The Party was atheist, and the KGB in Georgia decided how to bury her. My father cannot be blamed for that. She was a Christian, and attended church all her life. But it was not his decision. All of us are the property of the Party. Even she.'

The many attempts made to define Stalin's personality have eluded any real sense of dimension – usually because those who have tried did not know the man personally. Colleagues and contemporaries have given snippets, glimpses and epithets; but the person most qualified to talk about Stalin's character is his daughter.

'My father had a very negative view of human beings in general. He would see them as what they are good for, what he could make them do. That showed the influence of the life of a revolutionary. He was rough and tough: when he saw potential, he would go out of his way to attract it. He could be very charming when he wanted to attract and impress people; he would give them all that they needed so long as they worked for him.

'Aunt Eugenia was always telling me, "Your father was a charming man. We knew him well, and he could charm anybody flat when he wanted to. But people who he believed to be his enemies, they had to be destroyed. That was his psychology: black and white, with no grey between. They had to be wiped out: 'Until their heads are chopped off I can't live' – this is very Asian."

'He had a staggering capacity to inspire love, tremendous charisma. He spent his first twenty years in church education and they were *taught* to be charismatic, to attract people. The education of a priest in a seminary in eastern Russia was based very much on how you talked and how you looked, and he learnt there how to talk to people. Without faith coming into it, for him.

'Everyone has love, the last criminal has love. Certainly he had love towards me and my children, I could see that, and towards my mother and his own mother. But for Russian people in general? He had his own idea about what was to be done after the long years of Marxism and Leninism. Generally he had a cynical point of view that "if these people are not useful for something, what else are they good for? What can I get out of them?" Or "they are good for nothing at all." When he saw that people could put something into society, then he could be absolutely charming. For example, during the war he was an inspiration to the army as their military commander.

'There are a lot of amateur psychologists around who think that they know my father. But they didn't know the man. He was extremely complicated. His mother played a very strong part in his life, although not to the extent that she could rule him or prompt him in any way. But he had a tenderness in him which he gave perhaps to nobody but myself, as a child.

'And to his first wife, who had quite an impact on his life for a short period. She died of typhoid fever when their son Yakov was two months old. She was the choice of his mother, who insisted that the wedding take place in church. Yekaterina Svanidze had a special place in his heart. I don't know how deeply her death affected him because he never talked about her. But his two wives must have affected him in a tragic way: both were beautiful women who died young.

'What was more disturbing to me was that my father

never visited my mother's grave – it was in Moscow, after all. He could not excuse her for what she did. It completely shocked him, he was *bouleversé*. He never visited it, never once, not even towards the end of his life when he began to talk about her for the first time, and to "forgive" her. In one "official biography" one so-called bodyguard claims that he would go at night and sit at her graveside. It is total fiction: he never went to the grave. This is the time for creating fiction around Stalin. But I must leave a record of the truth.

'He didn't see my son, his grandson, until he was three years old. We were leading separate lives, me in my own house, he in his fortress. Suddenly he arrived at the dacha and little Jo started playing with him. He was a lovely toddler with curls and big eyes and long eyelashes. I froze; I thought my father would hate him on sight because he was so obviously Jewish. But he melted completely and played with him. "Oh what a lovely boy, what lovely eyes!" He forgot all his prejudices. Jew or no Jew, he was my child, and his grandson.

'Yet he never showed any affection whatsoever to my brother's children, never gave anything to them. Nor did he believe, as time went on, that women in the family, even his own daughter, could be trusted. When I was adult he became adamant that I couldn't be present when he was sitting with military colleagues, or the politburo. He would say, "I want to talk business now, so go." I could not be trusted with state secrets. He would send me away feeling that my way of thinking was not right.

'But people who remember my father knew that there were other sides to him too. There was a lot there. My cousin Kyra told me again and again, "It was your mother I was always afraid of! I was never afraid of your father. He was all right!" And he was good with children, especially other people's. He was nicer to them than he was to his own sons. His sons were always doing wrong, especially Vasili.

'My mother had high expectations and high standards;

she was a perfectionist, a Virgo. Father was partly Sagittarius and partly Capricorn; he was ambitious, he was a leader. He also had the sight of the Archer; he had very good vision and always read without glasses.' Stalin was born on 21 December, the darkest day of the year.

Let his elder contemporary, Count Leo Tolstoy, have the last word, in a passage from *Resurrection*:

One of the commonest and most generally accepted delusions is that every man can be qualified in some particular way – said to be kind, wicked, stupid, energetic, apathetic and so on. People are not like that. We may say of a man that he is more often kind than cruel, more often wise than stupid, more often energetic than apathetic or vice versa; but it could never be true to say of one man that he is kind or wise, and of another that he is wicked or stupid. Yet we are always classifying mankind in this way. And it is wrong. Human beings are like rivers: the water is one and the same in all of them but the river is narrow in some places, flows swifter in others; here it is broad, there still, or clear, or cold, or muddy or warm. It is the same with men. Every man bears within himself the germs of every human quality, and now manifests one, now another, and frequently is quite unlike himself, while still remaining the same man.

*Chapter Twenty-Two*

# STALIN ISOLATED

I am finished. I trust no one, not even myself.
                                    — Stalin, as quoted by Khrushchev

One of the key factors in Stalin's personal life has, Svetlana considers, been overlooked by his biographers. The influence of women on his life and character, and its gradual decrease through the 1930s onwards, throws some light, she feels, on many of the seemingly inexplicable and dreadful events that stunned and continue to stun the world.

As the leader grew older he became more and more isolated from any feminine influence both in his personal and in his working life. He began to lose touch with his own feminine side, the receptive, the intuitive, the yielding. This side of him never developed and matured. More predominantly male qualities took hold of his personality, governed by a lust for power which made a deep-seated link with his increasing paranoia. 'The feminine influence was lacking, and much needed,' says Svetlana.

Most biographers date the beginning of the purges from Kirov's death in 1934. Kirov was a close friend of Stalin's and undoubtedly the blow was as emotional as it was political: he showed a rare warmth towards Kirov. But it is also possible to look further back, to the death of Nadya in 1932, and the gradual erosion of any softening influence in his life. After her death, the wives of the politburo members ceased visiting or attending evening sessions with their husbands, so they became stag affairs. Stalin's mother died in 1936, an event hardly acknowledged by most biographers, but according to his daughter it would have had a far deeper impact than has been recognised. 'He kept on talking to me about his mother, that he knew that she was supporting him. There was a strong link between them, and it was a big loss to him when she died.' Perhaps it is not insignificant that her death occurred in 1936, in the middle of the purges and just before they accelerated into a reign of terror.

Between 1938 and 1941 his sisters-in-law, Anna and Eugenia, were banned from Stalin's home. The Svanidzes were arrested in 1938, depriving the household of two lively women visitors. From 1941 onwards Stalin's relationship with his daughter deteriorated and the distance between them grew greater and greater. She has told the story of her break with Stalin, of her disillusionment with him and the Communist Party in general, in detail in her books, *20 Letters to a Friend*, and *Only One Year*. The first shocking revelation had come to her when she was fifteen, when, in 1941, she discovered through reading the *Illustrated London News* that her mother had not died of appendicitis as she had been told. Her father had lied to her, his beloved daughter. Coming at an impressionable age, this was a deeply emotional trauma. It was followed by her father's reaction to her first romance, which she also relates in detail: his response was to despatch her would-be lover into exile, where he spent ten years in spite of her supplications. 'I learned very early that the fact of who I am can ruin everything.

'My relationship with my father had been quite good before the war. Then I learned about Mother's death, and I immediately thought, "What was the reason? Did he do something to her? Was she upset? What was *his* part in it?" There was a big question there. And why hadn't I been told?

'Then about a year after that came the Kapler story; I fell in love with this man, and then Father ordered his arrest. These two events were a shock to the system. They brought about a change in the relationship. I saw that he was not always right, that he could obviously be quite wrong. It all happened very fast, and I was at a vulnerable age. I began to have grave doubts about my father, and I withdrew. A child in my class at school would suddenly be removed into another class. Why? Because his or her parents had been arrested. I couldn't understand what was going on, but he knew that I knew that he was behind it all, and he withdrew too. He felt that I was no longer reliable, because he couldn't hug me and kiss me as he used to – I was not his "clean little girl" any more.'

Then in 1941 Stalin had Yulia, his daughter-in-law, arrested and imprisoned for two years. Worse was to come. In 1947 and 1948 he arrested first Eugenia Aleksandrovna and then Anna Sergeyevna, who were sentenced to ten years' solitary confinement. 'They knew too much. They babbled a lot. It played into the hand of our enemies,' her father told Svetlana. Then Kyra, Pavel's eldest child, who was only eighteen, spent six months in the Lubyanka before being sent into exile for five years. These inexplicably brutal actions were his last word to the family who had supported him through his rise to power and who remained loyal to him to the end.

For two decades there were effectively no women around Stalin. The person by his side was Beria, whispering conspiratorially in Georgian. All Stalin's energy was channelled into his work and expressed through the exercise of power; power which was corrupted into the use of fear as a weapon, into violence and oppression as a means to secure his personal position.

'He moved in an entirely masculine milieu, because the married members of the politburo stopped bringing their wives; they felt that it was a bachelor home now. It was entirely male company in which I often found myself as the only girl. In the early thirties they all brought wives, to the New Year celebrations, to birthday parties, that was still the custom after Mother's death, and all the Alliluyevs would be around too. Then all that disintegrated and we saw none of those familiar faces.

'So in the end my father was subject to male influence. In Mother's lifetime Molotov, Kaganovich, Voroshilov and the others would come with their wives and they were friends of Mother's and of my aunts. After she was gone this gradually disappeared. Even at the big state dinners in the Kremlin for the great revolutionary holidays, wives were somewhere in a little flock, separated, segregated, and the men were sitting together. It was very changed. So the female side in Stalin – as we are all made up, yin and yang – that balance was gone, it had no nourishment.

'The influence of women in the family was very substantial, even on Father in the early days, when he was around to listen and talk to them all. It was a benevolent, good influence. They were, in their way, all very strong and good. Their going had a bad impact. It was a very strong side of the family, strong in its benevolence but not forceful in its influence.

'Eugenia Aleksandrovna was very loyal to my father. She always kept a picture of him, even after he was denounced in 1956. I remember her saying, "They are all guilty, all these people – Khrushchev and all of them were participants, and your father was the scapegoat for them all." Yet she had certainly lost many friends in the purges.'

The influence of the women was also related to their power in society at the time. 'My grandmother's generation was working towards emancipation: my mother's generation was entirely emancipated. They were young revolutionaries and they immediately became equal members of society; women took men's jobs, they kept their names on marriage and kept their individuality. Then slowly that eroded and female power dwindled.

'The feminine influence had disappeared on another level too, because there were fewer and fewer women in the higher echelons of the Party. They were still in industry, but in Lenin's time there were women in high places, and that was recognised as the scheme of things; they had a certain influence in the Party. But later on it was all wiped out and women's numbers were reduced. It was a step back from the ideals of the revolution, which started by bringing liberation for women in every field, then it was all gone. This is called "ageing revolution", with the restoration of previous values. It is the natural process with every revolution in history; its nature is cyclical. It seems inevitable, and we simply watched. It wasn't something especially Russian.

'I got this idea from my aunts about how much Beria was responsible for these things, how ruthless he was. It was not my observation, it came from them, and from the fact that Mother didn't like him and was afraid of his influence on my father. Grandma Olga and Anna used to say – which always sounded strange to me but now I don't think it so strange – "Your father could be influenced very easily. He could be influenced by good people: Kirov had a wonderful influence on him. Beria had a terrible influence." My father always *talked* about Lenin, but I don't know how deep his influence went. You don't think that somebody who was a pretty strong character could be influenced, but they believed that he could. Beria would come to him, always flattering, and get what he wanted.

'For example, Beria was extremely anti-Semitic and he knew how to feed Stalin's paranoia. They would be sitting at table talking about somebody, and Beria would throw one sentence across the table – "He's a Jew!" He knew which buttons to press. They were alarmed about him and kept saying so, but of course we were children so we couldn't see this. The women could see the effect that Beria had on him, but they could do nothing about it.

'My mother had influence for a time, and perhaps it cost her her life . . . In general terms, the women had a benevolent influence, but not enough to change politics, the course of events; they were not politicians. Besides, it is the course of revolution, which turns on and devours her own. Which is seen in the example of our family most clearly.'

★

209

With my father and myself there was a loss of trust, of mutual love. Later on, when I was the mother of two children, he began to see me as an adult and for the last fifteen years of his life he desperately wanted to communicate, to talk, and he was mad at me for not being forthcoming. I was always a little reticent with him. We had lost our family. If grandparents and aunts had all been around, with that lovely warm atmosphere with lots of laughter and jokes, it would have been different. Whether he missed it I don't know, but probably he did. They had all gone, and he was alone. It was a very hard thing for him, and this isolation certainly contributed to the Cold War. He was in a very depressed mood, and when your absolute ruler is depressed it is bad for the country. It is bad for the country even if he is constipated!

'His last years were very gloomy. When the war was over he fell apart and became very ill. They thought that he would die. But this was a state secret – they didn't even tell me at the time. I had no idea what was wrong. I was ordered not to telephone even. The war had taken a lot out of him. I learned it only from my second husband Yuri Zhdanov. His father, Andrei Zhdanov, was proposed as heir to the Party, which he dreaded like anything – he didn't want to take that on. But what my father was ill with I have no idea to this day – it was top secret. His medical records have never been divulged.

'He survived, but he was never the same again. He was depressed, he had high blood-pressure and a general feeling of deteriorating health. He said to me several times, "What will you do when I am gone? You will perish!" He had the feeling that I would be completely wiped out without him. His gentle word to me was always, "You little fool".

'Yet he clung to me, wanted me to be closer; but I couldn't understand it and shrank from it. He wanted me and my second husband to live with him, but I dreaded it; it would have meant total isolation because of the way he lived. This was in 1949. He needed this, but his needs were not met, and this splashed over into politics making the Cold War colder. Malenkov tried to persuade me to stay close to him. Both he and I saw that the feminine influence was lacking, and much needed.

'The final irony is that it is the female side of the tree that has flourished, my mother's side, the Alliluyev branch. The male side, the Djugashvili branch, has withered and all but died: Yakov committed suicide, and his son is deaf, handicapped and mentally retarded. Vasili died an alcoholic, leaving one son who is unmarried and childless, one daughter who is an alcoholic, another who died in a mental asylum, and a son who died in his twenties of a heroin overdose. There is an impostor, a young man who claims that he is a grandson, but he is not.

'Stalin needed people. All his life he was very good at finding people and promoting them, and this is why so many remained devoted to him, often young people whom he would pull out and promote over the heads of the old guard. He wouldn't hesitate to take a young man who promised something – an aircraft designer, an armament designer or constructor – from obscurity and put him in charge of some big deal. They always felt that they owed him this promotion.

'That was quite a part of him, his sociability and being with people, and this disappeared in later years when nobody had access to him. There was a wall around him and he was a victim of it. I don't know how much it was of his own making, how much it was Beria, how much a certain paranoia was involved. Or how comfortable it was for those people to have him away from everything. It is complicated; the last days of a court, the end of a monarch, is always the same – there are people around plotting, a lot of underground activity at which we can only surmise.

'But he was isolated at the end of his life, and that killed him. He loved people who talked to him directly, without fear – even those who criticised him. He had led a very sociable life, he had never been alone, even vacations were spent with lots of people around. But now he was becoming more and more isolated, more closed into his shell, which was no good at all for him. In those last years he wanted me to go with him on vacation to the Black Sea, to read aloud to him, to sit and talk with him. He even talked about my mother, with great pain. But I had obviously transgressed in some way and the relationship was never as easy as it had been.

He couldn't trust anybody, including me – Beria, anybody, even himself. In this state of mind, everybody was doing things wrong, and nobody was excluded.' This did not go unnoticed among the politburo, those closest to Stalin in his last years. Khrushchev said that towards the end 'Stalin became even more capricious, irritable, and brutal.' This brutality spilled over on to members of his immediate family; even his sisters-in-law were not exempt.

Stalin's elder son Yakov in 1939, when his daughter Gulia was a few months old. *(Alliluyev Family Collection)*

A press picture showing Yakov held as POW by the Germans, 1941-3. *(Alliluyev Family Collection)*

Stalingrad before the siege. *(Society for Cooperation in Russian & Soviet Studies)*

Fighting in the Red October Factory, Stalingrad 1942. *(David King Collection)*

*Above left:* Official picture of Lieutenant-General Vasili Stalin of the Air Force. Taken at the start of the war when Vasili was still only in his early twenties. *(Alliluyev Family Collection)*

*Above right and below:* General Georgy Konstantinovich Zhukov (1896–1974), Marshal of the Soviet Union, who played an heroic role in World War II. He was awarded the Order of Lenin in 1966. *(David King Collection)*

Churchill, Roosevelt and Stalin at the Yalta Conference, February 1945. *(Hulton-Deutsch Collection)*

Churchill, Truman and Stalin at the Potsdam Conference, July 1945. *(Hulton-Deutsch Collection)*

Stalin, Molotov, Beria and Malenkov bearing the coffin of Kalinin, one of the founders of the Soviet Communist Party, through Red Square in Moscow, June 1946. *(Society for Cooperation in Russian & Soviet Studies)*

The Alliluyev graves in the Novedevichy cemetery, Moscow. Olga, Sergei, Anna and Fyodor lie buried in line under dark marble headstones. *(Author's collection)*

Drops of rain run down bas-reliefs of Sergei and Olga embossed on their headstones. *(Author's collection)*

Joseph Vissarionovich Stalin, 1936.
*(Society for Cooperation in Russian and Soviet Studies)*

Yekaterina Djugashvili, Stalin's mother, in the 1920s. *(Alliluyev Family Collection)*

Stalin with his mother in 1935. *(David King Collection)*

Stalin's birthplace in Gori, Georgia, is now covered with a temple façade and kept as a museum in his memory. *(David King Collection)*

*Above:* A montage from 1934 depicting the reconstruction of Moscow by Lenin and Stalin. *(David King Collection)*

*Opposite:* Cover of February 1938 issue of *USSR in Construction* showing the vast Stalin sculpture at the entrance to the Moscow-Volga Canal. *(David King Collection)*

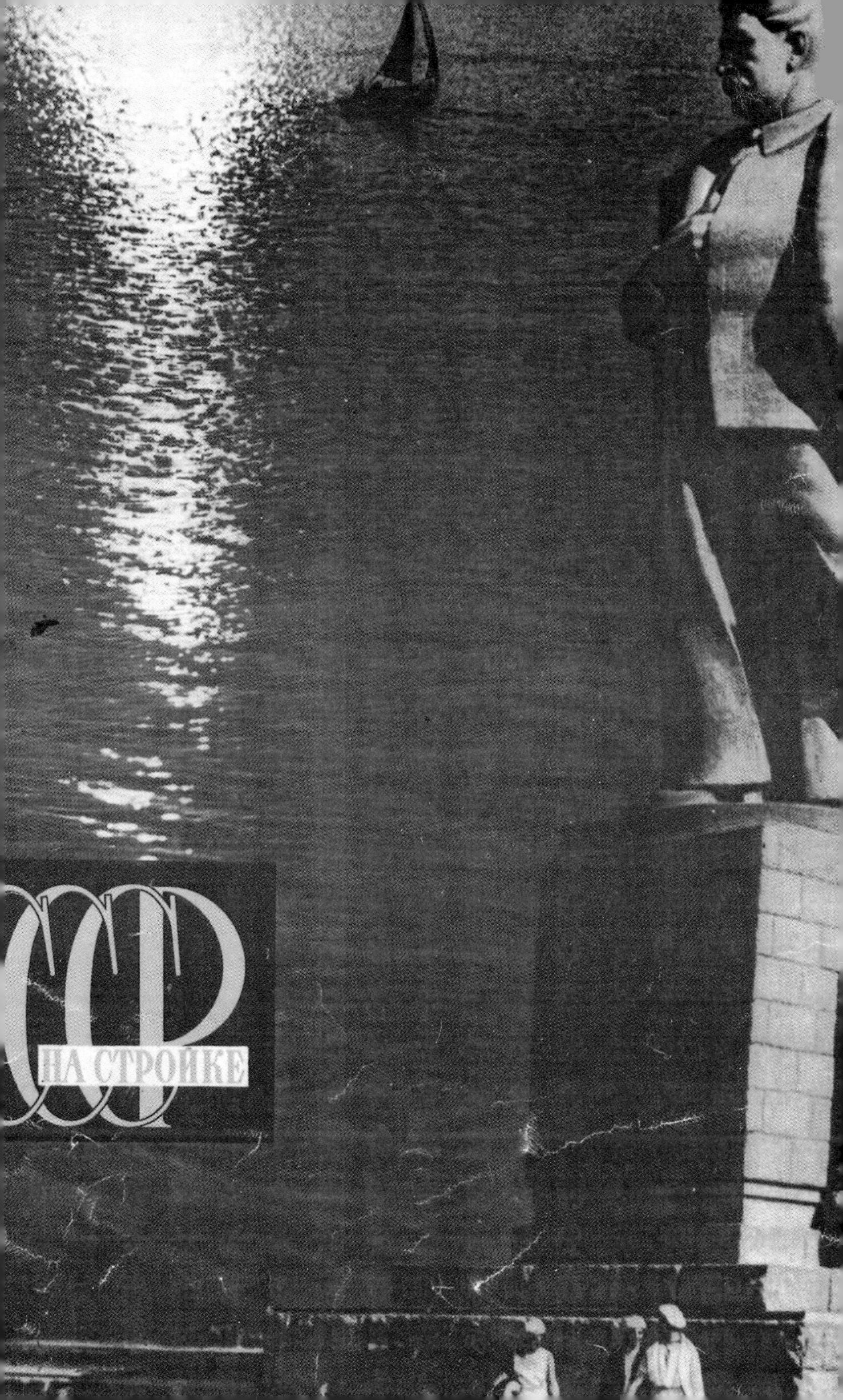
НА СТРОЙКЕ

Stalin in 1936. *(David King Collection)*

Khrushchev and Stalin in 1936. *(David King Collection)*

The Alliluyev cousins in their teens, relaxing together in the 1940s. Left to right: Sergei Pavlovich, Leonid Stanislavich and Leonid's brother Volodya. *(Alliluyev Family Collection)*

Kyra Pavlovna, Stalin's niece, daughter of Pavel Alliluyev and his wife Eugenia. Moscow, 1991. *(Author's collection)*

Leonid Stanislavich, one of Stalin's four nephews, son of Stanislav Redens and Anna Sergeyevna Alliluyeva. Moscow, 1991. *(Author's collection)*

Aleksandr (Sasha) Pavlovich, Stalin's second oldest nephew, son of Pavel Sergeyevich and Eugenia Aleksandrovna. Moscow, 1991. *(Author's collection)*

Sasha Pavlovich with his wife Olga. Moscow, 1991. *(Author's collection)*

Sergei Pavlovich Alliluyev, Pavel's eldest son and the oldest of Stalin's nephews. Moscow, 1991. *(Author's collection)*

Sergei Pavlovich Alliluyev with his wife Olga *(right)* and their daughter Aleksandra. Moscow, 1991. *(Author's collection)*

Vladimir (Volodya), the youngest of Stalin's nephews, son of Stanislav Redens and Anna Alliluyeva. Moscow, 1991. *(Author's collection)*

Photograph of Anna Sergeyevna taken after she came out of prison in 1954 after six years in solitary confinement. *(Author's collection)*

Eugenia Aleksandrovna in the late 1950s, some years after her return home from prison. *(Alliluyev Family Collection)*

Olga Leonidovna, Leonid Redens' daughter and Stalin's great-niece. Moscow, 1991. *(Author's collection)*

Party and government leaders at the bier of Stalin
in Moscow, 6 March 1953. *(David King Collection)*

Svetlana Alliluyeva at the author's home in 1991.
*(Author's collection)*

Svetlana Alliluyeva, summer 1991. *(Author's
collection)*

## Chapter Twenty-Three

# A RING AT THE DOOR

'Knock knock'
'Who's there?'
'NKVD!'
'You've got the wrong floor. The communists are upstairs!'
— 1930s joke

Nurtured by increasing isolation, Stalin's endemic paranoia assumed unprecedented proportions. He was approaching seventy and his health was not good. Unsure whether his Red Army generals, victorious over Hitler's armies, might establish a power base in peacetime, Stalin allowed them a short while to bask in triumph. Then he had General Vlasov, along with other dedicated officers who had been instrumental in winning the war, executed. General Zhukov, to whom the country was indebted, and who was immensely popular, was assigned to a series of obscure regional commands. Stalin, it appeared, was once again in the mood for purges.

In the years immediately after the war anti-Semitism became the militant official ideology. Says Svetlana, 'I knew all too well my father's obsession with "Zionist plots" around every corner.' His long-entrenched anti-Semitism had been nurtured by Hitler's holocaust, his paranoia nourished on imagined Jewish plots and infiltration. In 1948 he even arrested the wife of his foreign minister and long-serving comrade, Polina Molotov, who had been a close friend of Nadya's. She had hardly a trace of Jewishness about her; 'She talked Russian, she had blue eyes, she had completely forgotten that she was Jewish,' according to

Svetlana. When Golda Meir visited Moscow in 1948 Polina Molotov was spotted talking animatedly to her in Hebrew. Stalin chose to interpret this in his own way. 'The implication was that she was influencing Molotov along Zionist lines. To single her out and disgrace Molotov, who was known to the world as his foreign minister, was quite something.' But rationale was not the order of the day; Stalin had not forgotten that Polina Molotov had been the last person to whom Nadya had spoken before her death. She was sent into exile, and not released until after Stalin's death. After decades of being Stalin's right-hand man, 'Molotov became a nobody and faded from sight.'

The dark circle was closing around the Alliluyev family. 1947–8 saw the three shocking arrests of Stalin's close relatives whose reverberations are still felt within the family. No reasons worth the name were given; no need for an absolute dictator to give valid reasons. Three women, two of whom had been extremely close to Stalin in the early years, suffered at his hand. Svetlana still struggles to understand how her father could have turned on his sisters-in-law. 'They were declared enemies of the people; how could he permit that? How is it that he didn't protect them? Even as historic phenomena, I couldn't understand these purges.' The other was his niece of eighteen. 'No one,' says Kyra, now in her seventies, 'seemed to escape that chalice.' And with a delicate irony she laughs, able to see the absurdity in spite of the pain ingrained in the memory.

Kyra's attitude is reflected in her appearance; she looks much younger than she is, her vivacity and humour take years off her age. She is talkative, very warm, as expressive as the actress she once was. Her wavy brown hair is hardly tinged with grey, and she has the large brown eyes and deep eyelids that mark out the Alliluyev features. She is now retired, and lives quietly on her pension in a small flat in the outskirts of Moscow. The family likeness is as marked as her family loyalty, and like all the others she is convinced that her uncle was not at the root of all the troubles of the late 1940s. 'Beria hated all our family and tried to remove us from his path. We all believed that it was Beria who said bad things about us to Stalin. But of course we did not really know.' Yet there was no doubt in her mind that it was he, Stalin, who had ordered the arrests. 'We would not have been arrested if Stalin had not known about it. They simply would not have dared to do it.

'First of all they took Mother, Eugenia Aleksandrovna, on 10 December 1947. It was five o'clock in the afternoon, and I was rehearsing for Chekhov's *The Proposal* in the dining room. I heard the doorbell, and went to open the door. In came the Commandant of the House: "Is Eugenia Aleksandrovna at home?" I said, "Yes, come in." I went through. Mother was sitting with her dressmaker, and I said, "Mother, they want you." Mother went out and I went back to rehearse. Suddenly I heard Mother saying, "Well, prison and bad luck are two things that you can't avoid." She gave me a kiss and they took her away.

'Then the search began; they looked around for a long time. We had a great number of belongings, and lots of cactuses and flowering plants, and they went around tapping everything. I wondered what on earth they were looking for – it was obviously just an ordinary flat. They didn't find anything and eventually they went away.'

The three children, Kyra, Sergei and Sasha, were left alone with their devoted nanny Tatyana, and their maternal grandmother Zemlyanitsyn, very old and frail, who lived with them. None of them knew what was happening to Eugenia Aleksandrovna, and they were unable to make contact with her. 'One of Beria's rules was that the children had no right to correspond with their parents,' recalls Svetlana.

Kyra soon sensed that the circle was closing in on her. 'After this I was in a peculiar state of mind; I knew that something would happen to me. One day a few weeks later, between five and six in the evening, I was sitting reading *War and Peace*. Suddenly there was a ring at the doorbell. I had closed the door on the chain, and went to open it. The

Commandant of the House came in again with two men, and Sergei and Sasha jumped out behind me. I can't even remember the papers they showed me. Granny came out of her room and started to cry. I said, "Grandmother, don't humiliate yourself, don't cry, you mustn't." I went very courageously. I am surprised now at that, but it must have been the state of mind I was in. I didn't want to leave the boys – Sergei was nineteen and Sasha only sixteen.

'As we drove over the river I looked at Moscow and wondered whether I would ever see it again. I said farewell to the Kremlin and they took me to the Lubyanka. They took everything off me. Up to this point I had not wept, but in prison I cried all the time, my nerves were in such a state that I practically cried my eyes out. I simply couldn't understand what was going on.

'My only clue was that I was a relative of Stalin, and I knew that Beria was bound to say something to Stalin that he would believe. My mother was very outspoken, she was freedom-loving, she was forthright with Stalin and equally truthful with Beria. He had evidently taken a dislike to her from the moment they set eyes on each other. I realised that all this had been instigated by Beria. Stalin by this time was deeply under his influence.

'So I was not surprised, but I was both angry and offended. People told me to write to Stalin, but I never did. I felt that I had better not remind him of myself and that it was better not to ask him for anything. I did not want to humiliate myself. I felt that he had given his permission, so what was the point of my asking? So I asked for nothing; not a line. I didn't write anything to him, nothing about being guilty or asking for forgiveness and asking be saved. There was none of that.

'In prison they started accusing me of telling everyone about Nadya's death, that it had been suicide. I was completely shaken by this; I had not even known that it had been a suicide. At first they had said that she had died of appendicitis, that was the first story, then later on they said it was her heart. When my interrogator brought this matter up, it was the first time I learned about the suicide! Yet I was accused of "telling this to everyone around".

'I belonged to the kind of family where it wasn't accepted to talk more than necessary. There was no gossip. I was thunderstruck because I had been accused of the very thing I couldn't possibly have been guilty of. We were alleged to have talked a lot about how the people had been told lies, that she had not died of appendicitis or a heart seizure but in some other manner. They needed something to accuse us of, so that was what they pinned on me: I was supposed to have talked to everybody.

'I was in solitary for six months. I had no special treatment at all in prison, no luxuries, although when I once asked to have dry crackers instead of bread, they gave them to me. I always had stomach problems and needed a special diet. In every other way I was treated like everyone else. I cried a lot at first. Then I stopped crying and started singing. But they stopped me; it wasn't permitted to sing in prison. I can also whistle quite well; when I tried this they stopped me, and I never tried again. Finally I calmed down and came to terms with it.

'My salvation was in my memory: I kept visualising again and again all the good movies I had seen, Hollywood productions, and all the musicals. I kept re-living these in order not to lose my mind. I was allowed to read. And I could walk – seven paces forward, seven paces back. A jolly sort of life!' Again Kyra laughs with genuine humour, seeing the ridiculous side of the horror. 'To eat, there was that famous ethnic soup made of fish heads, quite pleasant. Our interrogators were fed on the same soup and always praised it to us; it was indeed good! And kasha of course – porridge – the national Russian meal.

'My feelings at the time? I was not so much angry as profoundly surprised. "What for?" I thought. I had always been a good "pioneer", a good *komsomol* [Young Communist]. I had never said anything detrimental about the system, and suddenly I was told about my crimes. "My god! What have I done?" I could not figure out what was going on. I just could not understand it. Slowly I calmed down. Only when I came out and returned home did I see things more clearly.

'After six months in jail I was exiled from Moscow to Ivanovo district for five years, and there, in the small town of Shuiya, I contacted the local theatre and got work. When I returned to the Maly Theatre in Moscow after my sentence was over, the director would not have me back because I had been in prison. He is a bastard. Meanwhile my mother and Aunt Anna were still in prison – they were there for six-and-a-half years. First of all in Vladimir prison, then later transferred to the Lubyanka in Moscow.

'When my sentence was finished I could go free, and I returned home. We all had our apartments in the House on the Embankment, the "House of the Government", so I returned there and slept first at my aunt's, and later returned to live with my brothers, as we always had. When Uncle Fyodor learned about my return from exile he came and danced like mad, and sang his French *chansons* with me; I was really surprised at the extent of his joy. It was some sort of relief for him, that finally justice came! That is how he felt, he was wonderful!'

Kyra was released in 1953, just after the death of her uncle. 'I cried when I learned that Stalin had died. I cried. I realised that after Stalin, Beria would come to power, and he was our great enemy. He had always hated us all. I was also crying as a relative of his. I did not know much at the time about history, or of his faults as leader. I was a cheerful girl and he loved this. I used to joke with him, and he would answer with a joke, and he liked that. I never had any fear of him – like "Help! This is Stalin!" as others had. I guess I was young and foolish!' Again this remarkable woman laughs, living proof of the survival of the spirit whatever the odds, so often demonstrated by her countrymen who had to undergo ordeals much worse than hers.

The traumatic events of 1948 that tore the family apart affected its members in widely differing ways. Leonid became, after the appropriate college training, a hydro-electrical engineer and worked on many important projects including the Aswan dam. He married a fellow engineer, Galina, and they have one daughter, Olga, who is now in her mid-thirties. Leonid is a slight, wiry man with large, intelligent eyes and a wide smile. He has a reputation in the family for being fairly reserved, although the opportunity to talk about his childhood appeared to loosen him considerably and he talked fast and willingly, albeit carefully, about the events that had moulded his life. He now lives with his wife, daughter and grandson in a pleasant, old-fashioned flat that hints of the *ancien régime*, in a wedding-cake building on the south bank of the Moskva river, not so very far from the House on the Embankment where he lived as a boy.

Leonid remembers the feelings that he as an adolescent had at the time of the arrests. 'Every night another person would be taken. First Eugenia Aleksandrovna, then Kyra, then neighbours. Everyone expected that they would be the one to be taken next. Yet through all of it Grandmother Olga was still there. I remember it all with a complex combination of feelings that is characteristic of the Alliluyev family.

'Despite the horror of the arrests and all that was going on, there was a kind of black humour about it all. Of course it was terrible, of course it was serious, all those late night visits. Yet there was something ironic, almost funny about it. Like it was unreal, a fantasy.'

And he looks up with a direct gaze, which is piercingly quizzical, yet not without an element of despair. This type of black humour has passed into the Russian culture Bulgakov-style, *à la The Master and Margarita*, a humour which has provided a way of dealing with the horrors of life under Stalin. How could anyone be expected to understand this parody, this tragic *comédie humaine*? We sip our tea.

*219*

## Chapter Twenty-Four

# EUGENIA ALEKSANDROVNA

There I learned how faces fall apart,
How fear looks out from under the eyelids,
How deep are the hieroglyphics
Cut by suffering on people's cheeks.
— Anna Akhmatova, 'Requiem'

Events of the late 1940s were reminiscent of the terror of the 1930s, when that ring at the door could mean the end of an already curtailed personal freedom, or even of life itself. In Leningrad, Stalin ordered Zhdanov to purge the artistic and literary world, and hundreds of talents were either snuffed out by shooting squad or dimmed in exile. Andrei Aleksandrovich Zhdanov, who was by now related to Stalin in that his son Yuri had married Svetlana, was thought by many at the time to be Stalin's natural heir as Party leader. His chief claim to fame was the carrying out of a policy that severely restricted Soviet cultural activities. After his death of a heart attack in 1948, the Leningrad Communist Party was purged of a thousand bosses, and many other associates and followers were accused of collaborating with the Germans during the siege of Leningrad. This purge was never officially mentioned until Krushchev's 1956 speech at the 20th Party Congress.

In the House on the Embankment members of the political and cultural elite waited sleepless behind their front doors listening to the lifts, to footsteps along the long corridors, waiting for that fateful ring at the door. Sasha Pavlovich's memory of those awful days remain vivid.

Sasha spoke with great frankness and warmth, at length

and in detail. He is a distinguished microbiologist, working as head of an epidemiological institute in Moscow. Bearded, brown-eyed like so many of the family, he possesses a remarkable resemblance to his grandfather Sergei Yakovlev-ich, especially on meeting. There, at the end of the metro platform at a prearranged time, stood a slim man wearing a peaked cloth cap and smoking a pipe. The likeness to photographs of his grandfather was uncanny.

Sasha has been married three times and had a son and a daughter. The difficulties of his early life were followed by what he described as the worst tragedy of all – the death of his son at the age of twenty-six, of which he spoke with evident difficulty. He regarded the sharing of his memories as cathartic, and spoke with a passion and openness that revealed a strong, deep character.

'I was still a small boy and never feared that I, too, would be arrested: when I saw Stalin for that last time at Zubalovo I was only nine or ten, and it was probably my age that saved me from arrest. I felt quite secure, but my older brother Sergei felt that he might be arrested along with the others. When at night the elevator moved up to our floor I did not care about it, but Sergei used to listen breathlessly, in terror. He suffered. After the arrests the family went quiet, hoping Stalin would ignore us, but we knew that Stalin knew something about what we were doing through Svetlana. To our surprise he watched us from afar. We believed that if we continued to live quietly and never "popped up" with anything, he might forget about us. But – not at all!

'I was at home when Mother was arrested. I cannot ever forget it. Mama was with a dressmaker, making a new dress, and Kyra was in her rooms rehearsing a play with her theatre friends. The doorbell rang and several people walked in. It was two military men – Colonel Maslennikov, a tall man with grey colourless eyes who looked like a Gestapo officer, and a Major Gordeyev – and two local "representatives of the community". Mother warned us that she was being arrested, that all would be well, since she had no guilt of any sort, and she tried to pull herself together. Then she left.

'After that a search was made of our flat, and anyone who visited us that day was not let out – it was like walking into a mousetrap. "Sit down, and stay there." They were searching until late into the night. All the photographs of the family with Stalin, with Vasili and Svetlana, were taken away, and all books with autographs as well. That started at about 6 pm and continued into the night. Kyra was arrested later, and that was late at night.

'It is difficult to describe my feelings at the time. There was no fear exactly. When Kyra entered the room while the search was going on and someone asked, "What are you looking for?" Kyra said with some irony, "They are searching for an underground passage into the Kremlin!" She even made a joke of it. Maybe that had bad consequences for her later.

'It became difficult later, but not at that moment. Later we did not even know what to tell people! After mother, Aunt Anna was taken, then Kyra, then her friends one after another. People were calling and asking to speak to them on the telephone, and we did not know what to say! The KGB told us to answer, "Our parents are on a prolonged trip." "But until what time?" "Until a special announcement." So we depended on someone's decision further along the line.

'I used this untruth wisely and got into medical college safely. I did not mention in my files that my mother was arrested, because I was told not to say it – and thus I was accepted into the college.' But his elder sister has further insights into the effects of the arrests on Sasha that he himself did not divulge. 'Our Sasha was not allowed to become a surgeon when he was at medical school, because Mother and I were arrested – so he was under suspicion, too! He became a microbiologist instead, which is OK, but it is not what he wanted.

'When the boys stayed on in the house after the arrests it

was not easy for them at all. They were still so young. Yet it is easier when people are young, things get restored, forgotten and resolved more easily. Not so for the older ones. Yet for Sasha it was quite a blow. Sergei took it easier: Sasha's whole character changed. He was sixteen – such a vulnerable age. Sergei was nineteen, and more mature. This is something that spoiled Sasha's life particularly.'

'When Mother returned home in summer 1954,' continues Sasha, 'her first phrase was "I knew it! I knew Stalin would release me!" And Sergei said to her rather abruptly that this was nonsense, because Stalin was dead. He said, "He did not release you, he died!" This is, you see, so typical! This shows the degree of faith that our family had in Stalin.

'All those years we were not totally cut off from her; from time to time we had some information – via Vasili and Olga Eugenievna – that our mother and Aunt Anna were alive. We could only surmise that there must be some minor guilt, something to do with purely personal relationships and loyalty to Stalin. We definitely thought that without Stalin's knowledge this arrest simply could not have taken place. And so far as he decided on such an extreme thing as to arrest his own close relatives, so, thought we, there must be a reason. It was a cruel step from our point of view. But from his point of view it had to be a legitimate one.

'My mother could not talk when she returned; all the muscles of her mouth had been idle for such a long time while she was in solitary with no one to talk with. But gradually the capacity returned to her.

'Mother did not talk much about her experiences so it is difficult to describe the psychological scars. But she said that reading a lot and knowing foreign languages were her salvation. Then she asked for some job to do and they gave her prison shirts to mend and hems to fix. Mother was a very active person all her life, with lots of energy.'

Eugenia Aleksandrovna signed all the accusations set before her: spying, poisoning her husband, contacts with foreigners. 'You sign anything there, just to be left alone and not tortured!' she told her daughter later. At night, she recalled, no one could sleep for the shrieks of agony coming from the cells. Victims screamed in an unearthly way, begging to be killed. Better to be killed . . .

'In prison there was a time she did not want to live and she swallowed glass; as a result she later had trouble with her liver and stomach. Later she also developed an oedema due to poor blood circulation and lack of exercise. In prison she had, for six years, only one hour of walking daily. But she had overcome all this, and began to read a lot, feeling that she must have hope to get out of there, that she would be needed. Then she decided to live.'

Kyra takes up her version of the story. 'When Mother returned we all lived in the same one big flat as we had done before. Sasha was married and had his baby daughter Zhenya by the time Mother returned. My mother's second husband was released from jail too, but she did not want them to be together again. She used to say that she was tired, and just wanted to be alone now with us children. Her second husband's children were already married and settled, but Sergei and I were still single, and she wanted to be with us, on our own.

'My mother was very sincere, and was always, as a relative, telling Stalin everything she knew. Maybe that was turned against her. But certainly to start with she never blamed Stalin for what had happened.'

Not long after her return from prison, Eugenia Aleksandrovna asked Svetlana to take her to Kuntsevo, to the place where Stalin had spent his last years and where he had died. Svetlana took her. 'Aunt Eugenia, the Novgorod priest's daughter, was a very strong woman, even after she had gone through all this. The first thing she asked me was, "Is it true? The first thing we heard is that Beria died." She and Aunt Anna almost danced! Then: "Is it true also that your father died?"

' "Yes."

' "Please take me to the house where he died" – because she always used to visit him at Kuntsevo in the thirties. "I want to see what remains." So I asked permission to take her there.

'The room was empty; they had wiped out all his belongings and furniture, taken everything away and put back other things which were not his. There was a white death mask standing there. She was in her mid-fifties, and after prison she was quite weak. She stood there holding my hand, and she cried and cried and cried. She said, "Everything is hurting. Everything. The best days of our life have gone. We have such good memories. We will keep those, and everything else has to be forgiven." That is how she felt, in 1954.

'Then in 1956 there was Khrushchev's speech with all its accusations against my father.' At a closed session of the 20th Party Congress Khrushchev made a six-hour speech denouncing Stalin. He spoke against Stalin's self-glorification, attacking the cult of the personality that had become central to his tenure of power. For the first time he exposed Stalin's crimes to the Party leaders who listened, incredulous, to the long lists of purges and sentences of exile. The nation went into shock over their fallen idol. Yet on a personal level the family remained loyal. 'Eugenia Aleksandrovna always kept my father's portrait everywhere she went, and she never forgot his charm. "Oh! Don't you tell me! If you want to know how it was, you can't tell me!" In the family they remained faithful.'


Sergei was a few years older than Sasha, and the events affected him in a different way. A tall man in his early sixties, he has upright bearing and thinning grey hair. His looks come more from his mother's side, fairer, with blue-grey eyes. He has a striking face with an aquiline nose, and there is a dignity about his defensive air. He has a huge collection of family photos in his little flat on the west side of Moscow, in a building whose fabric – like so many others in the city – is dilapidated. Sergei told us with regret that the entrance was a target for anti-Stalinist graffiti and vandalism.

He lives there with his wife Olga who is twenty years his junior, and their beautiful teenage daughter, Aleksandra Sergeyevna. The flat has a fifties feeling, more bourgeois than *ancien régime* – neither style a comfortable bedfellow of the communist ideology. Potted plants punctuate the bookshelves, the walls are decorated with prints and water-colours. A huge well-cared-for collie wandered around, Orlando. Sergei has a magisterial air that befits his post of Professor of Physics at the Technological Institute in Moscow.

His descriptions are more guarded than his brother's, but the photographs he showed me spoke for themselves. It was difficult to recognise the Eugenia Aleksandrovna who had come out of prison, so changed was she from the beautiful, elegant and evidently vivacious woman of the earlier pictures. The old woman looked dulled, as if somebody had switched her light off and knocked the vital energy out of her. Sergei chose not to elaborate on that, but to lay more accent on the practical arrangements that had to be made while the younger members of the family were left to fend for themselves.

'Up until the arrests, while everything was OK in our family, we used to visit Grandma Olga Eugenievna in her apartment in the Kremlin. But after the arrest of Mother and Aunt Anna we were not allowed there any more, although Leonid and Volodya were still visiting her. Then only Volodya was permitted, and after that we were all banned. So she came to us, and we saw Grandma every weekend until March 1951, until she died.

'Our flat and Aunt Anna's were in the same block, on the same entrance of the House on the Embankment. We had lived in those flats since 1938. We all stayed on there until our mothers returned home from imprisonment in 1954. So Grandma would visit Leonid and Volodya and we would all gather in their flat on the fourth floor; we lived on the eighth floor. She would also come to our flat to see my other grandma, Zemlyanitsyn, who was ill. And often we would travel to spend a weekend with Grandma at the dacha in the country. She loved to be visited by her grandchildren.

'Grandma would refer to the place where our mothers were confined as nothing other than the Gestapo, although she didn't say it to Stalin's face. She knew what that word was about! Her dark humour! She knew things, she had no illusions. She was not far from the truth, either, as we all realised later.

'She tried to contact Stalin, but she didn't succeed. We know that from the day of our mothers' arrests until the day of her death Grandma had no contact with Stalin.

'My mother's first words when she returned were, "I have only just learned that Stalin has died. I am full of sorrow." She did not know he was dead when she came out of prison. She was in tears, she was very upset. Then Svetlana arrived and again she was crying. I said, "It is only because he has died that you are let out of prison at all." It was only later that her views changed, and she began to think that but for him she would have spent less time in prison.

'As far as feelings went, it was very complicated for her. She had known him since 1918, just as Anna Sergeyevna had done; they had known him for a very very long time. This matters. This is very important: they knew him before he became a leader, before he began to run the country.

'In those early times Lenin would sometimes be with the family, and my mother had a glimpse of him – such were the relationships in those days! Of course Stalin already had a certain position in the Party, but he was not yet a leader. They knew that Lenin thought Stalin should never become leader, but it is not true that these two were always enemies. My mother felt so elated when Lenin pressed her hand that she did not wash her hand all day! My mother came from the provinces, the historic city of Novgorod, and she felt that way before the great leader. Yet she was very direct with him; she was outspoken.

'But six years in prison had changed her. First of all she had grown terribly old, and terribly thin. It is difficult even for me to evaluate the other changes – I have met so many people who have come out of prison and they have all been changed, everyone in a particular way. Mother was always an optimist and this quality helped her a great deal. It must have been very hard to be in solitary confinement for six years. But she loved to read and this was her salvation.

'She lived long enough afterwards – she was seventy-six when she died, so maybe prison did not shorten her life. Her own mother died at exactly the same age. But without a doubt she became less cheerful after her return.

'She was put in prison aged forty-nine, and came out at fifty-five. She lived at home with us for twenty years after she came out. For the last two years she was gravely ill; she had a stroke and was paralysed for a year and a half, she couldn't get out of bed. For a while she was in hospital, then she came home, she was in and out. Finally she died in hospital of a brain haemorrhage.'

Kyra describes how Eugenia Aleksandrovna's death marked the end of an era. 'My mother's death in 1974 caused us all to move to separate flats. Then Sergei got married and moved away from that area, but we still all get together for holidays and birthday celebrations, and we continue to see Leonid and Volodya.' But the close family fabric was now irretrievably loosened; Eugenia Aleksandrovna was the last of her generation to die, and with her death many of the threads of the past were relinquished and committed to memory. These memories influence the third and fourth generations today. Their lives have been deeply affected by these events and their consequences. A long shadow.

*Chapter Twenty-Five*

# ANNA'S FATE

No, it is not I, it is someone else who is
  suffering.
I could not have borne it.
        — Anna Akhmatova, 'Requiem'

Most shocking of all to the outside observer, perhaps, is the arrest of Anna Sergeyevna, Nadya's elder sister, Stalin's sister-in-law and erstwhile friend. Their relationship went back thirty years, through good times and bad – that sleigh ride in Leningrad, making tea and talking late into the night about the revolution, happy family weekends at Zubalovo, the birth of their children, then helping each other through the days after Nadya's suicide. The friendship had been a close one within a close family, and even though the Alliluyev family had 'fallen from grace' after 1938, the outrageousness of her arrest appeared to be unthinkable.

Volodya, Anna's youngest son, was twelve at the time of his mother's arrest. Now in his mid-fifties he lives in the centre of Moscow, a few minutes' walk from Red Square. His flat is tiny by Western standards, yet luxury compared with those families who in spite of professional status are obliged to share kitchen and bathroom with another family in the overcrowded capital.

Volodya is a tall, energetic man with a shock of wavy dark hair and the hooded brown eyes of the Alliluyevs. He worked as an engineer with Korolev, building spaceships, before he took early retirement. Quite accustomed to giving interviews to the media, he has become the spokesperson for the family and is writing a book on the life and times of his family. He is married to Svetlana who keeps their flat spick and span, and proudly displays a collection of rare china in a glass-fronted cabinet which stands in one of two sitting rooms hung with pre-revolutionary style dark-green velvet curtains.

The main sitting room is a shrine to Stalinism: around the walls hang portraits of the leaders – a good watercolour of Stalin, one of Lenin, a portrait of Dzerzhinsky, a bust of Lenin, a photo of Volodya's father Redens, a photo of himself when very young being visited by his Uncle Joseph, a photo of Anna Sergeyevna taken after she came out of prison, and a huge oil painting of Nadya. Red velvet hangings drape the settee and doorway, and there is a fine glass-fronted oak bookcase inherited from his mother. Tall windows look on to the square below.

Slightly incongruously, Volodya was dressed in a well-fitting denim suit decorated with US army badges. He described the events of that fateful night in January 1948. 'The arrest was at night, of course, at home, at about three in the morning. A whole bunch of people entered our flat, led by a very unpleasant colonel. He was short and small, wearing an astrakhan hat bigger than he was. They showed her the order for the arrest, and took her away. When she was leaving my mother said, "What a strange array of misfortunes come upon our family Alliluyev."

'After that we sat up all night while they did a search which lasted a day and a night. They found nothing interesting.

'She was arrested on 28 January 1948, very soon after her book was published. She was accused of slandering Stalin. Yet the people who wrote all kinds of things against her turned out to be "friends and well-wishers".

'My brother Leonid and I stayed where we were, with our nanny Tatyana who had taken care of us from early childhood. But then she died, quite soon afterwards, during the Easter holiday 1948. The mother of Eugenia Aleksandrovna, whose husband had been a Russian Orthodox priest, and who was the same age as Tatyana, envied her. We were left alone, Leonid and I, along with Sergei and Sasha plus two children of Aunt Eugenia's second husband, who all lived on a different floor. We all somehow carried on as best we could.

'On Sundays Grandma would visit us, as before. Uncle Fyodor lived in the same building, on a different entrance, and we saw him quite often. He suffered as everyone did. Everyone was shocked – shocked, depressed, surprised. But we all kept holding together, as we always had done, and even more so now.'

Svetlana made an attempt to stop Stalin: 'I tried to intervene at Anna's arrest but my father said, "They know a lot about our family and they are talking to potential enemies" – he meant Zionists – "to help them." My father had a "friend or enemy" mentality.' Binary logic, a monochrome outlook: yes or no, black or white, with no shades between.

'I asked my father, "What have they done wrong?"

' "They know a lot, they have been talking too much, and this is helpful for our enemies." They knew a lot about top politics and top family life, they knew the inner circles. They were talking a lot, he said, and they had the wrong friends. They didn't ever drop the families of people who had been purged, they remained close to them, and that was wrong.'

Svetlana describes her deepest feelings about her father's 'downward trend of the soul' in *20 Letters to a Friend*: 'My father's whole life stood out before me as a rejection of Wisdom, of Goodness, in the name of ambition, as a complete giving of himself to Evil . . . He had been destroyed by Evil, sunk deeper and deeper into the black chasm of the lie, of fury and of pride.'

This was Leonid's second experience of the arrest of a parent, for he had been ten when his father was ordered to Moscow from Alma Ata and never seen again. Now, ten years later, history repeated itself with his mother. He was impressed by her strength of will. 'When they arrested my mother they couldn't get her to sign anything, not even by force. She was stubborn, they couldn't break her, even by putting her into solitary. But when she returned she looked terrible, her clothes were torn, and she was suffering from the family illness that had afflicted Fyodor and touched Nadya.'

At Stalin's death the sentences passed on both women, ten years in solitary confinement, still had five years to run. However, Khrushchev was alerted to their situation and lost little time in helping the family to remedy it. Svetlana tells how 'Khrushchev made a special search of the prisons and found them. Otherwise they would have stayed there until 1958. Aunt Anna was very sick when she emerged, she didn't even recognise her children, or anyone else. She was just sitting there, and her eyes were not her eyes. They were fogged, misted. Later on it all cleared up and when she died ten years later she was relatively all right. She could laugh again, her children married and she had grandchildren. But in the first days she was almost incommunicado.'

Kyra remembers how 'She had hallucinations, heard voices talking to her, and talked to herself a lot. She did not wash her clothes, it was all the same for her, wearing the same dress all the time. It was very strange behaviour indeed.

'Aunt Anna loved Stalin so much, and she was very deeply upset that he would not see us all again. She could not understand why. She had known him since she was a girl in Petersburg, as all the others had done. This is why she became so ill later, I think. She absolutely could not understand why he turned away from us.'

Volodya describes her homecoming after nearly seven years in solitary confinement: 'In 1954 we received a telephone call and were told that she would be coming home. Kyra went to pick her up. Svetlana also came round. My mother looked terrible, she kept looking for me, because when she was arrested I was still a boy of twelve. Now I was the tallest of all of them, and nearly twenty. She did not recognise me. "Where is Volodya?" she kept asking, and I was standing next to her. She looked really bad. But slowly, slowly, things got better. But seven years is seven years . . .'

If the photograph on his sitting-room wall is anything to go by, Anna Sergeyevna was greatly damaged by her experience. Huge dark rings surround the sunken eyes whose expression is disengaged. A deep furrow runs down the forehead to the bridge of the nose, the face has become fleshy, florid, pasty, indicating considerable weight gain after her starvation rations in prison. The calm serenity and purity of the young Anna have receded under a mask of suffering. The hair is slightly unkempt, the face has a lost look about it.

'Undoubtedly she suffered immensely from being in solitary, but she didn't talk about it. We did not question her; everything was clear without words. It was a big lie, the whole thing, a big calumny. She knew the people who had spoken wrong of her. It was all well understood. She even asked forgiveness from those people; she would say, "Stalin did arrest me according to your reports – but it was not your fault, it was mine." She would not blame Stalin either. When one of the people who had made accusations apologised later on, swearing at Stalin, my mother said, "It was you, not Stalin, who made the accusation."

'This friend of hers, for whom my mother had done a great deal, asked for her forgiveness for having written the denunciations. At the same time, she was malevolent in her criticisms of Stalin because, she said, she had been forced to write these denunciations. My mother answered, "Who is more guilty, you who wrote the denunciation on the basis of which Stalin imprisoned me, or the system? It was *you* who was harshly treated by the system, being made to write them! Who do you think should feel offended with whom?"

'When she was arrested she perfectly understood that someone had betrayed her, but her reaction was, "What happened, happened". When she came back from prison I never heard her say anything bad about Stalin. She knew him well, she knew the kind of information he used to receive, distorted through the official channels. It was some intrigue of Beria's, although beyond any doubt Stalin did understand whom he was arresting and there is no way I can remove the guilt from him for that. Of course he is guilty. Beria was also without any doubt implicated, and he took all the measures he could to cut off the channel of information that the Alliluyevs had to Stalin.'

Svetlana bears out the remarkable lack of bitterness shown by either woman towards their brother-in-law. 'These two women, who had been sent to prison by my father, never had any bitterness. Everything was put on Beria's head, and that was how they felt about it. Anna believed in Fate. It had turned its dark side on us all, and that was how it was. Nothing you can do: so you accept it. Even so,' she muses, 'it's very strange that the family didn't show any anger.'

Leonid's daughter Olga was born the year that Anna came out of prison, and grew up with her grandmother for the first ten years of her life. 'I only knew her when she was already ill, and I remember being afraid of her. She was a very strange woman, she walked around the house talking to herself. But I never felt the tragedy of it all as my parents did.' Anna Sergeyevna's life was fundamentally changed by her experience in prison and she never fully returned to a normal life. Her son Leonid continued to look after her, but she remained an eccentric figure. Towards the end of her life the family illness worsened, and she had to be hospitalised. Svetlana describes what happened on Anna's last day. 'After six years in prison she was afraid of locked doors. She had ended up in hospital, very disturbed, talking all the time. She would walk the corridors at night talking to herself. One night a stupid nurse decided that she should not walk in the corridor, so she locked her into her room, even though it was known that she couldn't stand locked doors. In the morning they found her dead.'

*Chapter Twenty-Six*

# UNCLE JOSEPH

Asked whether he would like his people to be loyal out of fear or conviction, Stalin replied, 'Fear. Convictions can change, but fear remains.'

— Weissberg

As the family describe their ordeals, the sharp definition of their memories gives some indication of how intense the trauma was. The immediacy and vivid detail around events that took place over forty years previously are remarkable. Evidently the knife cut deep, and the wounds are hidden rather than healed. It appears that a complete coming to terms has not been possible.

These psychological traumas, however, can be seen in the context of the collective suffering of the entire Soviet Union; this vast country was undergoing unimaginable suffering, which went some way to make personal pain more supportable. Nevertheless, the Alliluyevs had to pick up their individual pieces and try to come to terms with their connection with Stalin, and with what happened to them personally, in order to lead reasonable lives.

Loyalty to Stalin, as a man, remains the outstanding and unshakeable feature of the family ethos – without, in most cases, denying the gruesome deeds that he perpetrated. There is an implicit understanding of how Stalin draws projections of evil to him on a universal scale, dark projections of the worst side of human nature. They see that for what it is: the power of the powerless, the only retaliation of the impotent.

Kyra, conditioned throughout her childhood to praise

and support the "glorious communist revolution", never at first questioned its leadership. On a personal level, 'I felt I had a good relationship with our uncle; he also liked Sasha and Sergei very much when they were small, and played with them like any uncle would. So it came as a shock when we learned the truth, when Khrushchev came to power, when we began to hear different revelations. But my mother Eugenia Aleksandrovna never blamed him for anything. My father Pavel Sergeyevich respected him, and my mother did too, so we never had such talks about him in the family. That was sincere with them – it wasn't that they "knew" and wanted to conceal it. No, they simply always thought well of him. And he always entertained us so well, he was so friendly.' Kyra remains loyal on this level, albeit not denying now that he was responsible for some terrible things; yet 'no one can understand that I cannot talk about him as others do now.

'I liked him, as a man. He was calm, and cheerful in good measure. I never heard him being rude. Now I read all these stories, but I never saw his anger or his rage, nothing of the sort! He was happy with us. He liked me – to him I was a jolly girl who never offended him. The last time I was in Sochi on vacation, in 1939, I was on the beach with Svetlana who was staying with her father. She said that he wanted to see me, so I went. I knew that Svetlana could not invite me on her own; it came from him. He said, "What a tan you've got!" – he was informal and friendly. That is why I cried when he died. While I was in prison I could not understand why I was there.

'I thought he was a very good-looking man. There was something very placid, very decent about him. Something very reliable. I heard later that he was "horrible", but that was not true. He had a good face with a long straight nose, he was well-dressed, and uniform looked good on him. He had bright eyes, his pipe in his hand – all very handsome. When my mother was in Paris with my father she bought him an expensive curved pipe, and he was very pleased with it and always had it in his hand. His relationships with his relatives were always very pleasant.

'I never saw him at his office, but he certainly had very good manners with us. We would always come when he invited us, which was when I saw him, and he was always glad to be with us. When he stopped calling us, after the war, then something was obviously on his mind that made him not want to see us. I never saw him after that time. But in general he liked to invite people around, although the initiative had to come from him. If we had pushed for a meeting he would not have liked that, so we never did. I think Svetlana is like that too. But this is a normal human quality, common to many. We never pushed ourselves forward or used our connection with Stalin, nor were his family ever snobbish with us.

'His character changed after the death of Nadya. He was offended and hurt by the way she left him. He lost his trust. The women in the family, who could have softened him, were becoming more distant from him, and this had quite an effect on what then happened. But it was he who had cut them off, and had them all arrested – it was not that they abandoned him, rather that he removed them from his life.

'My mother, Eugenia Aleksandrovna, who was always so direct with him, would even sing limericks to him – *Chastushki*, funny songs with a satirical content. They were often risqué, too. He loved all this, even when they were about him, they made him laugh. *Chastushki* were often about aspects of social life, and mostly against the regime. It always appeared that he enjoyed it all. But after we were all arrested, who knows, maybe he thought we were all against him? When he became so isolated he started thinking the same way his entourage was thinking. He did not know real life any more. Being so isolated he could not know what was really going on, who was good, who was bad.

'It is rather like a small child, pampered by mother, who when he is suddenly among grown-up people and goes out into the world cannot understand anything, least of all why people are criticising. He has been used to agreement. Those people kept him alone, pampered him, and like that child he became blind to the realities of life. He, Stalin, knew only "Hurrah! Hurrah for Stalin!" and he thought that was the Truth. We, his relatives, could tell him otherwise.

'When Svetlana's daughter Olga came to the USSR she was not so conditioned, she saw things here differently. But we are of our mould and upbringing.'

A constant and inseparable part of Stalin's domestic set-up was a large entourage of bodyguards, servants and a faithful personal assistant-cum-secretary. The longest serving of these was Vlasik, who attained the rank of major-general in the NKVD and who built up a personal empire in Stalin's name, running estates that the leader hardly ever visited. He was the family's official photographer; somewhere in the archives volumes of his pictures lie stored, testimony to three decades of Stalin's personal and domestic life, such as it was. 'Vlasik was with my father for thirty years, from 1919,' says Svetlana, 'and they were old friends. Poskrebyshev, his assistant and secretary, stayed for almost twenty years. As far as work is concerned, Poskrebyshev would have known more about Stalin than anyone. He left memoirs which were immediately impounded. Both men were arrested in 1952 at Beria's instigation, but released after Stalin's death the following year. I met Mrs Poskrebyshev who told me that her husband Sasha was writing his memoirs because he wanted to put it all down while he still could. When I met her again she told me that his writings had been taken away. The KGB could always obliterate what they didn't want or need, they were in charge of the state archives; but I don't know whether they obliterated them or stored them. Vlasik took volumes of photos over the years and they too have disappeared somewhere.'

Kyra became aware of undercurrents of conflict between the Alliluyev family and Vlasik and his staff, who were all under Beria's thumb. 'We had known Vlasik, too, for years, and all Stalin's entourage, but they did not like us! Because we were his relatives, we would bring to Stalin the reality of life as it was. He was isolated from the truth, he did not know about things as they were, but we kept the connections with reality alive. We were not welcome from the point of view of the entourage. My mother was so outspoken! She gossiped about everything, she was always criticising. They did not; they kept him apart from the truth, Vlasik and the others. But Stalin loved to listen to us. Eugenia Aleksandrovna would tell Stalin all sorts of stories; Stalin had great fun listening to them – and then sending her to prison. The relatives, it was thought, could do him damage if they weren't careful.' Kyra laughs yet again in hindsight at the cat-and-mouse games that now appear to have been going on. Her laughter is undoubtedly her chosen mask for feelings too deep for words.

In spite of all her traumatic experiences, she remains young not only in looks but in her heart, in her attitudes. She ascribes this to the example set by Eugenia Aleksandrovna. 'My mother was like that. We never saw her depressed or gloomy. I had to come to terms, and one thing that helped me greatly was my love for the arts. In exile, I worked for a local theatre for the first three years, then I worked with retarded children for two years – I love children! My work was in an international profession, and that was good. On stage I always had a part with singing and dancing, in musical comedies and vaudeville. It was all very helpful – not heavy stuff.

'I was still in my own creative atmosphere, although I was lonely without my family. But there were always good people who came my way! I was so lucky even there, always to meet good folk, people who never rejected me as an "exile" – they had been warned about that, yet still they were good friends to me.

'I remained in my own milieu in exile. If for example I had had to work as a cleaner or a sweeper, I probably would have felt angry and embittered. But I was still among actors. When I returned home I worked as an assistant director, and then an assistant producer on television – that again was my native element. So there was always a sense of mutual understanding around me. The arts bring people together, untie their knots, make them softer and kinder. Even different countries are united by arts. In my own country art certainly is a great healer and help.'

When Kyra was arrested in 1948 she was a married woman, but her young husband's parents insisted that he divorce her so as not to taint and possibly endanger the rest of the family by his connection to a wife sentenced to prison and exile. 'My first husband was an actor in the Maly Theatre, where I was an actress. After three years I was arrested, and his parents demanded that I give him a divorce. I did. He remarried and now has two children. That is how it was!' She ends with her customary good-natured laugh. Although such a step was not uncommon in those days, one can only guess at the personal emotions this may have aroused. However, some years after her return from exile, Kyra married again, although she never had children. 'I was married very happily the second time round. My husband, an architect, died in 1979 of cancer of the blood, aged sixty-five. He looked very, very young though. Now I am too old for a third time!

'I can say that I am supported by friends, and I have such lovely dear relatives. I want to live and be healthy because I see around me so many good people; this gives me the stimulus for living. I do not feel myself as the oldest, nor do I live with a vacuum around me – that would make me very gloomy indeed. I have always liked children, and played a lot with all my brothers' children, and now there are grandchildren and this is a great joy too. My brother Sasha asked me once, "Well, how many more years do you want to live?" I answered that I would like to see the wedding of his lovely daughter Sashenka, my niece. I want to dance then!'

Kyra's younger brother Sasha's feelings about the impact of his uncle's hand on the family are very obvious, if not explicit. He talked about pain, pain so deep and so hidden that he cannot even put words to it.

'After the arrests, the family just went quiet, hoping that Stalin would forget about us, but I know he knew something about what we were doing, via Svetlana, because I was at that point singing with the school jazz band. Apparently when Stalin heard of this, he said, "*Huh?* He's still singing! In spite of everything?" I was told this by Svetlana. However, we were safe, although many other children and relatives of the "repressed ones" went to jail as their parents did, or to special orphanages. We did not suffer total annihilation; we did get a pension from the state, and an apartment – somehow or other an exception was made, we assume by Stalin.

'By 1947, when my mother was arrested, I believe he was experiencing the beginnings of his illness – maybe a form of sclerosis, of vascular insufficiency. That was reflected in his change of character. Many people noticed it.

'Something happened around this time which was most remarkable. Svetlana got Sergei and me tickets to the Bolshoi Theatre concert of 6 November 1947 – the usual occasion of the celebration of the revolution. It was a closed affair for the chosen few, a government gathering at which Stalin always made a speech. Suddenly it transpired that a speech would now be made by Molotov, and that Stalin was not even in Moscow. Svetlana told us that "Papa was not feeling well and decided to stay in the south through the holiday." That was the most unusual and inconceivable thing to happen, that Stalin should not appear at this celebration. The family arrests took place from December 1947 onwards.

'Even after our mothers returned from prison, nobody in the family could believe Stalin himself to be an initiator of those arrests. They always thought the evil initiative came from somewhere else and they could not therefore blame Stalin directly, or alone, for their misfortunes.

'Maybe our fault had been in not speaking about Stalin

*241*

in the glowing terms that were the custom of those days. Etiquette demanded that everyone extol him. Maybe we did not do that enough; our parents could not permit themselves to speak about him in exclamations and exultation. But in those days that was enough to be accused of treason, by dint of what you are *not* saying! And this information was all flowing to him, via Beria, who could very well interpret all this in the worst way.

'Years have passed, and we kept it all inside, and suddenly now I see everything in a new light. As Freud says, unpleasant memories and impressions get slowly suppressed by others. I am very aware that a lot of highly unpleasant experiences are repressed – Freud describes how something that is too awful to bear comes out in another form later on. This keeps one from going completely mad, from losing one's mind, it is a natural protection. Later, after sitting there for quite a while, quiet and subdued, these painful impressions are suddenly called up, they surface, and then they look quite different.'

Sasha went on to talk of a personal tragedy that, he said, has affected him more deeply than any he has had to bear. 'I always thought the most difficult and traumatic times for me were those years when Mother was arrested. But worse was yet to come, when my son from my second marriage became ill with lympho-granulo-matosis, a form of lymph cancer, and I had to watch him fade gradually away. He was an adult, and in the last few years he was just slowly dying – the illness was lethal and there was no hope. As a doctor myself, and so was my wife, we tried all we could. Olga, my third wife, was a great support to me; she was very much a part of my life at that time. We have married fairly recently although she has been my secretary for thirty years.

'So twice in my life I have experienced great emotional shock. My son's illness was far worse. Not his death, because that was a natural outcome; but the moment when I understood that there was absolutely no hope of saving him, that he would not outlive me. That realisation was one of the hardest things of my life.

'I can't bring myself to write all this down, I keep postponing it. When I tried to write, not being a professional writer, I could see that my words on the paper were very clumsy. It is only in talking that I can concentrate and bring it all back from memory. So I am very grateful that I have had the opportunity to say all this. I hope that you will be able to use it in a form that brings it to a wider public. I am really grateful for this experience of remembering the past. It was good for me. We will never brace ourselves to write about it, so I have long hoped that this would be done somewhere else by someone else.'

Sergei Pavlovich, placed in age between Kyra and Sasha, is the eldest son of the third Alliluyev generation. His father, Pavel Sergeyevich, died at the age of forty-three when Sergei was ten. At some level that child may have realised, as he watched his grandfather's deep grief, that his father's legacy to him was the family burden. He was the eldest male; he must lead the family and follow in his father's footsteps. His comments showed a well-developed caution, a guardedness which was emotional as well as intellectual, and his responses came more from the head than from the heart.

He was noticeably frank about the Beria question, about attributing blame. 'In the family we see Beria's influence on Stalin as being very evil, because this way it makes things better for us. It would be much simpler to explain everything in this way. Yet we have to face the fact that Stalin himself initiated many things, that he made decisions and took the lead in many matters. At the end of his life, however, it is probable that Beria took too much power everywhere.

'It is perhaps striking to the outsider that members of our family were so loyal to Stalin. But how could they then express their lack of loyalty? It was not done by anyone. It just wasn't accepted, nor was it possible.

*243*

'My aunt, Anna Sergeyevna, was forgiving of Stalin, but only to a degree and maybe for the sake of his children, Svetlana and Vasili, whom she loved so very much. She could have claimed many wrongs, Aunt Anna, from Stalin. First of all, the arrest of her husband Redens. Then her own arrest. Nevertheless she came to forgiveness. She was in general a very kind-hearted person.'

Anna Sergeyevna had something else to hold against Stalin, another reason to be disillusioned about her brother-in-law. It has been kept a secret ever since it happened in 1941. Sergei confided it, on condition that it would not be divulged. Suffice it to say that Stalin perpetrated a further outrage on his relatives which was so offensive that they still cannot bring themselves to talk about it. 'Grandfather Sergei Yakovlevich suffered endlessly because of this. He was very, very upset. He knew perfectly well what was going on, and he had to live through this as well as everything else.' Stalin never told his daughter the truth about this dreadful episode; she was told a different version.

'After Aunt Anna came out of prison Stalin was dead, so although there was nothing to fear from him, she had never had any fear. It had nothing to do with fear. Stalin had been in the Alliluyev family for a very long time. She had been used to seeing him, from her childhood, as a person very close to the family. They had known each other from around 1915, and then they never suspected that one day they might become close relatives. Stalin never really thought he would become a leader of the country, so the relationships were based on kindness, on human values.

'My mother Eugenia Aleksandrovna had a very direct, outspoken relationship with Stalin too, in the early days, although Svetlana exaggerates this in *20 Letters to a Friend*. Of course they weren't prostrating themselves before him. At the same time, everyone knew what was permissible and what was not. It was the atmosphere of a court. Even I, a small boy, knew what was permissible. Nobody could do what they wanted. It was a court, and there were the rules of a court.

'Our lives during the hard years were not really so bad. Or maybe we have forgiven all? It looks as if it was so bad then, and so good now, but in fact it is just as bad now. Of course there were dreadful things then, but it is customary only to remember the good things. Our country is very complicated, and our family is also very, very complicated. We are talking here, using many beautiful words, but all the characters were strong and complicated.

'Once again things are all so bad in our country now, and we do not know for how long. In our family we are all fine now, with good jobs; I have a good job at an institute with a world-famous name. But life in our country these days is not all that simple; nor is the absence of food the most important thing. The euphoria of victory in August '91, when the *putsch* failed, means only that somehow we have to live on, and nobody knows how . . . We do not see many changes so far!'

Finally Sergei touched on the theme of complicity, the submission of the Russian people throughout the decades of communism and Stalinist rule, and the collusion of a vast army of informers and secret police. Was this collusion brought about by a collective hypnosis, a charismatic power that Stalin held over his people? Whatever the answer, Sergei felt that 'what was so terrible for the country in the thirties and forties is that when they started arresting people here and people there, people began to "get used" to this, as if this were normal. *That* is what was so horrible! Everybody believed that this was what had to be. That was the horror for our country. They say sometimes that it was "the punishment for our own sins". And people take it! This is the psychology of slavery.'

## Chapter Twenty-Seven

# STALIN'S DEATHBED

The great political criminals must by all means be exposed, and preferably to ridicule, for they are not so much great political criminals as the perpetrators of great political crimes, which is altogether different.

— Bertolt Brecht

On the night of 27 February 1953 Stalin attended a performance of *Swan Lake* at the Bolshoi Theatre, but left early feeling slightly unwell. The following evening, the 28th, he dined late, as so often, with four members of his politburo: Beria, Malenkov, Bulganin and Khrushchev. Stalin's working dinners, at which affairs of state were discussed and important decisions made, invariably started late and continued into the early hours of the morning. Stalin kept a strange diurnal routine and operated best in the darkening hours: he would go to bed in the small hours of the morning and sleep through until midday. Events of state were organised around his personal clock. In this instance the dinner ended when Stalin rose to go to his bedroom at about 5 am – as always, nobody else dared bring proceedings to a close, however late it grew.

Nothing was heard from him the following day, 1 March. Nobody had the courage to disturb him, to make sure he was all right. Nobody knew what was going on, and nobody dared do anything about it. Finally, at 11 pm his duty officer Starostin, accompanied by the maid Moizia Butusova, went tentatively into his quarters. They found him lying on the floor by a sofa in his undershirt and pyjama bottoms, unable to move much or speak coherently. His eyes spoke for him,

pleading and fearful. He had suffered a cerebral haemorrhage.

Panic-stricken, the two members of staff summoned help
from others on duty at Kuntsevo that night. They carefully
lifted him on to the sofa. He was trying to say something,
but could not articulate the words. Then he lost consciousness, and his power of speech never returned.

None of the household had authority to summon a phys-
ician. Vlasik and Poskrebyshev were no longer there, loyal
henchmen who had served their master for decades, and
who might well have taken an initiative. They had been
removed from the entourage at Beria's instigation a few
months before, arrested and sentenced to ten years' imprisonment. In his memoirs Vlasik says he is convinced that
Beria 'helped' Stalin to die after first removing his physicians
and the two men closer to Stalin than he was himself. He
believed that Beria was plotting to usurp power. Stalin had
himself sacked his personal doctor Vinogradov, and as
chance would have it Valya Istomina, his housekeeper for
twenty years, was off-duty that night. She alone might have
disregarded the red tape and summoned medical help.

'Valya Istomina had first appeared in the early thirties, in
Zubalovo, the training ground for people who looked after
the family. She worked as a waitress,' remembers Svetlana,
'bringing food from kitchen to table. She laughed all the
time and we really liked her – she was very young, with pink
cheeks, and she was liked by everybody. She was a pleasant
figure – others were more reserved or sour-puss. She was
typically Russian, like Eugenia Aleksandrovna, pug-nosed,
rosy, laughing.

'Quite soon she was taken to Blizhny to my father's dacha,
where at first she was basically a waitress, taking meals to
the table. I'm not sure at what point she was promoted to
housekeeper. Nor do I know how much he could trust her
and tell her, although she told me once that he said to her
that he didn't believe that the doctors' plot was actually a
plot, that the doctors had been set up, they were innocent.

But God knows how much conversation she had with him,' says Svetlana. Her father had had the Kremlin doctors arrested a few months previously, for allegedly conspiring to the "medical murders" of Zhdanov and others, and destroying the health of leading Soviet military personnel. This episode was a sinister portent of yet another purge, and it was suspected among the politburo that Stalin had plans to "finish them off" too – Andreyev, Voroshilov, Molotov, Mikoyan for starters. Perhaps only his death could avert another bloodbath.

'Valya looked after Father's creature comforts – his clothes, the food, the house and so on, and she travelled with him wherever he went. She was a comfortable soul, and devoted to him. But not as a companion, not to talk with. Yet he trusted her.' Kyra adds, 'He was very loyal to the personnel that worked for him, very good to them all, he never raised his voice or was rude to them. Stalin used to say that he liked Valechka, as he called her, to work for him – against Beria's wishes, who always tried to peddle some personnel of his choice. There was a big staff at the Blizhny dacha at Kuntsevo that worked shifts. Valya was not on her shift at the time that her master was taken ill.'

So the staff rang through to Malenkov to alert the politburo of what had happened, but they could do nothing without Beria. Beria could not be found, he was out carousing with women. After finally being tracked down he marched in drunk at around 3 am. Looking triumphant, according to the assembled group, he glanced at the comatose Stalin and summarily dismissed their fears telling them to leave him to sleep in peace. He forbade anyone to use the telephone, ordered the politburo to reconvene in the morning, and went away. He returned at 9 am, again with members of the politburo, to take another look.

Stalin had lain untreated for over twenty-four hours; it was ten hours since he had been found. Beria now ordered doctors to be summoned from the Academy of Medical Sciences, choosing intellectuals rather than practitioners presumably since the latter were mostly behind bars, but possibly also for his own reasons. The doctors nervously applied leeches to the back of Stalin's neck and head, took cardiograms, X-rayed his lungs and administered a series of injections. Meanwhile Beria dashed off to the Kremlin and spent some time in Stalin's study, his inner sanctuary, presumably removing from the safe documents that only he would have known about, which in his own interests should not be found. Instructions as to the political succession were never found, nor was a personal diary of Stalin's, a black exercise book in which the leader recorded his personal thoughts and plans. All this while Svetlana was trying to phone her father but was told she could not speak to him and that she must not call again.

Beria returned to the deathbed the next day, and according to Svetlana's account in *20 Letters to a Friend* started acting the crown prince. Not to be outdone, the other aspirant, Vasili, was reeling around drunk shouting, 'They've killed my father, the bastards.' Svetlana by this time had been summoned and stood immobilised amidst the frantic scene beside her father's bed. She is convinced that there was more to Stalin's stroke than met the eye.

'Beria finally plotted to murder my father. I don't know *how* he plotted it, and there is a lot of folklore about it. But they withdrew medical help for at least twelve hours; the whole politburo, Beria among them, arrived at the scene instead of the doctors. He was the one who had said hours earlier, "Nothing has happened. You are panicking. The man is sleeping." And then turned around and walked away.

'My father had had a stroke. I know he was calling me – it was a silent call, for he had lost his power of speech. At that time I was visiting him only once every two months or so. I had seen him in December, and it was now 2 March. I wanted to get to see him on that day, and I tried and tried – I felt that I *had* to get to him. The blasted guards wouldn't let me: they said, "No, you can't come now, and don't telephone."

'I was so frustrated that I went to see a friend; it was still winter, and I drove to her dacha. We watched some old silent movies. One of them was a Russian classic, a Pushkin short story set in the nineteenth century, when people travelled by sleigh. Horses had to be changed at various points along the way and the story was about an old man who was the keeper of one of the stations. A sleigh arrives with a young, beautiful hussar in it. He sees the old man's daughter, picks her up, and she goes off with him. She was his only daughter and this poor old man was left on his own. He never knew where she had gone.

'Eventually, years later, he went to try to find her in the neighbouring town, but with no success. Where she had gone with this handsome officer he didn't know. Exhausted and in despair, he fell down dead by the roadside, and was buried nearby. After a long while the beautiful woman comes with her children, finds his grave and weeps over it.

'I cried and cried that night, I wept over that movie.' Overwhelmed with emotion, Svetlana wiped her eyes, weeping again at the reawakened memories. After a while, regaining her equilibrium, she continued. 'I felt that I should have seen my father that night, but I wasn't allowed to. I felt that he was calling me. I was probably the only person in the world he would have called for.

'It was the maid who found him on the floor; she was a simple woman but she said immediately, "Call the doctor! I can see he has had a stroke!" Moizia Butusova had plain common sense, she diagnosed his condition immediately. Then the guards started messing around. They were frightened of calling the doctors, so they called the government instead, and asked the politburo what to do! Valya didn't arrive back until about three or four in the morning; if she had been there she might have requested that a doctor should come. She would have had the authority to say, "Listen to me, and do this." The other guards were younger, there was a hierarchy about who said what, and they had to report to their superiors, to the KGB, with Beria at their head. So they decided to call the government instead. That was the main idiocy.

'The politburo arrived and Beria said, "You are panicking. He is sleeping!" They did not call a doctor; my father's personal doctor Vinogradov was in jail because of the doctors' plot of 1952. They refused to let me in because it was a situation out of the ordinary which they didn't know how to handle.'

Many of the Kremlin doctors arrested were Jews. 'Vinogradov was removed as part of the Zionist doctors' plot. He was completely Russian, he had nothing to do with Jews; he was probably anti-Semitic, as many Russians were. But somehow he was buttoned up.

'I met Vinogradov after father died and he said to me, "Tell me, how did that all happen?" I said, "We don't know, so much time passed." He was incredulous. He just stood there, shaking. He thought there was far more to it than met the eye. Not to call a doctor for sixteen hours, while a doctor was there, available; the servants' and personnel doctor had been on duty that night . . .

'The politburo came back three times, and while they were thinking what to do the staff were on the point of revolution, of getting weapons into their hands in order to call the doctors. Then the politburo decided that, well, it's unsightly that he's in the living room on the couch, we have to bring him into another room and put him on another couch. He didn't sleep in his bed, he liked to sleep on a couch near the wall. So they carried him to it.

'They undressed him and put his nightgown on. This cannot be done with a brain haemorrhage! No doctor would permit that. With a brain haemorrhage, you stay where you are, flat, you should not be touched. But they did all that, with no doctor around! All these men, a bunch of guards and a bunch of politburo people.

'The next morning the doctors arrived, but they were not practising doctors; they were from the Academy of Medical Sciences, which was ridiculous. They were petrified. They tried to find my father's medical history and couldn't, it was somewhere locked up in the vaults of the Kremlin Hospital, and they never found it. Vinogradov had the records and he would have had a better idea about my father's health than anyone else. People arrived in dozens but they couldn't find the records!

'Beria certainly was very happy when my father died; he had worked towards that. He had removed my father's whole entourage, starting with Vlasik, who had been there thirty years. The doctor was arrested, the personal secretary was arrested, so something had been brewing there. I hate folklore and making guesses, but something was up.

'When I was called, on 3 March, they were behaving like a bunch of hooligans, in total panic, taking X-rays of the lungs and shaking the body. Why? When you have a brain haemorrhage? Just leave him alone, leave him quiet. My father had an extraordinary heart. He would have got over it.

'He died without regaining consciousness. I was there at his deathbed for three days, but I don't know whether he knew that I was there – he couldn't talk to us. But there had been that silent call to me; I had had absolutely no peace that night. My friend called me later and said, "We understand now why you felt so terrible that evening."

'My father cursed the people in the room with a final menacing gesture: he lifted his left hand as if he were pointing to something up above. His last glance was terrible – insane, angry, full of fear. It was not a peaceful death.

'The whole thing was hushed up and they do not want to talk about it to this day. I have written about it but it has been cut out of my texts. That is historical objectivity for you! The government was so distressed by the rebellion of the personnel at Kuntsevo that they reported to the whole world that he had had a stroke and died in his apartment in the Kremlin. He hadn't lived there for the past twenty years!

'The dacha at Kuntsevo was evacuated immediately. Everything was taken out and every member of staff fired or punished. Beria had it stripped. It was as if it didn't exist. Two of the entourage shot themselves; they were simple people and they just couldn't take it. It was done so that these people could not assemble the evidence to show that medical help had been withdrawn for such a long time. It is a very untidy story which they are still trying to falsify.

'The people who were there have all dispersed now, or they are dead; forty years later nobody can be found. So they put the words into the mouths of KGB dummies to give out their version of "history".

'One of the guards attended the autopsy, Vlasik's successor, a man called Krustalyov. They could not permit a post-mortem to go ahead unsupervised because by this time nobody trusted anybody. He sat there, and it made such an impression on him that afterwards he collapsed completely and drank heavily, and of course he was fired. He said that what hit him was when they opened the head, and he saw the brain. One of the medics said, "This is obviously a very fine brain, quite out of the ordinary." Krustalyov never got over it.'

Stalin's death was announced on 6 March 1953. According to the medical bulletins he had suffered a brain haemorrhage on 1 March and the stroke had partially paralysed him. He had lost both consciousness and the power of speech. On the night of 4 March a second stroke affected his heart and lungs and he died the next day at 9.50 pm, aged seventy-three.

'When my father died there was a tremendous outpouring of feeling from the people as he lay in state. It was all filmed by Sergei Gerasimov who had by then made a lot of documentaries and feature films. I knew him very well, and he told me, "I filmed mostly the ordinary people, not the official personnel. I am not making the official version!" That was in 1953. When I asked him, years later, what had happened to the film of the funeral, he said, "I showed it and it was banned. It was banned because it showed the truth of what happened. The later official story was that nobody cried."

'All his marshals stood nearby my father's open coffin, and Marshal Rokossovsky was weeping. He was Polish, and had been saved from prison by my father and had risen to high rank under him.' Rokossovsky had joined the Red Army in 1919 and had a brilliant career, being one of the most outstanding generals of the Second World War. He was twice awarded the title of Hero of the Soviet Union for his part in the defence of Moscow and Stalingrad. In 1949 he was officially transferred to the Polish army. 'I have never seen a man cry like this. Tears were rolling down his uniform, over his tunic and decorations. The others were weeping too, especially those who had been through the war with him. They knew that the war would probably not have been won without Stalin. When there was a need to hold everything in one pair of hands and pull everybody together to make the effort, he was there. They depended on him for that, and they had been through it all together. It was a powerful experience.

'General Vishnevsky told me, "When I was fighting in the war, I was not afraid of anything. I was under shellfire, I was wounded, and I didn't care. But when I saw your father in his coffin, when we all came to say goodbye in the civil farewell, and when I saw all those marshals sobbing, my knees gave out. I had to go looking for a chair and I sat down like a sack! I couldn't stand up. It was a very strong emotion." '

Crowds converged on Red Square in unforeseen numbers. Sergei describes going to the funeral: 'We were at the time "outcasts" and therefore, to tell the truth, nobody invited us. But we went to Red Square during the funeral day (not to the civil leave – we never got to see his coffin lying in state). We just joined the crowd of workers on Red Square. We were among these people who are usually invited to represent "citizens", standing in a restricted area near GUM, the department store opposite the mausoleum. We –

Uncle Fedya, Sasha, Leonid, Volodya and myself – were all there.'

The militia were unable to control the press of people, who stampeded, and many of them including women and children were trampled to death. Similar disasters had happened at funerals of the tsars.

'When the funeral was over,' continues Svetlana, 'there were so many wreaths in Red Square that they could not all be put on the mausoleum, but on the stone ramparts where the people came to watch. And it snowed. It was the sixth of March, and the wreaths were covered with thick March snow. Somebody took a photo of Red Square at night, and it looked like bodies beneath the snow.'

The coffin was carried to the mausoleum in Red Square and placed by Lenin's side. Stalin's name was engraved next to Lenin's on the outer wall of the mausoleum. 'They mummified him in a pickle solution for display and deification. Thank God, though,' says Svetlana, 'they gave my father a proper burial in the end.' But she had to endure the idea of people filing reverently past her father's preserved body for sixteen years, until October 1961 when, fallen from grace in the eyes of his people, Stalin's mummified body was removed from the mausoleum and buried. 'But I never visited his grave beside the Kremlin wall.' On New Year's Eve 1991 there were more flowers on Stalin's grave than on any other in sight.

The question as to whether those close to him plotted Stalin's death remains unanswered, although Svetlana is convinced of Beria's complicity, and by implication of others' too. 'I don't know whether Beria could have plotted that alone. He was executed very quickly afterwards. That was a rather mysterious thing too, how quickly they got rid of him. My father died in March. Within the year they wiped Beria out. It was rather like Kennedy: his assassin was shot immediately. They executed Beria, and with him many others, and some of the archives – it was a wiping out.

'Most of that time I was very shaky, I just sat at home

and saw very close friends. General Vishnevsky came to see me often, telling me news. "Beria is now in the basement under the Moscow military staff HQ", and, "The trial is going on", and then, "My God, they executed him." Then he was asking me, "Who will be next?" He said, "I think I should stay away from them all!"

'When Beria was finally tried he was begging for his life on his knees.' He was accused of being a British spy, tried by court-martial and shot. He fell to pieces under interrogation and displayed neither dignity nor courage as they led him to his death. 'They took him away to be executed. The people in the military squad who were supposed to execute him couldn't believe their eyes. Everybody believed that Beria was such a monumental force, putting everyone into jail, and there he was on his knees begging "Anything but death! Anything to save my life". They could not believe that he was so weak.'

For Sergei and the rest of the family the demise of Beria was the hugest relief. 'When he was finally arrested it was a great holiday for us! I may say that everybody felt this way, because it was the end of a certain era, an epoch. It was not the death of Stalin that was the end of the era, but the arrest of Beria. That was the turning point. Although of course we understood that all the dark deeds would be attributed to Stalin. But the end of Beria was the end of an epoch.'

## Chapter Twenty-Eight

# JOURNEY TO FREEDOM

I live, as I have always lived, in my father's shadow.
— Svetlana Alliluyeva

'The death of my father brought little change in my life. I saw him so seldom, I had been living separately from him and my simple way of life continued as it was after his death, but still within the limits of the Party.'

Father and daughter were effectively estranged by the time of his death; Svetlana would dutifully visit Stalin every two months or so, but describes in her books how uneasy she felt with him, how she could never wait to get away. The scales of early childhood conditioning had fallen from her eyes; she hated what he had done and continued to do. She despised his desperate need to hang on to power.

'When a parent dies we experience some kind of change in ourselves. But there was no sense of liberation about 1953: I had for years lived apart from my father, living my own life, with my own friends – real friends who separated me from my name. Yet there was a certain freedom in the air, and we all enjoyed ourselves that much more. It is not a question of the presence or absence of my father: it was still the same Party, the same ideology.'

Two years after the rift with her father in 1941, Svetlana entered the University of Moscow, emerging five years later with a degree in modern history and a doctorate in Russian literature. She married twice in those years, and had a son by her first marriage and a daughter by the second. In 1952, divorced and with her two small children, she finally moved out of the Kremlin into her own flat in the House on the Embankment.

She had mentioned to her father that she wished to take her mother's name – a common enough habit among Russians – instead of bearing the surname Stalina which she had grown to hate. Stalin was not pleased, so she did nothing more about it until after his death, when in 1957 she changed it to Alliluyeva. She was beginning to cut the ties. 'My whole life had been a withering away of shallow, unreal roots. I felt no attachment to my blood relatives, not to Moscow where I had been born and had lived all my life, or to any of the things that had surrounded me since childhood.'

In 1963 a spell in hospital provided an important personal encounter with an Indian man, with whom, two years later, she lived until his death in October 1966. His name was Brajesh Singh, and it was his death which indirectly enabled her to start on a journey that would take her, for only the second time in her life, outside the Soviet Union; she had made one short trip to East Germany to visit her brother Vasili in 1947. Mr Singh's explicit desire was that his ashes be sprinkled over the Ganges, so Svetlana applied for permission to go to India to fulfil this wish. After many difficulties she was granted an exit visa for two weeks, and she flew to Delhi to stay with Mr Singh's relatives.

Her first taste of living in freedom proved a heady experience. She managed to obtain several extensions to her visa and as time went on became convinced that she never wished to return to the Soviet Union. She wished to live in India. This embarrassed the Indian government who made it clear that such a request would not be granted. 'I came to India knowing about the culture, and I wanted to stay there. But it was impossible for them, the government wouldn't have me. They gave me lots of ideas, including going to the US embassy. But it was not my original intention to defect to the US from the Soviet Union.'

On 6 March, the day before her visa finally expired, Svetlana walked into the US embassy in Delhi and asked for political asylum. On 21 April, after being shuffled around by diplomats all over Europe like the hot potato she was, she stepped on to American soil at Kennedy Airport.

The long and uncertain journey westwards, described in her autobiographies, was an outward manifestation of an inner journey in search of an elusive psychological freedom. 'I was born his daughter': for all its simplicity this statement sums up her destiny. She had begun to search, by means of various religions, for an inner liberation – first the Russian Orthodox church, then catholicism, and then the mystical religions of the East which had long fascinated her. 'The kindly wisdom of India liberated me from my spiritual bondage. I now had to cut the physical and formal ties.'

When she heard the news of Svetlana's defection, Kyra was at first incredulous. 'I couldn't believe it had happened – something must have forced her to go against her will. I was completely taken by surprise. After that I felt worried that Svetlana had made a terrible mistake and taken a wrong decision. Mixed with these feelings was, over a longer period, one of regret: regret that she had broken with her past. I felt her whole life was broken by it. Split. And since then I have felt great sadness and pity for her, because her life has been so hard. From childhood her life had been tense and difficult.'

Kyra's brother Sergei agrees: 'Loneliness was always her lot; she lost her mother early, it was always hard for her. She lived under many pressures. Svetlana was regarded as a means of achieving a certain goal by all the pretenders to her hand for example, and she knew this. She was barred from the real feelings of people, she was regarded only as a stepping-stone to Stalin. This formulated her character, because she did not receive any sincere feelings from people.'

Kyra could see that Svetlana 'had always wanted to change her life, but I don't know whether that change in her life has been for the better. I still feel great human warmth towards Svetlana in spite of and because of it all, mixed with dissatisfaction that she can't be here with us now.'

Sergei was not greatly surprised at his cousin's decision to defect: 'It did not seem improbable to me, although many thought it to be utterly untrue and indeed impossible. Surprisingly, we immediately believed that it was true; we knew her resolute ways, we understood that it was a serious matter.

'Unfortunately for us as a family, though, we once again found ourselves the centre of attention, and that made us somewhat resent it. It is not always easy, attracting curiosity of an unhealthy and unpleasant kind. We discussed it among ourselves, hoping that after a while it would calm down – and indeed, in a few years it was forgotten.'

A literary friend brought a manuscript copy of *20 Letters* to Sergei's mother, Eugenia Aleksandrovna, asking her to spot any 'inaccuracies' in it before publication; Sergei advised his mother to have nothing to do with it and to leave that to the KGB and the government. 'I said to her, let them do it themselves, let's not meddle in this!

'Many greeted her defection, including the avant-garde intellectuals that we know. She was compared with Aleksandr Herzen, a writer of the nineteenth century, who left Russia to write about his country from abroad. Everybody knew that she could not write from here. The history of our family has always fascinated people, and they love to read about it. Even though her book was not a great act of politics, she still was not able to publish it here in those days. Many people believed she was a heroine.

'But at the same time many thought that it was bad, among them her children. I did not busy myself with the ins and outs – I am just saying that there were different opinions, and we were in the middle of it all! When in 1967 her son Joseph threatened to say something bad about her in public, I told him, "Please remember that she is your mother; and that public opinion is on her side." But at the time he took a contrary position, and he did say something publicly.'

Joseph was twenty-one and Katya seventeen when

Svetlana left Moscow to go to India. She knew that any contact between them would be forbidden, or at best be made extremely difficult. As events turned out, it became non-existent. 'The system brainwashed my children, it took them away from me. They did everything they could to put in their minds that I had gone to live abroad for money, for the good life; that I had dropped them and left them in misery. It was not so, they were not in misery at all. They succumbed to the idea that I was a very bad mother and had deserted them, which was not actually true. My son was a married student, and my daughter a high-schooler – it was the time when children go off on their own anyway. It was not as if I left them as babies! But they didn't take it like this and the system worked on them to feel abandoned.

'They had pensions from their grandfather until they graduated from their education. They had a very good education, then they got good jobs and their fathers were marvellous to them – they were both very good parents. So there was no misery there; they probably had it better than if I had been there! But the bitterness was planted, and has grown.'

When Svetlana returned to the USSR in 1984, in response to calls from her son from whom she had heard nothing for many years, the visit was not a success. She did not get on well with him, his wife or their teenage son Ilyich, her grandson. Her daughter Katya, then in her mid-thirties, refused to see her. Mother and son are now estranged and refuse to talk to each other. Svetlana's daughter has not seen or had contact with her mother for twenty-five years. She has a young daughter whom Svetlana has never seen. Katya is now a widow; her husband shot himself in his late thirties.

On her visit Svetlana did however spend many happy hours with her cousins in Moscow, who were all delighted to see her. 'I believed she would come back,' says Sergei, 'and we were so glad when she returned for her visit in 1984–6: for me it was a justification of my strong belief that she would return. We all wanted to see her so much.

However, I am sure that for the government her return was useful – whenever an émigré returns it is a form of support for the regime.' Svetlana now believes that the regime set up her return: that her son's wife was an agent of the KGB and had persuaded her husband to make phone calls to England in order to entice Svetlana back into the Soviet Union as a prime 'catch' – good for propaganda.

In those heady days of 1966–7 Svetlana believed that she was tasting true freedom, that a landscape of personal liberation lay ahead and that the games played by Soviet politicians were a thing of the past.

The US embassy officials in Delhi flew their precious charge to Rome, took stock of the situation, changed planes and flew to Geneva. Svetlana was at that moment 'a woman without a country, and no country wanted me. The first secretary of the embassy, who was travelling with me, said, "Where would you like to go? You can't stay in India, the government is afraid to let you. You have never lived abroad, you have never seen Europe, let alone the world. What is your preference? What kind of country would you like?" I said right away, "I like countries with an *old* culture. In Europe it would be Spain, because its roots are so old, and a mixture of Arab and European." He wrote it down, but I never was to go to Spain. He said I should go to America.

'I missed out very badly because I was so utterly naive; I didn't know how to talk to people, I didn't know what to sign and what not to sign. I could perfectly well have stayed in Switzerland with French friends who invited me to stay with them. They warned me, "If you want to travel to America you can visit it, but don't *live* there. If you go there you will never get out, you will be putting yourself into another cage. You have just arrived from one cage; you will be going into another. They are very possessive, they will keep you there." Which is what happened.

'I didn't know what to say; I didn't know how to do it. I

was sitting there absolutely overwhelmed. It was my first time in Europe, and I became completely dizzy. I am no good at making decisions quickly; I think many times and I still make mistakes! The next day I met with American people: "Sign this immediately. If you don't sign this we can't do anything for you." I really didn't know what was going on, or what it means when you sign powers of attorney and legal agreements. "Here, sign your will," they said. I could not understand why I had to sign my will. This old American lawyer was standing over me with words I could not understand. I had never had a will before! "Am I going to die?" I tried to make a joke out of it, and he laughed: "It's the way we work. It is because of this manuscript of yours, it's a literary property. Who will own it? Where will the money go?" They were planning what would happen if I died, it was very morbid. I thought, now *why* am I going to die? But then they said, "We are going to help you publish your book," and then I said, "Sign I will!"

'It was in that situation that I signed away the copyright. It was called an "assignment of rights". I had never heard of that. I was just out of the Soviet Union, where as a writer with a manuscript you had no rights; they belonged to the state. Of course I know now very well that I have rights to my work, but I didn't then. I didn't know what an assignment was: what kind of assignment? who is paying me? I tried to get them to answer that; they were offering me about one million dollars.

'I dreaded being impolite. I dreaded being stupid and showing that I didn't understand. "Leave me alone," I begged them, "give me a day. Until tomorrow." By then I felt some sort of commitment; the Americans had helped me out of India, they had brought me this far, to Geneva. Of course I see now that I should have taken the advice of the Swiss agent who was standing by the door, and they would have helped me to understand what was involved, and to protect me.

'That was my first experience of "freedom" in the West!

I was completely swamped by it, it took me almost ten years to understand what had happened. Then my lawyer explained it to me, and he was very outspoken. He said, "It was a terrible thing they did to you, they took advantage of your total ignorance. It shouldn't be done that way. You are bound here, you are bound there, you can't choose a publisher, you are all enclosed." I don't believe anything about being free!

'As for freedom of the press, my first experience was rather good. They met me at the airport taking pictures, and I read a statement saying hello and how pleased I was to be here and I would hold a press conference. I was told, "Please say that, otherwise they will follow you everywhere." So there was this conference at the Plaza Hotel three days later, and I still felt very good. I had come from India with wonderful equilibrium of spirit. I felt happy that I was not sent back to Moscow, happy to be there. I was in a very cheerful mood, I met very many people who were friendly and pleasant and outgoing. I was agreeing to everything that was offered, so everybody liked me. I was doing very well, and I didn't mind this first press conference at all. It was a great success because I spoke my English which was more limited then than it is now, more accented, but I managed. They offered me a translator but I said, "No thank you, I will translate," and that was appreciated. They liked what I said, and I think I did very well. So that first day I returned to Long Island quite happy and exhausted.

'Then the dark side started; I had no idea of the consequences of facing this mass publicity. My face was everywhere, I was not able to walk the streets, letters started coming, I was everywhere in the newspapers, they said this about me, they said that about me, they wrote a lot of nonsense about me – a book was already written about me! Magazines had a collection of fake photographs of our whole family, including me; I said whenever I could that it was not me but nobody listened. About a month passed and I was sitting there in a terrible state, thinking, My God, where am I? Almost on a stage, under the lights, dear God take this cup away from me! If I tried to go to the shops people recognised me and asked questions.

'There was a *lot* of bad publicity originating from right-wingers, red-necks, saying, "Send her back to the communists, we don't want commies here." From Russian émigrés, saying, "She says she believes in God and we don't believe her!" How she lived in the Kremlin and she was eating off gold plates, the golden dishes of the Romanovs; all the treasures of the Romanovs were in museums in my time.

'So this is freedom of speech! Everybody says what they want, regardless of the truth. My entrance to America as a celebrity, not as a writer and an intellectual, killed me for years to come. I was chased as a celebrity and I was not perceived as an intellectual, which was very sad for me.

'My lawyers in New York dictated everything. I was appalled; I was a sitting duck. Friends suggested that I should go to England, because it was no good for me in the USA. But my lawyers wanted me there, and of course my great patrons were the CIA, which is another aspect; they, I later discovered, were the ones who had got me there.

'They wanted me as big publicity and a propaganda tool: "She defected to us." I think they believed that I was a carrier of Kremlin secrets, which I was not. I knew a lot about Stalin's Russia, but my father was not the kind of politician who would share his innermost secrets with his daughter. It was not his style. I wasn't there with him every day to hear it with my own ears. They realised much later that I was not in that category, so as a Sovietologist or Kremlinologist I was a dead loss.

'Still, I thought with horror about going to a new country and starting there all over again, with the publicity and all. So I decided not to go.

'The CIA kept their tabs on me all those years, at all times. It was known to everybody but me that they were the main sponsors in getting me to the USA. They even sent me monthly cheques to keep me there. I still don't know who paid me the million for my book in 1967. Maybe the CIA paid it. The publishers didn't pay it, my lawyers didn't; who else?

'After ten years had passed the CIA sponsored my naturalisation, because there was nobody else to sponsor me. They were perceived as, and they were, my sponsors from the beginning. They knew more about me than anybody else.'

Svetlana stayed in the USA for sixteen years. During this time she married again, and gave birth to a daughter, Olga, in 1971. But the marriage did not succeed and once again she found herself on her own, raising a small child. 'Then, after all those years, we escaped to England. I did not tell the CIA my plans. When I was selling my property, our home, and somebody asked where was I going, I said China! I was not prepared to tell anyone. The British consulate in New York gave me the permit to come, so it was all legal. But I was not going to declare anything, because I could be stopped. I had had all these experiences, I had had so many battles, so I was cautious.'

The democratic freedoms that Svetlana had dreamed of from behind the Iron Curtain had turned out to be nothing like as ideal as she had imagined. She discovered that 'freedom' didn't have so much to do with place, culture and society as she had thought. 'Freedom is something inner, deep inside, and you have to find it for yourself. It is not a door that opens.

'I must say that the Western concept of freedom, whatever that means, was rather disappointing. Political and democratic freedom are one thing; the freedom within you is quite another. That's where my freedom is. I acquired it at a high price, and I would never be without it. When I returned to Russia in 1984, and stayed for eighteen months, I suddenly felt I was going to lose it again. People don't believe in it there. I felt cornered, I felt I had to get out. The feeling that I had I must call evil.

'What you have in the West is not freedom. The publisher

of my second book didn't like my title *Only One Year*. He suggested *The Sun Rises in the West*. I hated it! He was quite serious, he really believed it, he thought it was a great title. This concept that everything good comes from the West, that even the sun rises there . . . well, my experience of freedom was a little bit tarnished.

'I gave power of attorney to a law firm, so I couldn't do this and I couldn't do that, I couldn't choose my publisher, I couldn't go where I wanted, I couldn't travel. I had all the money in the world, yet I couldn't see the world because somebody else planned for me what I was going to do. So it was not so free. I spent ten years in America waiting for my naturalisation to go through – I had been a member of the Communist Party so it was ten years' quarantine for me. It was not all that free, I was very very limited in what I actually could do.

'This is how Western people live. They are limited by their income, they are limited by their family and social background, by their conditioning, by their job, by the sphere of their knowledge; their world is a very small place. If you are free inside it doesn't matter where you are living. Freedom should not be confused with democracy: a democratic free society means having free elections, freedom of speech and so on. That's all wonderful, but I didn't participate in it. I didn't go there to choose that political line; I chose freedom of speech, of course, I published my book. But all these years later I am living with no income, I have nothing from my books, I am completely stuck in one place. Yet I am still in the free world, and the sun still rises in the West . . . !

'I was always trying to escape my ethnic roots in America, not to stew in an émigré Russian soup. I wanted to lead a cosmopolitan life in America or England. English-language countries give you neutrality; you can learn anything you want, you learn to live with many peoples and nations of the world, with a mix of cultures and religions, and you are a little bit above the level of your emotions. I feel good with a lot of variation around me.

'I can't exist on the ethnic, national level, insisting that "this is the best". I want rather to be in some neutral spot where it doesn't matter who I am, where it is of no such importance. So this is the best thing that I have learned, to live apart from my roots. This is my inner freedom: and I want to be free.

'Many Russian émigrés that I know exist here but their hearts are back home. They gather every piece of information, they are in contact, they spend lots of money on phone calls to their friends and relatives. I don't do that.

'I don't feel Russian; I feel divided into many parts. The culture in which I was brought up, Russian language and literature and poetry, is in me very strongly. My ethnic roots are in Georgia. A lot comes from Asia, and this is where a profound love for India comes in, a profound respect for Asian culture and tradition. Russia doesn't speak to me in the same way as Georgia.

'Russia has a tremendous potential of talent, force, energy. How they survive! They are survivors, they thrive on lack of things, lack of comfort, they thrive on difficulties – and they come up with beautiful art. They should not be told what to do! They will find what they want. They don't have a democratic tradition because it was stopped by something else.

'Moscow was supposed to be my motherland, but I didn't feel it when I returned in 1984. Nothing resonated. I have always disliked the Kremlin, the fact of living there in my childhood with such memories. I hate Russia. I feel I am a citizen of the world.

'The Sun Rises in the West! It is believed that democracy can be taught from here, which is basically wrong. The sun still comes from the east! America puts herself over as the world's policeman. I didn't fit in with the American culture, but I came on my own, so my only way was to live in the culture, and to speak English, and so I did. I brought up my daughter in a perfectly American way, but there were many things that I really didn't like, and finally I didn't become part of it. This categorisation, that *we* are the best, our way is the best, insists that everybody has to learn our way and live our way and fry these hamburgers on the barbecue in the garden, with potato chips. What if I don't like to? And I feel sad when their cheap, plastic culture of hamburgers and Coke is imported to countries with their own beautiful culture. I almost cry for them: India, or the Arab world, or Africa, or even England which has its own tradition.

'My sheltered childhood was probably a bad preparation for later years, when things became difficult. I was often completely baffled about what to do. I had no mechanisms for survival or struggle. It is so to this day, like a Victorian lady who has led a sheltered existence. It gave me an idealistic view of the world, in spite of wide reading and a good education; this was learning from books, not from life. I simply was not prepared for the real world.

'But I have been made very angry by all the people who have written about me saying "oh she suffered so much, such a cross to bear, such a difficult life to cope with – she must have suffered as a child." Nobody abused me. My life was very good and happy until I was fifteen, and that is a long chunk of time.

'Nevertheless I live, as I have always lived, in my father's shadow.'

*Chapter Twenty-Nine*

# In Defence of Stalin

The horror which No. 1 emanated above all consisted in the possibility that he was in the right, and that all those whom he had killed had to admit, even with the bullet in the back of their necks, that he conceivably might be in the right. There was no certainty; only the appeal to that mocking oracle they called History, who gave her sentence only when the jaws of the appealer had long since fallen to dust.
— Arthur Koestler, *Darkness at Noon*

Apologists for Stalin invariably cite the war: Stalin, they say, won World War II for Russia and for Europe. If it hadn't been for Stalin, Europe would be under Nazi domination. Russian people are still, nearly half a century later, immensely proud of their Generalissimo. Three massive cannon-rests, now sculpturally arranged beside the main road from Moscow's Sheremetyevo Airport to the city, bear witness to the crucial battle of the war. A mere twenty-two kilometres from the Kremlin, the invading Germans met the Red Army, led by General Zhukov, on the outskirts of Moscow in 1943. Now both shrine and memorial, the cannon-rests are a chilling reminder of how close the German armies came to overrunning the city and seizing power over Europe. Huge sacrifices – millions of lives, and appalling devastation of towns and villages – had to be made for this victory.

The price was high, but in this case the means, in the view of Stalin's people, justified the end. But as for the millions serving time in the camps, or annihilated in the purges, that was a different matter, even within the ideological framework. Could this 'means' possibly justify the 'end' – in this case that of forced industrialisation and world-power status? That was harder to stomach, especially when the reward, for those who survived, was chronic food shortages, lack of consumer goods and inadequate housing. A widespread desire for improvements in the standard of living, and a yearning for personal security and greater freedom, were some of the legacies that Stalin left to his people.

Milovan Djilas, a foreigner and communist who had first-hand dealings with Stalin, takes an equivocal view of Stalin's rule, Stalin's revolution. 'If we take the point of view of humanity and freedom, history does not know a despot as brutal and cynical as Stalin was. He was one of those rare and terrible dogmatists capable of destroying nine-tenths of the human race to "make happy" the remaining one-tenth.

'But he transformed backward Russia into an industrial power and an empire . . . From the point of view of success and political acumen, Stalin is hardly surpassed by any statesman of his time.

'All in all, Stalin was a monster who, while adhering to abstract, absolute and fundamentally utopian ideas, in practice had no criterion but success – and this meant violence, and physical and spiritual extermination.

'However, let us not be unjust to Stalin. What he wished to accomplish, and even that which he did accomplish, could not be accomplished in any other way. The forces that swept him forward and that he led, with their absolute ideals, could not have been served by different methods.'

Djilas goes on to make the point about complicity. 'Certain strata of that society, that is to say the ruling political bureaucracy of the Party, needed just such a man – one who was reckless in his determination and extremely practical in his fanaticism. The ruling Party followed him doggedly and obediently.'

This begs the whole question of power, where it comes from and whether it is endowed or seized. The collective will of the people comes under scrutiny, an issue that Tolstoy attempts to resolve in his Second Epilogue to *War and Peace*:

> It is quite impossible to describe the movement of humanity without the conception of a force compelling men to direct their activity forwards to a certain end. And the only conception known to historians is that of power.
>
> If the source of the power lies neither in the physical nor the moral qualities of him who possesses it, it must evidently be looked for elsewhere – in the relations of the human who wields the power to the people.
>
> Power is the collective will of the people transferred, by expressed or tacit consent, to their chosen rulers.

A modern biographer of Stalin, Alec de Yonge, concurs:

> Stalin was not alone. It was not a question of one evil man dominating a country of the oppressed. He enjoyed nation-wide support at every level because he and his government were popular . . . The assent enjoyed by Stalin is reflected in the fact that no one has ever been put on trial for his crimes: to do so would require the indictment *en masse* of several generations.
>
> Stalin's popularity is deep-rooted enough to have survived some thirty years of official semi-disgrace. Even today his image retains an extraordinary mythic presence, radiating a blend of terror, love and authority.

Isaac Deutscher, in his elegantly impartial biography of Stalin, quotes the adage that Stalin undertook to drive barbarism out of Russia by barbarous means. He cites the growth in industrial production, which made the USSR second only to the USA in heavy industry and military power. He cites the growth of cities, and the investment in education. This resulted in a huge increase in the number of schools throughout the Soviet Union, and the subsequent excellence of its education and training system. Stalin's industrial revolution spanned thirty years; he achieved in that time more than many European countries had achieved in 150 years. At a price. Churchill commented that when Stalin took on Russia, 'it had only the wooden plough. He left it with nuclear weapons.' At his death, Russia was one of two major world powers.

Stalin put into practice a fundamentally new principle of social organisation on which other societies modelled themselves, if only for a term. 'The ideal inherent in Stalinism, one to which Stalin had given a grossly distorted expression, is not domination of man by man, or nation by nation, or race by race, but their fundamental equality . . . It is the community of the free and the equal, and not the dictatorship, that has remained the inspiration.'

Deutscher concludes, 'Stalin has been both the leader and the exploiter of a tragic, self-contradictory but creative revolution.' He had taken Russia from obscurity to world super-power within three decades, by means of the view, which he proclaimed, that everything was permitted for the sake of the idea. Thus did Stalinism represent a negation of human values, and become a system propped up by pillars of dogmatism.

Of the Alliluyev family, Volodya remains the most explicitly Stalinist. Icons of his uncle's era manifest his dogmatic adherence to the creeds and actions of the society in which he was nurtured. He eloquently defends his family's position, apportioning blame in no small measure to Beria, whose wish to control every channel of information 'was the reason for all the misfortunes of our family. At all times, even after the arrests of members of it, the family trusted Stalin completely, they continued to have a positive attitude to him. They knew Stalin and his character very well. I have come to the conclusion that it was Stalin's entourage who needed all the arrests.

'In history it was always like that, it is the usual unfortunate story of families close to supreme power to be the subject of slander. It will always exist; those close to the top man want to have him completely in their power. Of course the personality of the ruler plays an important role too, a leader's behaviour is determined by human nature, and so it was in our family. But as a phenomenon it is not unusual. As I remember, Grandpa and Grandma and everyone else respected Stalin greatly until the last day.

'Nowadays they deride Stalin everywhere, and of course this is not easy for the family. It is a burden, and not everyone is able to carry that cross with dignity. The shadow of the grandfather lies on the grandchildren. The shadow becomes bigger now, since they have started political investigations. How far do the shadows reach? That is a question of whether you see it as light or shadow. It is a light which has cast a shadow on their lives. I don't necessarily mean anything negative by a shadow: once the cloud has passed, it doesn't have to be sinister.

'Stalin was a man of hard, rigid character, he was tough. He had no time for personal life. We understood only too well both his strong characteristics and his weak ones, and the harshness of his character. Nevertheless, our relationship with him, as it started from the very beginning, carried on to the end of his life in our family.

'I have read a lot of contemporary books and I disagree completely with the way he is described. He was a man dedicated fully to his cause. He never wanted anything for himself – he left no possessions after his death. He gave his life to Russia, to the Soviet Union.

'None of us ever claimed anything special from Stalin. On the contrary, everyone else tried to use us and Stalin for their gains! My mother, Uncle Pavel – they never tried to get something from him for themselves. They respected him and regarded him as a normal man, on whose shoulders an unprecedented burden had been laid. Because to rule Russia is an unbearable burden, beyond measure, and beyond anyone's capacity. This is why they often pitied him, they tried to understand his enormous difficulties, his sorrows, his illnesses, and they always tried to help him somehow. One way of helping was to give him a supply of totally objective and unbiased information as to what was going on. This was not liked by others, who finally decided to weed us all out. That was as I see it the crux of the matter. Beria was annoyed that Stalin had other sources of information apart from himself.

'Plus there was all the political struggle in the country going on then, as it still goes on today. The internal and external battles of Russia! The country never evoked love; because of its rich resources, it has been regarded as a source of profit. You cannot hide from history. No wonder that to run such a country was an immense task. It is all too easy today to call Stalin a fool, a paranoiac and a mass-murderer. It was not so at all!

'I knew many people who worked for Stalin for years, those who served him, and his personnel. I have never heard from them one word of anything bad about him. This is quite remarkable. Those who write about him now have never known him at all. Those "authors" are creating his image from hearsay, from talk and gossip. But there is absolutely no resemblance to the real man. An idiot cannot create such a country, or win such a war. A fool can destroy a country, but not build it up.

'My personal view of the Stalinist revolution is this: nothing happens in the world without a reason, just out of nowhere. The Stalinist revolution was prepared by the flow of history. Our grandparents who went into the revolution, it wasn't their whim, it was their ideal. They followed their destiny when they took part in this battle. They gave their lives for this. With it they had to endure many difficulties, and they did endure.'

We were sitting in Volodya's dark, plush lounge, the gallery of family portraits around the walls. The light was not good, but a large bunch of flowers on a side table brightened the room considerably. A clatter of saucepans from the kitchen heralded the smell of sautéed onions, followed by the earthy fragrance of boiling potatoes. Volodya was not distracted.

'There is the question of the repressions carried out during the time of collectivisation; people now put the blame on Stalin. The first thing to say is that the Party fully supported the policy of collectivisation. The policy of the liquidation of the kulaks as a class was a policy which Lenin considered to be most correct; he considered the kulak the most malicious enemy of Soviet power beside the capitalist land-owner. He considered that as long as the kulaks continued to exist there would be a threat of the restoration of capitalism.

'Even at the 20th Party Congress, in Khrushchev's speech about the cult of personality, collectivisation was cited as one of Stalin's achievements, not used as a means of accusing him. Of course, it is another matter that in the course of this collectivisation mistakes were made. But in that case you have to look at the people who were carrying out the policy. Stalin's business was to arrange the general direction, but it was a question of how it was organised locally that affected how it was actually carried out.

'There are figures which suggest that ten million people perished at that time. I can't tell you the precise figure and so far no one has named it. There is probably data on how many were transported to the camps; I would think that far more were transported than perished. As for those who were transported, in the end they did have the possibility of going home! People talk a lot now about how it was not just the head of the family who was transported, but also his family and children. People consider this anti-humanitarian, but from the other point of view, to abandon the children to the vagaries of fate would be far less humane than to exile them and to provide them with a place to live in another region of the country.

'The repressions of the thirties touched our family, too. They were difficult years, the war was approaching, and Stalin was putting forward the theory of the class struggle, which had to be sharpened as the country made its way

*276*

towards socialism. I cannot agree that his theory was incorrect, because the war confirmed it. War is the most extreme contradiction, it is an intensification of the class struggle, that is to say that the country could not be knocked off the path of socialism in any other way. International imperialism had turned to open aggression; it was capitalist encirclement. Everyone knows that the country was surrounded by capitalism, and from the very first days of the war the country was under blockade.

'I think that Stalin had no doubt that Hitler would attack the Soviet Union. Stalin's aim was to win time. He saw it as his task to put off the beginning of the war with the giants of the imperialist world so as to wait until the contradictions between them had been aggravated, and win time in this way. Thus Stalin played the game of giving Hitler no motive for provocation.

'Stalin was in a position where, if they gave him documents against a particular person, he himself could not sort out all these matters. He had neither the time nor the capability, due to the structure of state power. He made many mistakes – if indeed it was he who made them – but I think that all the repressions were carried out by his executives, by those around him. Most of the repressions were not caused by him personally. If a special tribunal found someone guilty, the guilt lies in equal measure on Stalin and the tribunal. After all, Beria was judged by special tribunal and nobody will say that that special tribunal made a mistake! So it is a question of for what, how and why a man is being tried.

'Every man must be responsible for his every action. Stalin alone cannot be responsible for all of this. Responsibility must be taken by the people who took part. All the people who were close to power were in one way or another involved in the repressions; Khrushchev, Mikoyan, Molotov and Kaganovich, all of them. To say that all the repressions were unwarranted is, I consider, incorrect. There was a sufficiently high number of enemies in the country after the revolution, dissatisfied people – political criminals as well as ordinary criminals. There was also a good deal of banditry going on in the country; on the collective farms they had to put up with murders of activists and people taking up arms. There were victims, of course. The repressions about which so much is written and talked about today were not at all on the scale that is stated now. "Hundreds of millions of repressed", they say. Nonsense! All this idiotic propaganda has brought our country to where it is today, to the lowest level.'

Looking around at the portraits on the walls I couldn't help wondering if they were listening to all this, hearing their defendant as they stand trial by history. Were their consciences troubled, I wondered, or would they have regarded conscience as 'bourgeois', that much-used adjective that covered everything that did not fit in with the communist scheme of things? But perhaps one cannot speak of the conscience of a dictator; almost by definition he does not have one.

'Transferring all the guilt on to one person is stupid, just as it would be stupid to ascribe all credit to him. Stalin came to power as the bearer of a concrete idea. He maintained this position although he offered to stand down five times and was five times reappointed. A lot of fiction is written about Stalin nowadays, by people who did not know him personally. The people who knew him closely have disappeared. I have not met people who knew Stalin closely who would express such negative opinions about him as are expressed today. The Stalin that really existed is in my grandfather's book and my mother's memoirs, not the Stalin that is being drawn today. That is a terrifying half-truth which cannot explain anything. They are inventions which are unnecessary and harmful, and do not do any good to the history of our country.

'We mustn't paint him in black or white, or make him a giant. He was a very contradictory person but at the same time this person occupied his post for a period of twenty-nine years, because the policy he advocated was very close to the Party line and to the wishes of the people. What Stalin said and what was passed at the congresses was actually put into action, unlike under Khrushchev. It is true that this was at the cost of sacrifices, and unjustified sacrifices, but this was the situation of our country.

'Stalin continued the work of Lenin, and he was quite successful; we prevented the ruin of the country and its collapse after the civil war. We created industry, we collectivised the peasants, and to this day there is no desire among the peasants to leave the kolkhozes. We won the war, even though it was very, very tough. Hitler was armed for imperialism and the fact that our country managed to defeat him was to Stalin's huge merit. The economy of the country was restored, atomic weaponry created which has maintained peace for all these years. At the tail end of this the first Sputnik was launched into space, space rockets were built: and all this is due to the activity of one person. Stalin said he wanted to carry on Lenin's work, and under both Lenin and Stalin there was both repression and success.

'The revolution was victorious; first of all, above all, because industry was created. The Party became very strong and the peasantry very powerful. Stalin was a great man who had both a good side and a bad side, like everyone. What he did in our country was huge, his merits are enormous and he is not guilty of everything that happened in this country. All serious politicians say this. He was a great, great organiser. Even Churchill valued Stalin very highly.

'A gigantic task was accomplished in changing the face of this country: the second great world power emerged after his term in office – you cannot deny this fact! That power was so international in its essence that we did not know any "ethnic fights", so we were brought up knowing nothing of our "nationalist roots"; we could not care less. The ethnic fights are purely the result of present-day policies.

'I still maintain that the glorious revolution was successful. We are trying to put all our problems of today on the shoulders of the man who has been lying in a mausoleum for the last seventy years. Is that right? Every man must answer for what he has done while he lives. When dead, he will answer before God.'

Volodya ended his triumphant delivery with a flourish of his arms, sat back on the sofa and laughed, his passionate views articulated. Innate Russian hospitality came to the fore. 'Will you stay and eat with us?' and ten minutes later we were sitting over Svetlana's cooking in their tiny kitchen. While we had been talking she had been making an aromatic stew with wild mushrooms gathered from nearby their dacha that morning, served with a bowl overflowing with steaming white potatoes, and a cucumber and tomato salad. We talked about the hot topic of the day; it was September 1991, just three weeks after what has become known as the Second Revolution.

*Chapter Thirty*

# FULL CIRCLE: THE SECOND REVOLUTION

It would have been better if the experiment had been conducted in some small country to make it clear that communism was a utopian, although beautiful, idea.
— Boris Yeltsin on communism, *Newsweek*, September 1991

On the morning of Monday 19 August 1991 the world woke up to the news that a hard-line coup in Moscow had overthrown President Gorbachev. Vice-President Yannayev had declared a state of emergency and formed a committee to "save the country from extremist forces". Shortly afterwards dozens of tanks and APCs were seen moving into the centre of Moscow. After six years of *perestroika* and *glasnost*, it appeared that Gorbachev's liberalising regime had come to an end.

But Boris Yeltsin stepped into the breach, occupied the Russian parliament building, jumped up on to a tank with a heroic display of courage and became the focus of resistance. Within three days the coup had failed and the tanks returned to barracks flying the Russian flag. Gorbachev returned from his holiday dacha in the Crimea, and a new era began for the peoples of the Soviet Union.

On 6 November 1991, on the eve of the seventy-fourth anniversary of the 1917 revolution, Yeltsin banned the Communist Party in Russia. He had been swift to exercise his authority as the first democratically elected president of the Russian Republic; decrees flowed from his pen. On 9 December 1991, Russia, Byelorussia and the Ukraine

*281*

declared independence from the Soviet Union. On 12 December, an historic day which effectively marked the end of the USSR, Yeltsin's proposals for a Commonwealth of Independent States were agreed at Minsk by the majority of the republics. The agenda was kept secret and President Gorbachev was not invited. On 21 December, Stalin's 112th birthday, the USSR was formally dissolved, and the Commonwealth (CIS) recognised. On Christmas Day Mikhail Gorbachev resigned.

The communist revolution had turned full circle. The CIS now embarked on its perilous passage towards a free market economy. As the lid was lifted off the Marxist dream, ugly spectres of disillusion, deceit and bitterness floated out from the darkness of the past. The peoples of Russia and the fourteen other republics started out on an uncharted road of liberalisation, looking with a clear view, and for the first time, at the truth of their seventy-four-year-old legacy: that for all those years they had been prisoners of an ideology which had promised, but failed to deliver, a utopian state.

We sat – myself with interpreter – with Sasha and his wife Olga in his office at the Institute of Epidemiology and Microbiology. The quiet, gentle Olga provided tea with jam; I was getting used to this Russian habit, and getting to like it. You stir jam into your tea (no milk) instead of sugar. I was beginning to understand why they liked sweet things so much; it seemed to give me the energy to take on board everything they had been telling me, some of which had been almost too much to take. And regular meals had been scarce. Now, relaxing over an informal discussion, we ate cookies and sipped the sweet tea as we talked about the events of August '91.

'On 19 August the atmosphere was terrible,' said Sasha. 'The fear was that we would have to go backwards, to keep on telling everybody lies for many more years – again! The most dreadful thing that could happen would be a return to the past ways; that would be awful.

'But Yeltsin showed himself to be a very strong man, and

I feel hopeful about the situation, although for a while life will be very difficult regarding the basic necessities. In other countries where private property exists no matter what government they have, it is simple. But here we have to start all over again from scratch! The total overhaul of the economy to new basic principles will make everyday life very difficult for simple people.

'There are going to be terrible times ahead: unemployment, inflation, unrest. It is going to be particularly difficult for pensioners, and there are going to be a whole lot of bureaucrats in the apparatus who will be thrown out of work. But what are they doing anyway . . . ?'

Sergei, like his younger brother, feels confidence in Yeltsin. We sat with his young wife, also an Olga, and their teenage daughter Sasha, over a supper table elegantly laid with elaborate hors d'oeuvres, endless tea, with the ubiquitous sugary preserves. The placid Orlando lay at our feet as we talked and laughed: at all these encounters there was spontaneous mirth. They say that the Russians have a joke for everything; certainly they tell their jokes well and they are very funny.

'I believe in Yeltsin, I like in him what other people like so much: that he refuses to be part of the system, in the Party, or to take privileges. That is what is so genuine in him. I am an optimist in general about what lies ahead. Yeltsin said that it would have been better if the communist experiment had been conducted in some small country to make it clear that it was a utopian, although beautiful, idea. He is quoting Bismarck, who said what a good thing it was that communism had not first been tried in Germany!

'Even Stalin stressed in his works that the majority of the population, about 90 per cent, is always passive. Quite possibly, in his case, out of fear rather than apathy. Fear has become a prevalent habit with the Russian people.

'Even now, here in Russia people are saying that they joined and went on to the streets because they were sure that everything would end well. So they say. *Chance* has a great deal to do with history and often everything depends on chance.'

While Sergei was in general optimistic, it was clear that Olga was pessimistic. 'We agree that Yeltsin was a very strong man, and that a strong man was what was needed. There *is* hope. But the women have to experience the frightful daily grind of trying to obtain food and services, and it is a nightmare.' That morning I had walked past the queue for McDonald's, Moscow's primary venture into Western culture, and was moved by its pathos. People queuing, excitement mixing with their customary resignation, all for a Big Mac. They were prepared to wait three hours, standing, for this Sunday treat. Meanwhile the hard currency queue was short; if you had dollars you could get your burger and Coke in minutes. I was struck by the joylessness of it.

Olga described what it was like for the women. Things, she said, were terrible. She has to queue for everything; her day starts with a walk around the neighbourhood finding which shops have goods that day, and whether it is anything worth having. Then queuing for everything separately: carrots, potatoes, onions. Even after all the queuing you may miss the goodies if supplies have run out, so on you go to the next place in the hope of better luck.

One day, queuing for vegetables, the shop assistant was rude to her when she asked her to wash some mud off the tomatoes. The woman standing behind her started to criticise Olga, who turned around and said, ' "Are you *always* going to be slaves?" The people are getting very angry, there is a great deal of tension around, and that is not how it used to be. People were much more relaxed about the situation, even though it has got worse. Feelings have changed.

'There is a Russian proverb that the peasantry traditionally believe that their next tsar will be a great leader. The Russian spirit lives on hope, it is a strong spirit, it has survived through all odds, it is nurtured, and grows, through suffering. But for now, it is hell living as we do, and sometimes I just don't want to go out of the house in the daytime, it is all so awful.'

Olga was warming to her theme; she had been shy to start with, and left most of the talking to Sergei to whom that was no problem. Now she came into her own and began to sparkle, her irony and humour giving me a taste of that Russian way of joking about the most desperate matters. As she told us this joke, she was finding it difficult to finish, she and Sergei were laughing so much. Their mirth infected us with a sense of the ludicrousness of a great revolution whose characteristic achievement was this comedy: 'Nobody in Russia produces canned dog food; it is forbidden because they fear that the people would buy it for themselves.' Here the merriment started. 'You have to laugh, don't you,' snorted Olga. 'For people who have dogs and cats, particularly pedigrees, they have dog clubs and you can get your canned food through the clubs. *But* – the animals have to eat it supervised, at the club. Can you believe that this is one of the fruits of the communist revolution?' We laughed until the tears rolled.

Equilibrium restored, Sergei became more serious again. 'People don't want to work; they have been told all their lives, for generations, when to work, how to work, where to work. Thus inculcated in their attitude is getting away with as little work as possible because the system is going to reward them in any case. Or not: deliver a stab in the back, as the case may be . . . It is impossible to get people to work, even as entrepreneurs in business, except possibly on the black market.'

Olga wanted to insist that 'there is something in the Russian spirit that always finds hope.' She paused, then turned to me and said, 'In the West your life is easy. In our country life is interesting.' She laughed, quite happily, neither bitter nor envious. She has a point, I thought . . .

It occurred to me that I was witnessing the end of a line. As we spoke, Sergei was still a member of the Communist

Party: now the Party is dead. He was the end of a line that had started over a century ago with his grandfather, in great idealism and for laudable motives. For a week I had been looking, with them, at its course, and seen what terrors it had wrought not only on the immediate family but on the entire country. There was a sober dignity about this man whose grandfather's legacy was so closely linked to his life, and whose destiny it was to bury it, along with millions of fellow Russians.

A note of sadness tinged with bitterness crept into Olga's voice as she pointed out that they had all worked so hard for the past seventy years because they had believed in the ideology in which they had been educated. They believed what they had been told: that they were better off than any other country in the world. They had more goods, they lived better, they were freer (they were not allowed of course to go and see for themselves). When they found out the truth they felt profoundly and irrevocably cheated. It was her life she was talking about.

Her sadness was as infectious as her humour. I wondered as we talked, in this world so different from affluent, insulated Western society, what lay ahead for this powerful people, this strong and articulate culture with its extraordinary spirit. Would its flame be smothered by a blanket of wealth? Images of what a free market economy would do to the Russian culture floated into my head: the shops full of consumer goods; Benetton chains and Pizza Huts everywhere. Could the Russian spirit be overwhelmed by a Western monoculture? If so, it would take a long while. But quite possibly material wealth, and the opportunity to make money, would do what it has done in most wealthy capitalist cultures: make people greedy and shallow. Yet seeing their lives as they are now, who could blame them for wanting these things?

But there were more jokes to cheer me up. Had I heard the one about *glasnost*? 'There's freedom of speech but the question is whether you have your freedom after your speech . . .' And 'a bite of freedom is more important than a bit of sausage' – this one circulated the hungry queues outside the food stores. And the well-known story of the little Russian boy visiting London, who walks through the city streets one evening with his father after the shops have closed. They pass a supermarket and the little boy asks his father, 'Why is it closed while there are still goods on the shelves?'

As we sat in Volodya and Svetlana's tiny kitchen in Gorky Street we heard a different point of view. Huddled four around a table large enough for three, I noticed that a small sofa-bed was jammed up against the oven door; presumably it had to be moved every time the oven was used. Every surface was covered with jugs and ornaments, the walls were smothered with pictures and a minuscule television on the windowsill remained on, its volume down, as we ate.

'All that we see today, all of this mess, is nothing to do with the revolution,' declared Volodya. 'The crux of the matter is that we have abandoned those initial principles on which the revolution was based. And it was Khrushchev who started this abandonment. Brezhnev continued the process, and it was put to an end by Gorbachev. Now we are reaping the mess of it. But this is not the end yet! I believe that we are going to follow the pattern of events which we see in 1991 in Yugoslavia.

'The workers' lack of personal responsibility is the main scourge of our system; while we do not have personal responsibility, the system will never work. A person must be answerable for his actions in the workplace; without this, there will be no forward movement. This is the case in every developed civilised government.

'In order to build a capitalist society, as in England for example, you needed hundreds of years; and we want to do it in one year! It has taken you the efforts of generations to achieve life as you enjoy it now. We want somebody to give us a hundred billion dollars, as if it is going to help us. And if someone does, who will be the recipients?

'We want to create Western farms instead of our collective system, but it cannot be done easily. All this needs technological equipment, management and a lot of time. For the time being we have destroyed everything: to destroy is easier than to create. Add to this the grave embitterment of our people. And we have lost time, which we might have had in the beginning of *perestroika*, so the problems are still here. I am not anticipating anything good.

'Now we have chaos. After that may come a backlash to the right wing. I do not see another way to stop the chaos – there is more and more every day. Whether there might be a return to the "old ideals" is difficult to say, but I cannot exclude a situation where the working class will get fed up and might return to the old order. Imagine: we are told that we may expect to have 30–40 million unemployed. When the people see what that means, I do not think they will rejoice! I used to buy potatoes, carrots, onions in the greengrocers all for one rouble. Today I have to pay thirty roubles for the same thing! Judging from this I do not see any joyful perspectives.

'Yeltsin has disappointed us; he seemed strong and democratic but now we think it was empty words. He was just like all the others: jumping through the same hoops but coming at it from a different angle and calling it democracy. We thought Yeltsin was hopeful, but he has failed – he is not a strong dictator, he has gone hand-in-glove with Gorbachev. His words of democracy are empty words. There is chaos now, and it will get worse. All the republics will go independent and there will be war between ethnic groups, and mega-unemployment of forty million people! Already people are milling around, not working; in the old days you would never have seen that, people had to work, and do what was needed.

'I saw Yeltsin's tanks coming down the street brandishing the Russian flag that August morning and said that in the old days there would have been none of that nonsense. They would have obeyed their command. The tanks didn't kill the three young men, they were drunk and fell over in front of them. Obviously we want to return to a strict disciplinarian regime with a restored KGB. Every strong state needs a secret police. I know there will be a backlash.

'The coup was an operetta: if you want a *putsch*, do it properly. It was so ill-thought-out; of course they should have got Yeltsin, he was the key figure, and they didn't. I think that Gorbachev was implicated, that he knew it was going to happen. There was no reaction to the coup for two days because everyone thought, "Good: we hate Gorbachev anyway, he has seduced the West and betrayed the USSR." '

There was a certain irony in what Volodya and Svetlana were saying. These staunch supporters of the communist system were living the comfortable lives of the privileged, of an elite which in theory was not supposed to exist. Their lifestyle belied their ideology. They supported the system, it seemed to me, less out of ideological fervour than because it had supported them.

By contrast Volodya's cousin Kyra, three years younger than the revolution itself, subscribed to the idea that communism was a chimera, a 'beautiful dream that does not accord with human nature'. The views of this likeable septuagenarian are, ironically, closer to those of her nieces and nephews of the fourth generation, who delivered their epitaph on the demise of the Party with an articulate clarity inspired by deep feeling.

*Chapter Thirty-One*

# EPITAPH: THE FOURTH
# GENERATION

We brought you truth, and in our mouth it sounded a lie. We
brought you freedom, and it looks in our hands like a whip. We
brought you the living life, and where our voice is heard the
trees wither and there is a rustling of dry leaves. We brought
you the promise of the future. But our tongue stammered and
barked . . .

— Arthur Koestler, *Darkness at Noon*

Olga Leonidovna, Leonid's daughter, is in her mid-
thirties. She is a frail, pale creature with high cheek-
bones, slim to the point of fragility. Long fair hair
frames the fine bone structure of her face. She speaks good
English with a lively intelligence, although she was modestly
dismissive about her ability. She is highly trained in Italian,
and no doubt was comparing her professional skills with
this conversational English. We sat in a small room in her
father's flat, around a low table on which she had placed
elegant teacups and a bowl of apricot preserves, home-made
by her using the most golden of Georgian apricots on the
market. Around us were bookcases, a sofa-bed, and some
enormous pot plants that stretched over the furniture and
towards the ceiling.

Her statement is a poignant epitaph on the idealism of
her great-grandfather. She felt deeply pessimistic about how
things were, and the way they were going. Weighing up the
situation in terms of Russia's long history of oppression and
suffering, however, she felt that it might have equipped the
people to endure yet another period of hardship while the

economy righted itself and the nationalities sorted themselves out. 'We have had to overcome a lot of difficulties, and a Western citizen can't even imagine what kind of difficulties. So for us it is all alike – for us it just became our environment, the culture in which we live.

'The 1930s and 1940s were a tragedy for almost all the people of our country. But I never suffered the tragedy of our family as my parents did; for me it was the tragedy of a generation, it was never a personal loss, it was not my personal tragedy. My father's father, Redens, never felt like my grandfather, because I never saw him. I saw him only in photographs, so for me he is just a person of that generation.

'It was a tragedy for all Russians. When I was young I knew that my grandfather had been killed, but even now I don't know all the particulars. My father is a very reserved person, and he never told me much. Although I read a lot of history, I first discovered what had happened from Svetlana's book, *20 Letters to a Friend*. I don't remember my father telling me the story of the family; he never said to me, "Sit down, I will tell you our story."

'To my way of thinking, the communism of the Bolsheviks was certainly not a glorious revolution. Even ten years ago I didn't think so. But I thought, as did many other Russians, that it was something progressive. Personally, I always thought that we have something more than Westerners. I was in Italy for three years, from 1981–3, and I felt very proud of being Soviet, of having something extra, something which they didn't have. Maybe they had wealth, but we had something they didn't: our ideology, our future.

'Towards the end of those years I saw that really we have nothing. I thought our morals were higher than their morals. But now I see that our morals are the lowest: because the communists are amoral. They don't *have* morals. They don't know what the word moral means. They are hypocrites, they are liars. They deceived the people, they deceived me, and there is no excuse for that.

'For example, they never told the truth about the Second

World War. The war was always, for me, something *holy*. During the last few years we have found out the truth about the war and we can't celebrate the victory as we used to do. This victory was bought by twenty million lives; there is no excuse for that. Yes, we won, but twenty million died, Twenty million. In tank warfare the tanks usually go ahead into battle, and the soldiers follow. But in our war we now know that the generals, just to make economies with the tanks, let the soldiers go first and the tanks afterwards. To make economies with the tanks rather than with the soldiers, this is their morality. We learn this now through the reminiscences of that generation, published in the papers. We haven't the right to celebrate it as a victory, we must celebrate it as the day of remembrance for those who died.

'There are so many different opinions about Stalin's part in all of this. Stalin's fault in it is that he didn't want to hear. He wanted to play with Hitler, he was acting out some strange joke – or else he was afraid of him. His fault is that he didn't believe it when everybody was saying that the war would begin.

'But we can't deny the role of Stalin in this war: at that time, the ordinary people, soldiers and the Soviet people, believed in Stalin. He inspired them. Yet at the same time we know that in the blockade of Leningrad the Party hierarchy, Zhdanov and others, they had everything they wanted, they were never in need. They even received fresh fruit while millions died of hunger in the city. Yet still the role of Stalin as a leader cannot be denied.

'As far as the purges of the 1930s are concerned, it's obvious that this is the morality of the Communist Party. In the past I've never been anti-communist, nor anti-Soviet, but now I have become so. Lenin was an absolutely immoral type, as Gorky pointed out; he was a rogue. He even rode in a Rolls Royce. Lenin had nothing to do with the proletariat, or with the peasants; he was a party politician, an intellectual, he made his policy and wrote his books but he was miles away from the needs of the poor people. Stalin was the perfect pursuer of his policies. They were both good representatives of that Party.

'As for Gorbachev with his *glasnost*, he seems very sincere, but there are many things that don't add up. Yet his role is really significant, even if I don't like him very much. He gave us *glasnost*, and reduced the power of the KGB. This changed our lives. Gorbachev has given us the possibility of going abroad, to meet with people and to talk freely.

'When I was doing my language training course in Italy in the early 1980s the KGB were flourishing. As representatives of a collective organisation we didn't have the right to have personal contacts. We lived on a reservation, and were not allowed to leave. I was always looking over my shoulder, I was always being followed to see where I was going and who I was meeting. We were controlled, we were puppets. Special agents came in the evening to ring our doorbells to find out if we were at home. I stayed with another secretary in our apartment; we were never allowed to live alone, only in twos, threes or fours. I was lucky to live in a twosome. But I found it impossible to live in a country and never meet the people, so I did – I could not have behaved otherwise. I risked a lot. So when I returned to Moscow I had trouble getting work; it took some months before I found a job . . . But now things have changed; when I returned to Italy recently there was none of that.

'I am for independence, I am for freedom, but for seventy-four years we were one country, so I really don't know what will happen. I am very far away from this Communist Party. The Party is all doctrine, all ideology. I can't understand those people who sincerely believe in that: how it is possible, with what we have now, to believe in communism or socialism with all its hypocrisy, all its stupidity, when our standard of living is so low. But at the same time I am against the banning, the closing or prohibiting of the Communist Party. They shouldn't do that.'

Yeltsin's stand against the August *coup d'état* and its subsequent collapse were proclaimed in the Western media as a great liberation for the peoples of Russia; democracy had at last arrived. But the evidence there, on the spot, was that these Western concepts were overlaid on a wholly unprepared and disintegrating society. It was the view through Western eyes; the view from the streets of Moscow looked entirely different.

The standard of living, even in the capital with its glorious Kremlin and national treasures, is third-world. A dual economy has operated for years to divide society into them with dollars, which will buy you anything, and them with roubles, which won't. Them with roubles is poor. Goods of any kind are difficult to obtain except through the select stores for the rich, and the food queues are world-famous. It is almost impossible to buy good boots for winter with roubles, let alone coats or anoraks, or household linen. And much of what *is* on offer looks as if it has been sitting there since the 1950s.

The people have, in material terms, so little. After three generations of hollow promises they feel betrayed. What they have left is a little hope that the future might get better, and not much of that. All this in a land of plenty, one of the richest countries in the world in terms of its natural resources. An official at the British embassy summed it up succinctly: 'The only thing in Moscow that works is the metro.'

'I liked Yeltsin very much,' Olga went on, 'we all did, but now we see that he speaks before he thinks; he is this kind of person. I am afraid we could end up with the same totalitarianism as before, in this case from Yeltsin. They are saying that when he was secretary of Sverdlovsk, then in Moscow, he was rather dictatorial.

'Whereas in the Western media his stand was portrayed as "liberation, democracy and freedom for Russia", this freedom is on paper only. Let us see what will happen next. There are many people in the KGB for example, millions of them, and what are they doing now? What will they do in the future? They are used to giving orders, to dominating, to being in command.

'The idea of a free market economy seems to have released a free-for-all. Even the wonderful Western ideas are reduced here to absurdity. Take the stock exchange: in the Western world the stock markets show the level of the real prices. Here they are artificially raised by the Moscow mafia; the brokers sell to each other to manipulate the market, their contracts are not real transactions. A very high price is then fixed on the stock exchange, but it doesn't tell you anything about the real price of the market. I don't know how much time will pass before we have a real free market economy. The people who want to speculate and make a fast buck have got in there. It's very sad, it's tragic.

'But I don't know what the alternative is. I don't know what will happen to this country. Many generations may have to pass before it changes. I'm very pessimistic. The people here have lost the desire to work. In the office where I work we are very well paid, including the secretaries and interpreters, and they have certain privileges. Even so, they will do *anything* to escape from work. They'll have a coffee, a smoke, they'll put on make-up, they'll pop out somewhere . . .

'In the villages on the periphery of Moscow the people are very apathetic. They also hate each other. Muscovites hate those who come in, those who come in from outside hate the Muscovites because they think that we are having a wonderful time. Workers and peasants hate the intelligentsia, everybody is hating everybody.

'This has been going on for many years, and it is our poverty that is the basis of our hatred. It is the conditions of our life. When the *coup d'état* took place, many people were glad. "At last we shall have order, at last we shall have wealth." They were ordinary people who supported the hard-liners and I personally know such people. I don't know whether it was a large number of people, but many were angry about it, they became indignant when it failed. They were looking back to the "good old days" when somebody took charge at the top, and controlled the system so that people got fed.

'If people don't believe in communism or God, where can they turn? In the present situation the spiritual side of life is quite the fashion – they have returned to the Russian Orthodox church to baptise their children, and you see a lot of them wearing crosses. According to the Orthodox church the cross should be worn against the skin, not over your clothes, but people are going around with their crosses on top! Wearing their hearts on their sleeves . . .

'Many are simply indifferent, and I find that frightening. They don't care about communism, or about anything in particular . . . It is very good when a person believes in communism or God because it means that he is thinking. But many people don't believe in either, and I can understand their point of view; they have to find something to eat. You can't begin to understand what our lives are like.

'They are now writing about the bad harvest, the cold winter weather coming, and maybe it's all exaggeration. But our lives are really terrible. I am afraid for my child, who is now four-and-a-half. I am just thinking about sending him to kindergarten and I am afraid of it, for many reasons. Our kindergartens are very bad, in all ways. My son has to have special meals because he has stomach problems. But their meals are not clean, and they don't care very much about children. The groups are always full and the children are always ill there.

'In the old days, before Gorbachev, everything was very bad, it was black black black; but at the same time, there was something that could be white. It was possible to count blessings. But now, in the last few years, I don't see anything that could be white. Especially this last year or two. Before, we had something. We thought that our lives were terrible, but now, looking back, we think that it was paradise. It doesn't mean that I want the regime of Brezhnev to return, but I really don't know what will happen next. I don't know how we are going to come out of this situation. Everybody is thinking about Western aid, but I don't believe much in this help. For me it is just throwing away millions of dollars. There's a massive infrastructure to build, and it is difficult to be optimistic. We are in a blind alley, a dead end. I would like to say that I am exaggerating.'

The Alliluyev star has touched Olga's personal life. Her marriage to Valerii, according to her aunt Kyra, was a love match, and they were very happy together. He was a commercial representative who travelled a great deal, and earned enough to support her. So she gave up her work to look after their baby son. In 1990 Valerii travelled to Spain on business, and while alone in his hotel room succumbed to a heart attack and died. He was only forty-three. Olga, then in her early thirties, was forced, from economic necessity, to return to work, leaving her son in the care of her mother during the day. Bearing her grief as well as the strain of financial responsibility has taken its toll, and her views are tinged with pessimism.

'Valerii was alone in his room. He must have had a heart attack, and the next day he was dead. I don't know what happened. I received his body back after ten days. He had suffered a bit from ill health, but he never went to doctors, he never looked after his health. He used to say, I am safe, I am not unhealthy. But he had a heart attack, aged forty-three, alone in his room. His firm said he was very valuable, a very good man, everybody is saying so still. I still meet partners who remember him, and even if they met him fifteen years ago they still remember my husband and offer me help and hospitality.

'So now I have to work – and I was lucky to find my job. If I had not found it I do not know what would have happened to me. When the coup happened, I was terrified; if it had succeeded I would have lost my job, because I am employed by a co-operative venture and when the *coup d'état* took place the major joint ventures were closed. I would have been unemployed.

'My son doesn't know the truth about his father, not for the moment. He's too small. Maybe when he's six years old we will tell him. It was terrible for me, and it is terrible for my son. He keeps asking for him. He remembers everything about him, he knows that his father went abroad to work, and he keeps asking me when he is coming home. I don't know what to do, how to tell him. For the time being I can't tell him anything. I just have to invent. My husband's mother is very ill, but still she is alive, and her son is dead. She is suffering, and I feel very sorry for her; his father as well, who is a very old man. It is terrible for them.'

The light was fading as evening changed, imperceptibly to dusk. Olga turned on a lamp in the corner of the room and I could see the sky darkening over Moscow. Our conversation ranged widely over social and cultural topics; we discussed the 'Russian spirit', that inner strength and resilience of the Russian peoples that has survived ordeals and terrors for so long; that collective soul that finds expression in great literature, music, film, ballet, circus and gymnastics; a fire that refuses to be extinguished.

'Yet it's very sad that all these things are for export only. They are not for us Russians. You can only buy the circus tickets for dollars, so not many people can afford to take their children. It's awful. Same thing with the Bolshoi Theatre. When I was a child we had these possibilities – I have been to the Bolshoi Theatre with my friends; I can count the times on my fingers, but still I went to the Bolshoi. Now it is impossible. If you don't have dollars, you can't go, and it is the same for the circus.'

We returned at last to the subject that was not far from the lips of most Muscovites in those days: what now, now that the communist machine had finally broken down? Olga was not optimistic.

'The idea behind the reforms is to take away the central control and give people the chance to run things for themselves. But at present we see the reforms on paper only; nothing has really changed and the same people are in charge as before. We don't see results. Maybe we want it to be too quick. It is true that before, there were people impeding the reforms, so let's give Yeltsin and the democrats time. Maybe. Everything is possible. I wish it would be so; you need a glimmer of hope. But now a lot of people are very depressed. We hoped, we believe in democracy, but there are some symptoms which are not very good. We shall see.'

We talked of the collective responsibility of the Russian nation, that collective that had been called upon to serve its own higher interests in the early days of communism as it repeatedly sacrificed the part for the whole. Was there some kind of inevitability about the necessity for the people to experience their own darker side? It appeared that, historically, they had chosen idealist, not to mention extremist, leaders.

Olga's pessimism turned to a deeper shade of gloom; her summary echoed not only the words of her uncle Sergei Pavlovich, but also the shadow that lay over the people of Moscow whose eyes spoke of trust betrayed; trust in a system that had not only failed them, but crushed them. 'We are like children: we are used to doing what we are told. We are slaves.'

While Olga's cousin, Volodya's son Sergei, agreed with her that the ideology of the Communist Party had served to crush its people for three generations, he in contrast felt that life in Moscow was now perfectly reasonable and that the family had much to be both proud and grateful for. Sergei Vladimich is in his early thirties, has been married twice and has a young daughter. He organises international sports competitions and has therefore had first-hand experience of Western cultures. He started by talking about his personal heritage, and delivered a telling epitaph for his great-grandfather, Sergei Yakovlevich.

'I am proud to have such a person as Stalin in the family. People like me for myself, not because I am a relative of Stalin, although some people are afraid. He made mistakes but he was a great political leader. History will judge: the future will tell, it will pass its sentence.

'The great October revolution was a historical experiment: Lenin worked out the ideas, Stalin followed them through to the letter and put them into practice. It took the people seventy years to understand that it was a crazy idea; it was a crazy idea of Lenin's to make an ideological statement into an organisation. It was fiction. It's impossible to organise such a statement in our lives. But they believed it, and they believed *in* it. This idea corrupted and crushed the nation.

'It is impossible to do that here; people have different characters and you can't impose a norm – some lie, some cheat, some steal, some are good, some are bad. It's poetic fiction, it's a crazy idea.'

Talking about the Second Revolution, it became clear that Sergei Vladimich's views were not unlike his father's, and that he too spoke from the position of relative privilege. For one thing he was earning dollars, which put him in a different league from people who earned roubles.

'Gorbachev is popular in the USA and the West, but he made his career in the West and not in the USSR. He is not popular here. He is not a real political leader. Maybe he did good for the USA, but he gave nothing to the USSR. As for *glasnost*, I don't believe in it. Things have changed, but that's not *glasnost*. There are documents, yes, but it doesn't mean that it's true. It is *glasnost* on paper only. What I am doing now I was doing ten years ago.

'But life here is OK for me and my wife, it is not difficult for us. What it boils down to is that every person in any country has their own problems. I lived here before the *coup*, and I didn't feel that it was difficult to live here. It hasn't made any basic difference. Time will tell whether it will.

'The *coup* was a good piece of theatre. Although it destroyed the KGB and the Communist Party, its aim did not succeed. But I am not sad. I think everything will be

OK here. It will be impossible to keep the Soviet Union together and Russia will split off from the other republics. One big problem is the nuclear weapons. Another is the economic connections between the countries – these must survive, they cannot live alone. They will form democracies modelled on the USA and the GDR. Probably the Asian republics will turn towards Iran and will organise themselves as religious states.

'Yeltsin is a real politician. Time alone will show what kind of leader he is. But he is tough. The history of Russia shows us that the USSR always needs a strong political leader, a dictator. Perhaps it is in the character of the people to need it. The country, after all, is *very* big. You have to look at the story of Europe where there is experience of democracy; the USSR doesn't have that experience. The USSR will have to study it: in Europe the laws work, in the USSR the laws don't work.

'We will have to take the best things from the Western countries. It is impossible to live separately any more. I cannot live and go my own way, doing what I want and what I think. I have to speak with people, share with them, get information from them, and learn from history. How long that will take is perhaps the same period of time as the European countries took – it will be a very long process.

'You cannot impose a culture in a decade. You have to bring up a new generation of young people. The present generation will not understand this system; they have their own stereotypes, their psychology, their education. It will take longer than one generation – two, three, even five generations.

'War and chaos are both possibilities. That is one way things could go, but a totalitarian regime is now impossible. Dictatorship, yes. It is necessary to have dictatorship for stability; otherwise there will be chaos or war – even the end of the earth. The nuclear threat is immense. We are a *huge* country. If we have massive unemployment I don't know what will happen.

'The KGB is still necessary, we need a secret intelligence service, like any country. In Canada the intelligence service used to operate through the CIA, now they have their own organisation – and that is a "democracy"! There is not democracy here now. Russia is under some kind of dictatorship; they may have destroyed the Communist Party and the KGB, but this is dictatorship, not democracy.

'I don't believe in democracy anyway. It is impossible to live in a democracy. I have lived in Canada, and OK I had some rights, but for example the press in the West is not a free press. You have an editor of a newspaper, or an owner, who has his opinions, and the journalists on that paper write to suit those opinions. Otherwise they lose their job. Is that democracy?

'Whether the Russian soul will be smothered by capitalism and wealth depends on the individual. I hope the psychology of the Russian will survive. This is a difficult question. The other big question is, do we have a destiny of suffering? It would seem so, but this is our history, it is our life. Maybe this is the reason for the Russian soul; life here is difficult, and this has nurtured the Russian soul in the people. It is up to the individual whether that inner light survives.'

# INDEX

# INDEX